THE EXPANDING LANDSCAPE

South Asians and the Diaspora

The Expanding Landscape

South Asians and the Diaspora

Edited by
CARLA PETIEVICH

MANOHAR
2021

First published 1999
Reprinted 2021

ISBN 978-81-7304-279-9

Published by
Ajay Kumar Jain *for*
Manohar Publishers & Distributors
4753/23 Ansari Road, Daryaganj
New Delhi 110 002

Printed at
Replika Press Pvt. Ltd.

Contents

Foreword

There are many questions surrounding the term 'diaspora'. In addition to the 'hows' and 'whys' of leaving (emigration), there are the questions of how migrants end up where they seek to go. The statutory and regulatory changes of the US Immigration and Nationality Act from 1965 to the present form the underpinning of the South Asian migration to the United States; these developments and the immigration-related changes of the Departments of Labor and State have defined the shape, size and nature of South Asian migration to the US.

It was the statutory changes to the US Immigrations and Nationality Act in 1965 which first made immigration possible for South Asians in significant numbers. In addition to establishing immigrant visa quota numbers for those seeking to immigrate to the United States from the world's Eastern Hemisphere, the US Congress developed ceilings on immigrant visas to be allocated at 20,000 per country per annum, and a Preference (or category) System against which these numbers would be allocated. (Later revisions to the US Immigration and Nationality Act included a Preference System for the Western Hemisphere as well; and a final revision to the Act articulated a worldwide ceiling on immigration visas rather than one for each hemisphere.)

This new Preference System, now made available to such countries as India, Pakistan and Sri Lanka, included six categories of immigrant visa eligibility defined by law. Two of these preferences (specifically, the third and sixth) did not require the sponsor to be a citizen or Permanent Resident of the United States. Rather, these two categories were employment-based.

For the third Preference, in most cases, individuals in the sciences, arts or professions could enter if there were (1) proof of their professional expertise in the form of credentials and experience and (2) the promise of employment from a US employer whose *bona fides* were verified. Immigrant visa-seekers would go through procedures involving both the US Department of Labor and the

Immigration and Naturalization Service (INS) in order to verify their eligibility to obtain Permanent Resident Status (the 'green card'). In some cases, verification procedures also involved the US Department of State.

The sixth Preference, which included skilled workers, became an option for those whose skills and backgrounds may not have fit the definition of 'profession' in US immigration law. In addition, in the early days of this new system, it would also serve to catch the spillover from third Preference when that category became oversubscribed.

For graduate students and professional school students from South Asia who were studying in the US, permanent immigration now became a serious option. For professionals already established in South Asia, whether educated abroad or not, the new laws made immigration to the US a viable professional opportunity.

What was significant—both for the US and for South Asia—was that without benefit of pre-existing family ties in the US, South Asians with requisite professions, skills, training and experience could be immigrants. In a very short time, it became clear that these individuals were part of the United States' 'new seed'.

Quite different from the traditional American mythology of immigrant beginnings (which were, in fact, related to other US immigration laws of an earlier time) this was not the migration that came to the US in steerage alone or with one's family or to join already established relatives. This was not a 'Horatio Alger' arrival starting with nothing and working one's way up through the ranks. With the 1965 changes, one didn't necessarily have to start from professional scratch in one's new country. The early South Asian immigrants, coming in largely under the third, and sometimes the sixth Preference, tended to move horizontally across cultures and nations before they moved further up the vertical ladder. Such a migration would not merely be a new chapter in US immigration: it would be a whole new story, an American first.

According to the most traditional immigration myth of the United States, one comes to the US leaving one's past behind, never to return again. However, when one migrates to the US with a professional US starting salary, one's past is merely as far away as the price of a plane ticket at vacation time. Clearly, there are important implications here for both the sending and receiving cultures.

Until 1976, when US law began to seriously restrict the immigration of foreign medical professionals, the delared shortages in medical personnel in the United States only facilitated South Asian immigration (or, as it was often described from the South Asian side, the 'brain drain').

A significant impact of these new laws and the subsequent wave of South Asian immigrants to the US was that 'family' and 'household' would now be defined by the restrictions of US immigration law, rather than by culture or custom. What is more, Permanent Residents would find themselves severely limited by law as to the kinds of relatives whom they could sponsor under second Preference: only spouses and unmarried children were eligible. Under the Preference system, second Preference was the only preference available to Permanent Residents seeking the reunification of their families in the United States. Additionally, the more permanent residents who apply for eligible family members, the quicker the allocations for this preference will be used up and the longer will be the queue for this category of immigrant visas.

One way to resolve this, and to finally fulfil one's obligations to a brother or sister, regardless of their professional qualification; or to a parent; is to become a US citizen. US citizens may file immigrant visa petitions for a spouse or parent, or an unmarried child under 21 years of age, without these being subject to annual quotas. (This category, known as Immediate Relatives, is outside of and not subject to the worldwide immigrant visa ceiling). A US citizen is additionally able to sponsor a child who has reached the age of 21, whether married or unmarried; and siblings (also regardless of their marital status).

The questions which have been part of these migrations all along—questions of just how permanent this immigration to the US really is—certainly begin to rear their heads when the issue turns to citizenship and its relation to keeping families together. To the new generation born in the United States (who are thereby automatically citizens) it also begs the question of just where 'home' really is.

The US Immigration and Nationality Act has not stood still since 1965, nor has the demand for immigrant visas. Whereas twenty years ago the wait for siblings' visas was about five years, it may now take up to ten or even twelve years. Most recently, the Immigration Act of 1990 eliminated the traditional third and sixth Preference designations of the 1965 Act, developing two different preferences for worldwide application. The first, Family-Based Preferences, is largely the same as before: unmarried adult children of Permanent Residents now fall into a separate, special sub-category of the second Preference, with a separate numerical limitation. The second, Employment-Based Preferences, include five different kinds of access to the immigrant visa system, depending on levels of education, expertise, renown and skill.

Each month the Department of State publishes the *Visa Bulletin* which is a kind of tracking sheet. It shows the allocation of immigrant visas by country and by preference category for each of the two current preference systems (Family- and Employment-Based) within the annual worldwide allocations. A country only shows up on the list by name when its allocations have a particular configuration of oversubscription that varies from the backlogs shared by all other countries. (Countries which share the same backlogs are described in the *Visa Bulletin* as 'All Chargeability Areas Except Those Listed'.) For more than ten years, India has had its own month's entry. Since the Immigration Act of 1990, India now has two entries: one for its own configuration of Family-Based immigration visa backlogs, and another reflecting the demand for Employment-Based immigrant visa by applicants from India.

With only certain exceptions—bringing to the US Asians who were expelled from Uganda by Idi Amin in 1972, admitting Afghan refugees (1979-92); and certain grants of asylum to members of particular groups or communities from India, Pakistan, Bangladesh and Sri Lanka—South Asian migration to the United States has been conducted largely through the regular categories of the Immigration Preference System.

A full comprehension of a Diaspora must include how groups may be changed by the demands and criteria placed by the receiving countries upon those who seek admission. These changes involve such explicit permissions and prohibitions as the demands of immigration law (who and which family members may or may not be admitted) and the far more subtle implicit cultural values and demands of a receiving country, which may often be hinted at in the legal code.

ESTELLE F. STRIZHAK

Introduction

CARLA PETIEVICH

The papers in this volume were originally presented at a conference held on 5-6 March 1993 at Columbia University. The conference was organized by the Independent Scholars of South Asia in conjunction with Columbia's Southern Asian Institute. While the phenomena of migration, exile and displacement have been of concern to cultural critics and scholars of South Asia for perhaps a decade now,[1] this conference was, as far as we know, the first of its kind.

The conference brought together independent persons, institutionally-based scholars, and younger scholars completing their training. Among us are firmly-rooted South Asianists, adamant non-South Asianists, and those grounded in a variety of academic disciplines (the heavy social science orientation that has characterized this field of study to date was complemented here by fair representation from scholars in the humanities). This conference was an opportunity for all of us to examine questions of culture and identity among people of South Asian ethnic origin who live outside South Asia. Organization of the papers into panels was generally structured along three thematic lines, those of transnational identities; the re-creation and (re)construction of culture in the diaspora; and the displacement of South Asian communities such as Bangladeshis and Ahmadiyya Muslims into new, but still minority, positions within the dominant cultures.

One of the most dramatic and stimulating achievements of this conference was formulation of a many-sided and complex notion of 'diaspora' and 'identity'. This emerged at the outset and remained central to the ensuing discussion. How does diasporic experience connect up to class, ethnicity, race, gender, generation and other social divisions or to technologies and renegotiated spaces? How are we to understand transnational cultural flows in the context of this diaspora? And most of all, who defines and represents the myriad people, places, identities and other concerns implied by the phrase 'South Asian Diaspora'?

Participants and audience were challenged to consider the

geographical extent of, what we often so casually refer to as 'the South Asian Diaspora' and the wide range of sub-ethnicities implied. Some people identify themselves sometimes through religious community rather than town, region or country of origin,[2] as 'Muslim' and express their identity through activities centred around mosques;[3] sometimes identification is primarily geographic (see Leonard on Hyderabadis, Angell on Bengalis); or yet again, self-identification may be expressed in terms of more than one 'place' and experience of migration ('multiply-migrant British Sikhs from East Africa' a la Bhachu). Significantly, though almost all of us bear some nationality, these choices of self-identification often take precedence over nationality.[4]

Transnationality and Diaspora permit of choice in the expression of identity, and this conference underlined in eloquent fashion the range of cultural performance through which identity can be expressed. Cultural performance can be understood as the celebration of festivals, as discussed by both Hansen and Petievich; in the claiming of territory and marking of space through construction of temples or mosques, as discussed by Waghorne or in the arrangement and orchestration of wedding celebrations (Leonard) and dowry exchange (Bhachu). The reader is invited to explore some of the nuances of 'performing culture' in the ensuing pages.

Transnationality is about more than culture, and Johanna Lessinger focused on the experiences of a particular occupational group, Indian businessmen in New York. We may not perceive engagement in business to be primarily an expression of culture, but it cannot be understood as separate from the forces of class, racism and family. Arguing persuasively against accepting easy notions of 'model minorities', Lessinger exhorts us to acknowledge and pay attention to the impact of class on any migration experience and to resist totalizing notions of 'culture' that threaten to erase class.

Gender was acknowledged as a profound factor in how migration, resettlement and (re)articulation of culture are experienced. Some research projects had been designed explicitly around gender (Bhachu, Sanyal). In every paper presented, the data seemed to mandate some discussion of gender difference (Angell, Hansen, Waghorne, Walbridge & Haneef): Sanyal looked particularly at the experience of South Asian immigrant women identifying themselves with the Islamic Circle of North America. She describes the empowering effect re-embracing Islam can have as a person adapts to exile and displacement in North America. On the other hand, Haneef and Walbridge's survey of Ahmadis in New York shows how cultural difference, even within a theoretically universal religious community, can challenge group unity. The point on which each 'problem' of difference or adaptation pivoted was the different experience of migration dictated by gender.

No less crucial to any discussion of diaspora is the issue of generation, especially in 'host' societies heavily oriented toward assimilation (North America or Britain). Development of complex cultural identifications on the part of their children is often viewed with dread on the part of migrant parents, who see it as 'loss of culture'. This tension is central, though not exclusive, to the phenomenon of cultural patronage and performance; and cultural performance takes myriad forms (Bhachu, Hansen, Leonard, Petievich, Srinivasan, Waghorne).

On the second day was held a panel discussion entitled, 'The Second Generation Speaks'. The panelists were four younger scholars, raised in North America by one or more immigrant parent(s) of South Asian origin, whose academic work is concerned in some way with the South Asian Diaspora. The session became an occasion to explore questions about the enterprise in which we were engaged. Reiterating other participants' reference to South Asian global migration in terms of a 'diaspora' (cf. Leonard, Lessinger, Bhachu), these panelists also problematized the term 'second generation'. Debate remains wide open concerning whose term 'diaspora' is, or which particular experience of migration ought, or not, to serve as a model (cf. Lelyveld's introductory remarks to this panel). Problems of language remain unresolved; but this panel provided a valuable reminder that academic engagement with identity politics is more or less inevitable.

To my mind, the implications of generational difference on determining or describing the experience of diaspora remain the most vexing and the most compelling.[5] While this area of inquiry appears to be extremely sensitive and, therefore, particularly challenging to researchers, it is my hope that the Independent Scholars' three-year project on the South Asian diaspora will yield some important insights into the generational aspect of cultural transformation and adaptation. The excellent, growing literature on Asians in Britain, will be of tremendous value (though the differences in demographics between British and North American

South Asian populations will likely impede facile comparison).

Independent scholars and others who have been studying aspects of South Asian diaspora for a decade and more, talk of the difficulties of engaging in scholarly exchange: diasporic South Asian culture has been deemed 'inauthentic' by other South Asianists; and those cultural critics who have taken more seriously the culture of migrants and who recognize the importance of the large global population of people of South Asian origin have tended to come from an academic orientation that views South Asian studies with skepticism (at best) or scorn (at worst). The decision of the Independent Scholars of South Asia to embark on a three-year intellectual project with the South Asian diaspora as its focus reflects our perception that the present time is ripe for bridging some of these gaps. This volume is the first of three which we expect to see result from our now-completed intellectual project on the south Asian diaspora. In particular we hope that the pieces in this volume will help to advance dialogue among scholars of diverse disciplinary and intellectual orientation who share an interest in peoples of South Asian ethnicity.

NOTES AND REFERENCES

1. Cf. Anzaldua, Gloria, ed., *Borderlands/La Frontera: the new Mestiza* (Consortium Books, 2nd ed. 1999.
   Bhabha, Homi K., ed., *Nation and Narration* (Routledge, 1990).
   ———, *The Location of Culture* (Routledge, 1994).
   Metcalf, Barbara D., ed., *Making Muslim Space in North America and Europe* (Comparative Studies on Muslim Societies, No. 22), Berkeley: University of California Press, 1996).
2. This has been observed to occur most often in the case of an 'Islamic identification'.
3. See especially Sanyal, Walbridge and Haneef for both simpler and more problematic manifestations of this phenomenon.
4. In Dorothy Angell's work the apparent cultural notion of what it means to be Bengali renders almost irrelevant the national boundary between India and Bangladesh.
5. Since this conference, Homi Bhabha too has addressed this issue in *Nation and Narration*; and in remarks as a discussant on a diaspora panel at the annual conference on South Asia, Madison, Wisconsin (November 1994).

Class, Race And Success: Indian-Americans Confront the American Dream

JOHANNA LESSINGER

This present collection of papers is a welcome sign that it has finally become academically respectable to study South Asians living outside the subcontinent. Perhaps we can now do so without having to face the implied criticism that these populations are no longer authentically Indian, Pakistani, Bangladeshi, or Sri Lankan, and therefore of only secondary concern to South Asianist.

Part of this altered scholarly outlook can be traced to global changes which have weakened the analytical importance of national and cultural boundaries. International flows of people, capital and culture have broken down whatever isolated entities existed in the past and have gone on to create new definitions of nationality and ethnicity (see for instance, Sassen [-Koob] 1988,1991; Schiller, Basch and Blanc-Szanton 1992). It is hard to argue any more that the only authentic South Asian experience takes place in South Asia itself. Indian society, for instance, can no longer be properly understood without considering the vast impact of outmigration and return by important sectors of its population; these migrants, commonly known in India as NRIs (Non-Resident Indians), are important agents of social change in Indian society, whether they return 'home' or whether they simply send remittances or sponsor the further migration of relatives. The same processes have profoundly altered the societies which play host to immigrants. Countries such as the United States, Canada and Great Britain are not only growing more ethnically diverse than they have ever been, but are being forced, by ethnic militancy, to acknowledge the fact in both the political and cultural arenas (see for instance, Takaki 1989; Portes and Rumbaut 1990; Werbner and Anwar 1991; Omatsv 1994). South Asianists need to account for these changes as well.

In parallel with these changes there has been a shift in the way in which social scientists approach the phenomenon of migrant communities. There is now less concern with cultural essentialism and more attention to immigrants' roles in the labour market of a restructured world economy (see for instance, Sassen 1988, 1991; Robinson 1990; Lamphere 1992: 12-13; Waldinger 1995). We no longer seek to pin immigrants somewhere along a single point in the assimilationist continuum and are less preoccupied with asking 'how Indian (or Chinese or Korean)' they are. Instead of gradually shedding their Indian-ness or Pakistani-ness and 'becoming Americanized', it is possible to see immigrants as constructing new identities for themselves, built out of various elements of old and new, creatively combined. Parminder Bachu (1993 and in this collection) offers particularly compelling examples among Indo-British women but the process is global and parallels can be found anywhere.

The newer focus in social science on constructed identity and personal agency allows us to understand more clearly the kinds of social and cultural differentiation that emerge within any immigrant population, as people coming from a variety of social backgrounds create a range of new identities built around their particular experiences as migrants. At the same time new identities are constructed within a social arena containing other, often competing, ethnic groups so that the question of assimilation to a single dominant culture is replaced by questions of accommodation between groups (see Lamphere 1992: 14-17; Goode and Schneider 1994).

If we abandon notions of ethnic authenticity and ethnic uniqueness it becomes easier to examine the parallels and differences in the experiences of different ethnic groups who have ended up in similar immigrant situations and to ask what South Asian immigrants do or do not share with, for instance, Mexican or Korean migrants. This comparative stance may be a particularly bitter pill for traditional South Asianists (and for many South Asians themselves) to swallow, since both South Asian culture and South Asian studies have for many years reveled in the implicit assumption that South Asian society is incomparable—and probably superior. Yet all over the globe once-homogeneous societies are becoming multi-ethnic and cultural uniqueness is being dissolved and reformed. As South Asian immigrants fan out around the world and become part of such societies, whether in the United States, Britain, Malaysia, Canada or

Fiji, this kind of comparison, along with a focus on cross-ethnic relationships (rather than assimilation into the hegemonic culture) is an increasingly powerful analytical tool.

This paper argues for the importance of class and racial stratification in understanding the kinds of identities Indian immigrants in the United States create. The data is drawn from a study of immigrant business people in New York and a larger study of the general New York Indian population (Lessinger 1995).[1]

The heterogeneity and size of the Indian community in New York City (according to the 1990 US Census 94,590 individuals out of a national total of 8,15,562) makes the issue of class particularly salient. At the same time the vast mixture of new immigrant groups in the city makes a comparative approach inevitable and renders questions of inter-ethnic and interracial relationships unavoidable. The question of assimilation into 'American culture' is undercut in a city like New York by the frequent plaint of new Indian arrivals: 'But who *are* the Americans? *Where* are they?'

Three kinds of issues emerge from this data. First is the role of pre-existing class differences among migrants from a single country; these differences, often relatively minor to begin with, may have enormous influence on the way individuals can position themselves within the employment structure after immigration and on their subsequent access to class resources. Second is the issue of emergent class relationships within an increasingly stratified immigrant community as some people 'make it' economically and socially while others do not. Finally, the material suggests some of the ways in which class, ethnicity and race interact as Indians position themselves within a multi-ethnic local and national context.

To make this kind of analysis, however, a scholar must first move beyond an ideology of ethnic group homogeneity, economic success and smooth assimilation into a dominant (white) culture, vigorously propogated by the Indian immigrant community,[2] more particularly by its elite. This ideology is constantly on display in the immigrant media, in speeches by immigrant leaders and in public events staged by 'the community's' elites. The intended audience for this message is both the outer world of 'the Americans' and an inner world of fellow Indians. Concern is often expressed that any doubts and demurs over universal prosperity or easy assimilation (see for example Motwani and Barot-Motwani 1989) expressed from within the community not reach the outside where they might tarnish the shining image of the entire ethnic group. It is wholly understandable that immigrants, in the process of creating themselves anew, prefer to stress the positive aspects of their new lives. Yet this particular form of self-identification also has less positive consequences.

Some previous research on Indians in the United States has also been influenced by this ideology as well as by the strong tendency to examine each ethnic group individually and to stress assimilation as an unstated but presumed goal of immigration. Saran (1985) and Helweg and Helweg (1990) highlight that sector of the Indo-American population which is urban, professionally employed, affluent and economically integrated into mainstream US society without apparent dislocations. In contrast, Leonard (1992, 1997), La Brack and Leonard (1984) and Gibson (1988), studying particular local groups of California Sikh farmers and farm workers, devote more attention to poverty, economic struggles and tense inter-ethnic relations. This semi-rural population, made vulnerable by its class position, does not coincide wholly with the Indian community's ideal vision of itself. A group of Indo-American scholars now present a more nuanced view (see Mazumdar 1989, Radhakrishnan 1994) while Bacon (1996) offers a sophisticated account of assimilation and the second generation.

The proud claim by Indians that their community in the US is made up of professionals and business people is at one level a statement of fact about an immigration wave shaped by post-1965 US immigration laws. These favoured the arrival of those with professional skills, business interests here or sizeable amounts of capital to invest. In insisting so vehemently on what one community leader called 'a healthy image' (Abraham 1984: 5) of prosperity, self-sufficiency, middle-class lifestyle, political influence and smooth integration into American society, there is anxiety that non-Indians 'see the community as a whole',[3] that is, identify the community as undivided, unmarked by internal cleavages. By distancing themselves from other new immigrants and other ethnic minorities here, Indian immigrants deny that they experience parallel kinds of social and economic problems. They reject any suggestion that they are a source of social pathology or share a common marginalized and often racially defined status with other groups. By implication Indians have tended to embrace the 'model minority' image which Chinese-Americans have begun to critique as destructive (Kwong 1987: 57-80; Takaki 1989: 474-84).

As social scientists we need to look at immigrant Indian self-created identity more closely, to pick apart issues of class and economic versus cultural assimilation. We need to trace the roots of the success-through-employment ideologies around which these immigrants construct their identities and note their reactionary implications. In advocating a more nuanced view of the Indian community here, I am not denying the central fact that many of its recent immigrants have been extremely successful in finding work and making money. Nor, in citing instances of difficulty and failure do I wish to denigrate the large numbers of energetic, optimistic, courageous people who have built new lives for themselves and their children here.

Nevertheless, it is clear that some of the prosperity gained through professional employment and business activity is achieved rather more painfully than the official community ideology would suggest, and that racial and anti-immigrant prejudice is sometimes at work. It is evident that the community is internally divided, not only by linguistic region and religion, as Fisher (1980) noted two decades ago, but also by class. These class divisions stem both from pre-migration class status (and the statuses which relatives still occupy in India) and from occupation. My own fieldwork suggests that relatively small differences in class background confer differential advantages in terms of finding US employment. Consequently existing class differences are further amplified after migration as people's differential access to the job market sorts them, sometimes brutally, into different sectors of the US class structure, determining where they can live, where their children can go to school, who their friends are, and what kind of ongoing access they can have to India.

Interestingly, one potential form of cleavage suggested in discussions with Indian community leaders—that between 'the businessmen' and 'the professionals'—is less profound than it might initially appear. My data suggest that a great many Indian immigrant professionals are, at least on the East Coast, simultaneously deeply involved in entrepreneurial activities alongside their professional employment. Some choose investment in real estate while many others become the financial partners of fellow Indians setting up businesses. For professionals the primary motivation is an increase in income, although there is clearly also an effort to extend social networks through business and to create social capital. There are, in addition, a sizeable number of professionals who have abandoned salaried jobs to start their own businesses, either because they had difficulty in finding suitable jobs or through frustration with existing employment. Thus in terms of class position and ideology the two groups are more closely intertwined than might first appear.

Finally, it is evident that the kind of professional/occupational self-identification the Indian community has chosen for itself, and the accompanying respect for success and 'making it', shape the ability to respond to social, economic and political problems within a society which is simultaneously pluralistic, racist and nativist. This difficulty has become particularly apparent in situations where Indians have been the victims of racial attack, such as the notorious 1987 'dotbuster' attacks on Indians living in several working-class New Jersey communities.

SUCCESS AND THE AMERICAN DREAM

The roots of the Indian immigrants' commitment to what might be called the American Dream are complex, drawn both from the experiences of the Indian middle class over the last fiorty years and from homegrown American ideologies of individualism, self-help and success. Any discussion with people about why they migrated to the US will evoke similar refrains: the freedom American society offers individuals to make their own way in life; the ability to 'be one's own boss', and the fact that hard work brings financial reward. Status, money and the material advantages they confer are frankly valued. Within this ideology, entrepreneurial activity plays an important role as the means of simultaneously achieving independence and wealth.

Some of this concern with 'making good' is created by the circumstances of immigration itself. Most immigrants are slightly defensive about having left India, for which all retain strong, if ambivalent, emotions. They justify migration as the search for a better life for themselves and their families. Thus prosperity and success are seen not just as good in themselves but as the validation of the decision to leave. It is no surprise that business and the professions—the major routes to wealth and status in both societies—become the centrepieces of the entire community's ideological identity.

I began by labelling such an ideological stance part of the American dream of success, but it has its parallels in India itself. The Indian urban middle class, and an allied semi-urban rural elite, groups which have contributed the majority of immigrants to the US, have long been interested in money, status and the visible signs thereof. India's present generation of middle-aged adults, and even more markedly a younger generation now in its twenties and thirties, have both tended to abandon the prestige and security of government service or professions favoured by earlier generations, entrepreneurship as the way to quick wealth. (Indians are hardly alone in this new orientation.) Money and what it can buy are increasingly the main source of status in a country recently opened to a flood of consumer goods and the assault of foreign mass media. Cultural commentators in India tend to blame these trends on creeping Westernization and a loss of Indian identity, rather than on modern capitalism encroaching as the Indian government makes active efforts to integrate the country more closely into a world economy.

Indian immigrants have also absorbed another, more negative aspect of the American dream. Although there are honourable exceptions, much of the community has adopted the hegemonic ideology in the US which stigmatizes the poor, the socially dependent and the 'deviant' as well as the non-white. (Often these categories are conflated.) Such an ideological stance often slips over the edge into overt racism. Most Indian immigrants express open prejudice against African-Americans, Hispanics and non-white new immigrants, while thinking of themselves as sociologically white and native-born. As one man (himself rather a failure in economic terms) said in 1986, 'If I were Simpson and Mazzoli [authors of a then hotly-debated immigration bill], I would have thrown out all those immigrants, made them all go home. They are just tearing this country down.' Such attitudes have well-documented foundations in indigenous Indian caste/class prejudices as well as in American race/class prejudice. In fact, Indian immigrants are rarely seen as either white or native-born by Americans. At best, many Asians in the US form a kind of intermediate category between the two polarized groups, white and black. Interestingly, many South Asian immigrants in both Canada and Britain have chosen an alternative strategy, identifying themselves as 'black' and as part of a multi-ethnic grouping (see Werbner and Anwar 1991) in opposition to whites.

The effect of stigmatizing American attitudes about poverty and class, part of vigorously promoted Indian immigrant group identity, creates both pain and social marginalization for those Indians who falter in their push for success and money. A harsh moralism is brought to bear on those who fail in business. Those who work hard yet never manage to earn much, never own cars or buy suburban houses, are viewed with open contempt. Even recently arrived siblings who fail to fling themselves aggressively into the job market and become self-supporting soon enough are castigated. Increasingly, one hears complaints about 'the third wave' of migration, relatives sponsored through family preference quotas. These, described to me privately by one community leader as 'our stupider younger brothers and cousins', are people whose qualifications are often not good enough to land them immediate professional positions here. Thanks to individualistic ideologies of success, the community blames fellow immigrants rather than the US economic system or the prolonged recession which has narrowed job opportunities and probably increased anti-immigrant discrimination in the job market.

The difficulties of 'making it'

The career histories[4] collected from numerous businessmen suggest that achieving success in the US is more of an effort than the community mythology acknowledges, and that the path is strewn with frequent failure. Ethnic small businesses operating within the ethnic economy (catering to, and employing, primarily Indians), generate sharp competition. 'We drive each other down', one such entrepreneur confessed ruefully. Restaurants, sari shops, electronics stores and Indian-oriented groceries cluster together and then compete fiercely for a finite number of customers. In other kinds of businesses, limitations on success may have to do with inability to grasp American social patterns, unwillingness to deal with American workers or suppliers and—in some cases—racial/ethnic bias. Few Indian immigrants will admit to having been victimized by bias when asked point-blank, yet work histories suggest that it does operate. The first case involves somebody operaring in the ethnic economy, running a grocery store catering primarily to Indians. His case reveals a very common thread—the trained Indian immigrant professional who started his own business because he could not find work here in his profession.

> Mr. D came from Gujarat in the early 1970s to get a master's degree in engineering from a small American university. Although his father was a farmer, Mr. D. and all his five siblings are college-educated.
>
> For eigth months after receiving his degree he searched in vain for an engineering job. Finally in 1975 he accepted an offer from a childhood friend to become a partner in a small grocery store. His older brother, teaching in

West Africa, contributed the initial capital D needed to begin. D also contributed his own labour to the partnership and began to learn the grocery business. Subsequently he and several other men became partners in a franchised Indian sweet shop.

In 1978 the uninsured grocery burned down. D managed to relocate, but the financial drain was great. In the same year a Mexican restaurant in which he was a partner went bankrupt shortly after it was purchased, refurbished and reopened.

Now D has a new grocery store in an Indian shopping area, and two more smaller stores in other locations. The latter are operated by partners. He has recently lost a sizeable amount of money which he had loaned to another Indian entrepreneur. That person went bankrupt owing money all around the city; he now works in a candy store. In spite of this embittering experience D says that he prefers informal loans from fellow Indians, but admits that he also has difficulty getting a formal bank loan.

Mr. D can be considered successful: after initial setbacks he has managed to attract partners. He has expanded his business, and is a welcome investment partner in other people's enterprises. To do this, he works seven days a week and worries constantly about declining trade and competitors springing up around him. Much of the time not spent in the shop is spent checking up on his partners and in a restless search for other investments in bigger businesses. He cannot get bank loans easily. Furthermore, D's business associates, customers and personal friends are all Indian, despite his residence in a largely working-class suburban town. What he was unable to do was to enter a white collar profession here, as he and his provincial family had hoped.

What does not appear in D's account, but emerges in the work histories of others, is the degree to which such small businesses depend for their profitability on economic exploitation of fellow Indians. D's shops, as well as those in which he holds a partner's interest, hire Indian men at subminimal wages. So do dozens of other Indian-owned shops, restaurants, hotels and newsstands (Lessinger 1990). Indeed, very low wages are inevitable if small businesses are to yield profits to several partners. For women, babysitter/housekeeper positions for working couples provide a similar field of exploitation since the relatively high household incomes Indian immigrants report often depend on both husband and wife working—sometimes at more than one job.

Such low-wage workers are usually people whose visa status is irregular, elderly people who cannot hope to find better work in the

US, and younger people in the process of searching for better jobs.[5] Female domestic workers are often widows or divorcees brought from India for the purpose of housework. Contrary to the mythology within the elite sectors of the Indian community, these workers are not necessarily uneducated country bumpkins. Many of the younger and middle-aged men are relatively well educated and may even have finished college. A survey of newsstand workers indicated that some even had postgraduate degrees (Lessinger 1990). Their misfortune is often simply that they have attended less prestigious universities in India, or that their fields of study were not scientific ones which might have won them an immediate job or sponsorship in the US. Some lack well-connected relatives or friends here to help place them. Some seem simply to be victims of economic recession, having arrived not in the booming 1960s and 1970s but in the 1980s when jobs were scarcer.

Such employees commonly put in twelve or more hours a day, seven days a week, for very low pay and no benefits. The employee may be doubly at the mercy of the employer if immigration sponsorship is involved in the employment. A babysitter remarked that she was 'living in slavery', without time off to visit the temple or make new friends.

'I'm under him entirely', says J, a restaurant waiter about his owner. 'Whatever he says, I must say 'yes sir'. And this will go on until I can get my 'green card' [a process J envisioned as requiring several years.] As is typical, J shared a tiny apartment with several other men in similar situations. But he had to spend most of his free time (which fell in the middle of the day) in a tiny room back of the restaurant. He and his fellow workers watched Indian videos, American TV, played cards and slept. Although dreadfully bored and lonely, they had neither time nor money for more. J earned the minimum wage (he claimed he had to threaten legal action to get that) and the kitchen staff earned far less. J shared his meager tips with the kitchen staff, but none were able to save much.

In some instances the economic exploitation cross-cuts kinship lines, like the unhappy man managing his brother's card shop, or the groom, a man with an M. Phil. degree, who found he was expected to support his wife and baby by work in a newsstand owned by his new in-laws, themselves both doctors.

This group of workers, exploited because they find it impossible to move out of the ethnic economy, are important in two respects. On the one hand, their presence (along with an unknown number of Indian workers in small factories and women doing sewing or assembly work at home) undercuts the Indian community's image of itself as prosperous and middle-class. Rather than acknowledging the practical and psychological difficulties such individuals face, the tendency of many prosperous Indians here is to castigate this group for stupidity or laziness. Some people dismiss the complaints of poorer immigrants by citing their own early struggles: 'When I was a college student here, I mopped floors and waited on tables to pay my tuition. These fellows also have to struggle in their turn.' There is no recognition that the situation of 'these fellows' may not be a temporary one. Nor is there any recognition of how closely the wealth and economic success of some is dependent upon the largely invisible cheap labour of others within the same community.

This experience of poorly-paid wage labour is not uniquely Indian, but is common to large numbers of new immigrants. Professionally-trained Russian, Central American and Caribbean migrants frequently find themselves employed as domestics, shop helpers or sweat shop workers at substandard wages. Similar patterns of intra-ethnic exploitation can be seen among Chinese and Koreans, where poorer men and women work for more affluent fellow immigrants in extremely oppressive situations. What this means, therefore, is that some Indians also form part of the new low-wage immigrant labour force which characterizes a city like New York (see Sassen 1991: 299-319).

The Indian-owned import businesses which are a major feature of New York City are less embedded in the ethnic economy but are closely tied to India's low-wage labour market. They serve non-Indian customers here but rely on Indian social networks and cheap labour Indian to produce the goods they sell. Importers of clothing, carpets, costume jewellery, diamonds and gem stones usually come from traditional business families; many operate here as the US branches of firms in India or of transnational firms now spread around the globe. The diamond importer Z, for instance, says his important business decisions are still taken in consultation with his brothers and cousins who run the family firm in Rajasthan. Mr. L considers his cloth importing business his own, but is still closely tied to the family firm in Hong Kong, where he got his training and where he buys most of his goods.

T, a garment importer and real estate magnate, comes from a former land-owning family. His parents fled from Pakistan to Bombay after Partition. Left impoverished by his father's death, T dropped out of college and went to work for a Hong Kong garment manufacturing firm which paid very poorly but allowed him to learn the business. Feeling that they needed to break into a new field, T's brother came to New York and opened a tiny one-man office to sell garments and cheap jewelry in the late 1960s. Much of the time he had to support himself by working for other Indians since the business yielded so little. For a number of years he scraped by, living in a small room, subsisting on rice and dal. In 1970 T and his brother began to take turns coming to the US for six months at a time, sharing the hardships. Unlike many other clothing importers, they did not have a Hong Kong or Singapore firm and its capital behind them.

Eventually they accumulated enough to open a larger office and to hire a few employees. 'Having our own employees was a big thing for us', recalls T.

In the 1970s the market for cheap, bright Indian clothing expanded and T's business boomed; the brothers abandoned jewelry imports. They put effort into buying and stocking retail clothing shops in New York and in other states. Within five years they had sold those shops, finding them too risky and hard to manage at a distance. The garment import business also began to yield less profit as the US government erected import quotas against clothing imported from India and as still more importers flocked into the business.

Instead the brothers turned their efforts to US real estate. New York was in the midst of a real estate slump with office and apartment buildings for sale relatively cheaply. Real estate is now the major source of their income. T's brother now invests exclusively in motels in southern states. T concentrates on New York area real estate and is also involved in financing other businessmen who want to open retail shops.

This case illustrates the kind of flexibility successful Indian entrepreneurs here adopt. They shift from area to area until able to find something which yields a profit. Their primary skill is in managing a business, any business. T is perhaps unusual in that he has moved out of a traditional form of import trade into a business where he competes directly with Americans. Yet he is typical of many traditional business people in that his social circle is almost entirely Indian and heavily weighted towards people from his native region. Only in the past few years has his real estate business begun to bring him into contact with American entrepreneurs at his level. He indicates, however, that he does not mix with them socially, citing his own vegetarianism and teetotalling as barriers to easy socializing.

Many such businessmen also express reservations about employing an American workforce, even when it might be economical to do so. An importer of ready-made clothing described the elaborate, expensive steps he must take to control quality and keep his fashions up-to-date in Indian factories. He had, he said, considered getting his clothes made locally in New Jersey. Higher American wages might be offset by the fact that he would not have to fly trained American fashion coordinators to India several times a year and keep them in luxury hotels for weeks at a stretch. However he was not ready, he said, to manage working-class (and non-white) American employees, whom he characterized as 'too rough for me to manage. Even my son couldn't handle them'. Mr. T added that he prefers workers in India, who are 'softer' and prepared to work harder than Americans. What this suggests is a high, if unacknowledged, level of Indian immigrant unease with the ethnically varied New York area working class. Just as many Indian immigrants remain ensconced within a largely Indian social world, others prefer Indian employees, either fellow migrants or workers in India.

Some of the most profitable Indian businesses operating in the larger 'American' economy are those owned and operated by technically trained former professionals. These people, after sojourns in US universities and US firms, have founded businesses which utilize their professional skills as engineers, computer experts, managers or financial analysts. This group has moved relatively smoothly into the 'American' occupational structure, thanks to Western-style education at India's premier institutions or in the United States itself. Ironically however, many of these businessmen explained their decisions to launch their own firms in terms of their inability to rise any higher within American organizations where they had worked. As one man said, 'When I realized that I would never be chairman of the board, I decided to form my own company.' A few people identified the barriers to their advancement as racism or as prejudice against foreigners. Others saw themselves as excluded because they did not belong to a network of people who had gone to the right colleges together or who socialized at the same club after work. Many others, however, denied the existence of any barriers.

Mr. H comes from a highly educated professional family in a large city in Maharashtra and attended a first-ranked college in Bombay. After a B.A. in economics and a year of graduate work there, he transferred and received an M.B.A. from a respected school of management. He then worked in one of India's major conglomerates, as a manager and marketing executive. He emigrated to the US in 1970, sponsored by one of his wife's relatives. He remarked that, well before he actually left India, others within his social network had already made the voyage, 'and we all discussed these things, we all knew what to expect'.

H had friends working in banks in New York and got a bank job on arrival. He became an executive in finance and in corporate planning, eventually rising to be a vice-president. H describes the eleven years following his emigration as years of uncertainty and turmoil, in which he frequently wanted to return to India. Part of this was homesickness and part was frustration at slow promotion. He thought his situation typical of that of many Indians in the US: 'We feel blocked. We rise rapidly but we then find we can't be one of the top ten [executives] in the company.' During this period H's highly educated wife also worked in a well-paid professional position, so that the family always had two substantial incomes.

After a brief, unhappy return to India to work as a top executive in a multinational company, H returned to New York, to his wife's vast relief. He established his own firm with two American partners (one a former colleague). The firm buys and resells real estate and manages construction projects. It is still small, with only two American office workers, but H mentions having recently completed two projects in Manhattan, each worth $40-50 million. H's wide connections in New York banking circles are of great help to him. Like many Indian entrepreneurs at this level, he had formed his own firm with encouragement from former employers.

H has already done some exporting to India and plans to branch out by establishing some kind of factory there. He is actively researching the question of what products will sell, and what kinds of Indian government assistance will be available to him as an NRI investor (see Lessinger 1992a, 1992b).

H's story is one which probably most closely approximates the Indian immigrant success story enshrined in community legend. He had little trouble finding employment, has worked steadily at well-paid jobs and lives very comfortably in a wealthy suburb. He is poised to become an international capitalist if his NRI ventures in India take form. Like many at his level, his social circle includes Americans as well as Indians.

H's story is also a striking example of the role played by Western-oriented elite education and elite social networks in immigrant success. The education and the networks predisposed H to migrate, then eased his transition when he arrived here, again when he returned to India, and yet again on his return to New York. As a result of his elite, urban, semi-Westernized upbringing and the kinds of jobs he has held, H considers himself socially more liberal than many Indian families in his social circle, permitting his teenaged daughter to go to a disco, for instance, as long as she goes with a group rather than with a single boy. He recalls with amusement the uproar of discussion and debate when this fact was innocently revealed at an Indian social gathering. In fact, however, people as successful and well-able to handle the demands of two cultures as H are not the majority within the immigrant community. He himself acknowledges that he has been extremely lucky, both in his career and the ease with which he was able to move back and forth between India and the US with no major loss of status or income. If he has sometimes been unhappy in the US he discusses it only with a few close friends who hold similar feelings.

Class divisions

If we were to look at the preceding case studies simply in terms of assimilation, we could say that H was the 'most assimilated' into American culture and the importer T the least. Indeed all of these people are economically assimilated, in that all are active participants in the host economy, albeit in very different capacities. However the rubric of assimilation is not very useful in distinguishing these people's varied cultural styles, their different relationships with 'the community', with American society and with the home ocuntry.

An alternative approach to the question of difference is to examine the way class has mediated, and still mediates, these immigrants' experiences. Class differences, often subtle ones, endow individuals with particular advantages, resources or disabilities, shaping the ways they can enter the US job market, their fortunes within it and the subsequent course of their lives. In examining individual life histories, class resources seem as vital as the qualities of hard work, frugality and family loyalty which Indian immigrants usually cite as the secret of their success. It is also these class resources which set Indian immigrants apart from members of other immigrant groups (and members of native-born minorities as well). Yet Indians who lack some of these resources end up in low-status, even menial, jobs, clinging precariously to the edges of the US lower middle class. Sometimes this is genuine downward mobility when compared to pre-immigration class positions. Their experiences are much closer to those of other new immigrant groups or of native-born American minority groups.

Probably the most important of the class resources Indians bring with them is education, usually college or post-graduate education from English-medium institutions with Western-derived curricula. Other immigrant groups, among them Koreans, Russians, Haitians and Chinese, have many highly educated people in the ranks of the newly-arrived, but members of these groups usually have had to struggle against their lack of English and lack of recognition of their educational qualifications by US employers. In contrast to those Indians who have graduated from the most prestigious Indian universities, or from equally prestigious American universities, are Indian immigrants coming from small vernacular medium colleges. These people find it as hard to get work in the US as immigrants from other parts of the world. Indians who are able to arrange admission only to smaller American universities may, like American graduates of these institutions, find it just as hard to get jobs, particularly when the US economy is floundering.

Although the actual education people have received is important in helping them enter the job market, uptodate familiarity with Western ideas, attitudes and career opportunities is also crucial, a point Ilsoo Kim (1981) has made in regard to the migration of Korean professionals. Mr. C, a Bombay-born construction engineer, credited his 'cosmopolitan' family and classmates with orienting him toward migration. Mr. H, whose story is presented above, remarked that he felt confident in looking for work in the US because he had already worked in India for a firm with American-style management techniques. That job came to him largely because of his education at a management school with an American-style curriculum. Both men were describing upper-middle-class Indian environments where foreign migration and its employment demands are common subjects of discussion and the latest shifts in the overseas job market are keenly followed. This is also the social group in which essentially Western ideas of personal fulfilment through professional employment are common, and migration to the West is seen as a route to such fulfilment. Such people are well aware of the moment when engineers become a glut on the US job market and precisely what kinds of computing or genetics are now in vogue. If they use the migration strategy of enrolling in an American college prior to seeking employment certification, sophisticates know that not all American colleges are equal in reputation and prestige. They insist on the top foreign universities—Indian and are well-enough prepared to gain admission. In contrast, people less wealthy or well-connected also have less accurate information about the workings of a foreign education and employment market within their social networks and less access once they arrive here. They may flounder for several years after arrival until (if lucky) they are befriended by somebody who can help and advise. The narratives of many Indian immigrant businessmen focus in great intensity and detail on the critical moment they finally met somebody able to give them concrete advice in advancing their careers here.

The obvious advantage of class is entrepreneurial capital. Virtually all those who have made it in business in the US have done so because they are part of social networks with access to large amounts of capital. For some, particularly those from traditional merchant families, financing is routinely supplied by the extended family in India which will eventually profit from the overseas establishment. For people without this kind of support system, capital may come from the savings of professionally-employed friends and relatives in India, in other immigrant locales such as the Middle East, or in the US. One New York advertising executive described laughingly how a friend had launched a business venture in the 1970s by getting six former classmates, also working in New York, to each lend him $500: 'We all had Visa and Mastercard. That was the first thing we all applied for [when we got our first jobs]. He asked us to each charge $250 against each card, then we just all prayed he could repay us before the bills came due.' Much of Indian immigrant socializing in New York involves a search for contacts who can finance business ventures, or for promising entrepreneurs in whose businesses one can invest. Indian friends and acquaintances remark that they have only to express a casual interest in forming a company to be besieged with phone calls from would-be investment partners. In this web of overlapping investments, credit-worthiness is judged informally but sharply. Those who come from well-known families, those known to have had first-rate educations, and those with prior work experience in 'good' firms are the most favoured.

The less affluent, although they too yearn to open their own businesses, are excluded from such networking. People who work long hours in others' shops or restaurants complain that they cannot attend community events, the receptions and large parties where contacts are made. They charge that the major immigrant organizations are dominated by rich people who disdain them. Certainly many of the public functions are expensive dinners, dances and fund-raisers held in suburban locations difficult to reach without a car. The poorer and less successful immigrants can hardly expect to join such organizations or to help shape their agendas, let alone make use of the informal contacts they offer. Much of this exclusion also bars the poorer members of the community from participating in such symbolic affirmations of Indian identity as concerts, dance recitals and dance dramas. For the less affluent there are instead free entertainments such as the India Day parade in Manhattan, and a Diwali street fair in Queens.[5] In terms of entrepreneurship, although some poorer immigrants do eventually manage to move from employee status to proprietors of their own small businesses, usually retail shops, they have more trouble amassing the capital, rely heavily on family labour and have less of a financial cushion against failure. In doing so they are replicating a classic US pattern of immigrant small-business formation.

Political implications of Indo-American community identity

One of the effects of Indian immigrants' insistence on their successful middle-class image has been to shape their political participation. People who are politically active complain that their fellow Indians are politically apathetic. Many Indians still feel that the best avenue to success in US society is for the group to 'keep quiet, don't attract attention'. Certainly there are few issues which have mobilized the community as a whole. Lobbying around the inclusion of Asian Indians as a separate category in the census, or around the Simpson-Mazzoli immigration bill have briefly engaged the entire community but have also caused unease because such campaigns necessarily emphasized Indians' minority or immigrant status. On a more long-term basis there are efforts to win greater US government support for India (and less favour to Pakistan), an effort that has occasionally brought the Indian community to support right-wing politicians. In general the leadership of the Indian immigrant community is politically conservative,[6] thanks to its commercial orientation, firm belief in an individualistic, self-help ethos and fear of non-white minorities.

Since Indians do not generally see themselves as other immigrants, because immigration itself is not problematized in their view of the world, and because there is a stern denial of internal social problems, they have not been particularly interested in seeking social service programmes or support as other immigrant groups have done. Indian parents will lobby for advanced computer training in public schools but will often reject ESL classes or bilingual classes for their children. Community leaders tend to share the view of middle America that social welfare policies encourage shiftlessness and dependence. For similar reasons Indians have not sought to form alliances with other ethnic groups. In the late 1980s, for instance, Chinese and Koreans in the New York area took tentative steps toward a pan-Asian political alliance because both groups felt victimized by a largely unrecognized racial discrimination. Indians were not interested in such an alliance, making it clear that they felt they had little in common with other Asian migrants.

Because Indians in the US have tended to conflate the categories of race and class, blatantly racial attacks, such as the 1987 dotbuster attacks in New Jersey or attacks on Long Island, have left the community frightened and bewildered (see Sethi 1993). The New Jersey incidents in particular forced many affluent Indians in the New York City area to confront for the first time the reality of racial hostility. People were obliged to recognize that some sectors of American society see them as outsiders, both foreign and non-white, despite their professed middle-class self-identification. The situation in New Jersey was further complicated by the fact that some of the Indian victims were a distinctly unprosperous group of marginal small shopkeepers, service and factory workers living and working in decayed working-class areas, in close proximity with African-Americans, Hispanics and poor whites.[7] The Indian community's political response to the situation was slow. When protest rallies were eventually organized, there was great hesitation in accepting the support of African-American activists, who identified a familiar scenario of racist attack and official inaction and advised protest and agitation in the civil rights tradition. Among the Indians who did campaign for protection and better police investigation of the crimes, there was an eventual split along class lines.

The most recent evidence of Indian-American conservatism is tied initially to Indian, not US, politics. The ferociously right-wing Bharatiya Janata Party, responsible along with various fascist groupings in India for the destruction of the Ayodhya mosque and pogroms against Indian Muslims, has been doing intensive propaganda work and fund-raising among Indian immigrants in the US,

Britain and Canada. The BJP, adept at tailoring its appeal to its audience, has brought to uneasy overseas Indian immigrants a message of renewal in Hindu identity. To a generation covertly unsure of its place in these new societies, the BJP message of cultural revitalization and religious renewal has seemed comforting, true and ultimately harmless. Unfortunately it is not harmless, since the heart of the BJP's Indian political programme is anti-Muslim racism and a reactionary social programme that seeks to reassert caste stratification and the subjugation of women. And as the world becomes increasingly unified into a single political arena, the implications of this social movement will not be confined to India's borders.

CONCLUSION

I began this essay by noting that immigrants shape new identities for themselves, both individual identities and the identities by which they constitute ethnic groups and communities. Yet new identities are never inscribed on a wholly blank slate. Pre-existing social relationships, importantly those of class, impose constraints on how people can remake themselves and filter how they experience their new lives. Immigrants from South Asia come from highly class stratified societies, and they move into new societies which are differently stratified on the basis of class and increasingly on the basis of race. Immigrants then have to negotiate where they fit in, individually and collectively.

For the Indo-American community I have pointed to the importance of class-based ideologies. An elite immigrant leadership defines the group almost entirely in terms of economic success and economic integration into the American upper-middle professional and entrepreneurial classes. This formulation obscures certain aspects of Indian immigrant reality; social scientists need to be cautious in appropriating this emic model uncritically.

One problem with this model is that it mistakes economic integration for cultural assimilation. Another is that it ignores the implications of internal class stratification within the immigrant community. While some Indian-Americans become extremely wealthy via high-paid professions and/or business, others settle into the hard-pressed lower-middle class and still others have become part of an exploited immigrant labour force—a structural position which links the experiences of these poorly-paid Indians with the experiences of many other recent immigrant groups. This economic polarization partially caused by the restructuring of the US economy (Sassen-Koob 1989: 61; Leonard 1997: 76-85) needs more careful consideration; it also emphasizes the need for a comparative approach when studying South Asian immigration.

Adherence to the model of universal professional success advocated by Indian immigrant leaders, combined with many social scientists' penchant for examining each ethnic group in isolation, serves to obscure the location of South Asians within the increasingly complex racial/ethnic configuration of the United States. As neighbours, students, employers, or potential economic competitors South Asians are forced to interact with other ethnic groups, not just with a generalized 'American culture'. For the Indian community this conceptual blurring of class/ethnic/racial categories has political consequences in terms of its inability to make political alliances with other ethnic and immigrant groups, to react effectively to prejudice and discrimination or to demand legitimate kinds of governmental support. It also makes the group vulnerable to various kinds of right-wing political ideology emanating both from US and from South Asian society.

I have argued here for is a more detailed analytic focus on class and labour force participation in the study of South Asian immigrants. We need to look at both the kinds of resources people bring with them, which are as much class-based as cultural, and at class differentiation which occurs, and is sometimes amplified, once people arrive here, depending on their location within the labour market. To do so will help us develop a far more nuanced vision of South Asian immigration. We may then be able to understand not just the kinds of jobs people get, but many of their subsequent experiences: where they can live, what kinds of friendships they can have, their tastes in music and food, where their children go to school—in sum their relationship with US society and with India itself.

NOTES

1. The research, funded by the Rockefeller Foundation programme on immigration, was carried out intensively from 1984-6, but has continued in less organized fashion since then. The data in this study were collected from immigrants born in India (in some cases in pre-Partition India), but

the generalizations are probably valid for other South Asian immigrants as well.

2. 'The community', the term by which Indian immigrant leaders refer to Asian Indians living in the United States, is itself ideologically laden and part of the attempt to construct a unified identity. I use it here as a convenient shorthand but am aware of its sometimes misleading implications. It is usually contrasted in private discourse with 'the Americans', meaning the non-Indian population. However, some Indians argue that Blacks and Hispanics and recent immigrants aren't really 'Americans' either.
3. Unattributed direct quotes are drawn from interviews.
4. Although none of the individuals whose case histories are given in this section can be said to be 'typical', they are chosen as representatives of certain groupings visible among the city's Indian entrepreneurs. The narratives of their work/life histories, taken directly from interview material, reflect the dichotomy they all invoke implicitly or explicitly between 'Indians' and 'Americans'. Thus, although I call this dichotomy into question elsewhere in the paper, I use it here as my informants did.
5. This kind of exploitation of fellow countrymen seems to exist throughout the Indian community. For instance Indian-trained doctors, waiting to take their US certifying exams, are taken on as poorly-paid or unpaid paramedics assisting certified Indian-American doctors with large practices.
6. Poverty also bars these immigrants from that ultimate affirmation of Indian identity and immigrant success, the holiday trip to India to visit relatives. Such trips are very expensive; in addition to airfare gifts are required. Even the well-to-do shudder at the prospective expense. As one man remarked, 'They know all the brand names, Nike and Jordache. We can't bring them just anything. It will cost us thousands.'
7. It was amusing to watch leaders in the Indian community who had supported New York City's race-baiting mayor, Edward Koch, scramble for new alignments when the mayoral election was won by a mildly liberal African-American, David Dinkins.
8. The 'dotbuster' attacks presented a complex mix of racial, class and ethnic hostilities. Although the original 'dotbusters' were white, many of the attacks, including one in which a young Indian professional man was beaten to death, were carried out by Hispanics or Blacks. Unemployed youths in the affected towns were quoted in the press as blaming Indians for being foreign, different, but also for their mysterious ability to set up small retail businesses in decaying areas. The sloppy police investigations and trials which followed some of the attacks never clarified the mix of racial, ethnic and class hostility involved. The most effective mobilization was that of the anti-racist group YAAR led by Indian-American students in New York City.

REFERENCES

Abraham, Thomas, 1984. 'Preface', in *North American Directory and Reference Guide of Asian Indian Businesses and Independent Professional Practitioners*, Thomas Abraham (ed.), New York: India Enterprises of the West Inc.

Bachu, Parminder, 1993. 'Identities Constructed and Reconstructed: Representations of Asian Women in Britain', in *Migrant Women, Crossing Boundaries and Changing Identities*, Gina Buijs (ed.), Oxford: Berg Publishers Ltd.

Bacon, Jean, 1996. *Life Lines, Community, Family and Assimilation Among Asian Indian Immigrants*, New York: Oxford University Press.

Fisher, Maxine P., 1980. *The Indians of New York City*, Columbia, Mo.: South Asia Books.

Gibson, Margaret, 1988. *Accommodation Without Assimilation: Sikh Immigrants in an American High School*, Ithaca, N.Y.: Cornell University Press.

Goode, Judith and Joanne Schneider, 1994. *Reshaping Ethnic and Racial Relations in Philadelphia, Immigrants in a Devided City*, Philadelphia: Temple University Press.

Helweg, Arthur W. and Usha M. Helweg, 1990. *An Immigrant Success Story, East Indians in America*, Philadelphia: University of Pennsylvania Press

Kim, Ilsoo, 1981. *The New Urban Immigrants, the Korean community in New York*, Princeton: Princeton University Press.

Kwong, Peter, 1987. *The New Chinatown*, New York: Hill and Wang.

La Brack, Bruce and Karen Leonard, 1984. 'Conflict and Compatibility in Punjabi-Mexican Immigrant Families in Rural California, 1915-1965', *Journal of Marriage and The Family* 46: 527-37.

Lamphere, Louise, 1992. 'Introduction: The Shaping of Diversity', in *Structuring Diversity, Ethnographic Perspectives on the New Immigration*, Louise Lamphere (ed.), Chicago: University of Chicago Press.

Leonard, Karen, 1988. 'Ethnicity Confounded: Punjabi Pioneers in California', in *Sikh History and Religion in the Twentieth Century*, Joseph T. O'Connell, Milton Israel, W.H. McLeod, Willard G. Oxtoby and J.S. Grewal (eds.), Toronto: South Asian Studies Papers 3, South Asian Studies, University of Toronto.

———, 1992. *Making Ethnic Choices, California's Punjabi Mexican Americans*, Philadelphia: Temple University Press.

———, 1997. *The South Asian Americans*, Westport, Conn.: Greenwood Press.

Lessinger, Johanna, 1990. 'Asian Indians in New York: Dreams and Despair in the Newsstand Business' in *New Asia*, special issue of *The Portable Lower East Side*, 7.2: 73-87.

———, 1992a. 'Investing Or Going Home? A Transnational Strategy Among Indian Immigrants in the United States', in *Towards A Transnational Perspective on Migration, Race, Class, Ethnicity and Nationalism Reconsidered,* Nina Glick Schiller, Linda Basch, Cristina Blanc-Szanton (eds.), New York: The New York Academy of Sciences.

———, 1992b. 'Nonresident Indian Investment and India's Drive for Industrial Modernization' in *Anthropology and the Global Factory,* Frances A. Rothstein and Michael L. Blim (eds.), New York: Bergin and Garvey.

———, 1995. *From the Ganges to the Hudson, Indian Immigrants in New York City,* Boston: Allyn and Bacon Publishers.

Mazumdar, Sucheta, 1989. 'Race and Racism: South Asians in the United States', in *Frontiers of Asian American Studies,* Gail Nomura, Russell Endo, Stephen Sunida and Russell Long (eds.), Pullman, Wash: Washington State University Press.

Motwani, Jagat K. and Jyoti Barot-Motwani, 1989. 'Introduction', in *Global Migration of Indians, Saga of Adventure, Enterprise, Identity and Integration,* Jagat Motwani and Jyoti Barot-Motwani (eds.), New York: Commemorative volume released by The First Global Convention of People of Indian Origin.

Omatsu, Glenn, 1994. 'The "Four Prisons" and the Movements of Liberation, Asian American Activism from the 1960s to the 1990s', in *The State of Asian America,* Karin Aguilar-San Juan (ed.), Boston: South End Press.

Portes, Alejandro and Ruben G. Rumbaut, 1990. *Immigrant America, A Portrait.* Berkeley: University of California Press

Robinson, Vaughan, 1990. 'Boom and gloom: the success and failure of South Asians in Britain', in *South Asians Overseas, Migration and Ethnicity,* Colin Clarke, Ceri Peach and Steven Vertovec (eds.), Cambridge: Cambridge University Press.

Saran, Parmatma, 1985. *The Asian Indian Experience in the United States.* Cambridge: Schenkman Publishing Co.

Sassen, Saskia, 1991. *The Global City, New York, London, Tokyo,* Princeton: Princeton University Press.

Sassen-Koob, Saskia, 1988. *The Mobility of Labor and Capital, a Study in International Investment and Labor Flow,* Cambridge: Cambridge University Press.

———, 1989. 'New York City's Informal Economy', in *The Informal Economy, Studies in Advanced and Less Developed Economies,* Alejandro Portes, Manuel Castells and Lauren A. Benton (eds.), Baltimore: Johns Hopkins University Press.

Schiller, Nina Glick, Linda Basch and Cristina Blanc-Szanton, 1992. Transnationalism: A New Analytical Framework for Understanding Migration' in *Towards A Transnational Perspective on Migration, Race, Class, Ethnicity and Nationalism Reconsidered,* Schiller, Basch, Blanc-

Szanton (eds.), New York: The New York Academy of Sciences.

Sethi, Rita Chaudhary, 1993. 'Smells like Racism, a Plan for Mobilizing Against Anti-Asian Bias', in *The State of Asian America,* Karin Aguilar-San Juan (ed.), Boston: South End Press.

Takaki, Ronald, 1989. *Strangers from a Different Shore, A History of Asian Americans,* Boston: Little Brown and Company.

Waldinger, Roger, 1995. 'The Other Side of Embeddedness: a case study of the interplay of economy and ethnicity', in *Ethical and Racial Studies* 18(3): 555-580.

Werbner, Pnina and Muhammad Anwar, 1991. *Black and Ethnic Leaderships, The Cultural Dimensions of Political Action*, London: Routledge.

Construction of Identity in Diaspora: Emigrants from Hyderabad, India

KAREN LEONARD

This is a report on a research project on emigrants from the former princely State of Hyderabad, in the context of migration (specifically diasporas) and the construction of identity. I report some preliminary research findings from Hyderabad itself, and form Pakistan, Great Britain, the United States, and Australia. Finally, I focus upon second generation marriages, again reporting preliminary national and cross-national findings but relating these back to the theoretical issues set out in the first part.

THE RESEARCH PROJECT

I have studied emigrants from Hyderabad, on the Deccan plateau of southern India, and compared the construction of personal and national identity in their places of settlement abroad. Most of the emigrants or their ancestors were once citizens of Hyderabad State, the largest princely state in India, ruled by the Nizam. Soon after Independence, the Indian Army took over the state in a 1948 'police action'. Some citizens left then for Pakistan, and later, people left for other destinations. These destinations now include strikingly different nations: Pakistan, Great Britain, Canada, the Middle Eastern Gulf States, the United States, and Australia. The project involves delineating the international networks that emigrants from Hyderabad have built, and the images they have retained and constructed of their Hyderabadi culture and homeland, and, most importantly, their constructions of personal and national identity in the Diaspora.

We begin with the assumption that there was a distinctive Hyderabadi culture back in the days of the Nizams. Variously labelled a cultural synthesis (the 'Deccani synthesis') or a plural society,[1] this was a Mughlai court culture in which Hindus, Parsis, Anglo-Indians, and others participated along with Muslims who dominated the ruling class. In spite of the presence of the British Resident after the mid-nineteenth century, Hyderabad's urban court culture basically continued to be a combination of the north Indian Mughal culture and that developed earlier by the Shia Muslim Deccani kingdoms. Persian was the state language until 1884, when it was changed to Urdu. Also, the Urdu spoken in Hyderabad drew upon its Deccani roots and was more informal than the standard Urdu of northern India. The elaborate courtesies and ceremonies characteristic of a fundamentally feudal society continued in Hyderabad into the 1940s.

Before the 1940s, Hyderabad was a destination for immigrants from elsewhere in South Asia. It was seen as a place of opportunity and culture, a magnet which drew talented people, both Muslims and Hindus, from British India. Indigenous or *mulki* Hyderabadis (countrymen) used to have to fend off *non-mulkis* (outsiders), particularly those who arrived in the late nineteenth century from Madras and North India.[2] Hyderabadis themselves seldom left their city even for a short time, and when they did everyone wept at the railway station; a daughter married off to Lucknow seemed to be going far, far away. Even the Anglo-Indians who served primarily in the Nizam's army felt that British India was a foreign country, that 'Indians' were distinct from and inferior to Hyderabadis.[3]

The Hyderabadi civic culture highly valued cosmopolitanism, secularism, courtesy, and love. Such a culture could presumably flourish in and contribute to other nations (and it is being redefined in interesting ways abroad). Most first generation Hyderabadi emigrants *do* retain a collective memory or myth about old Hyderabad, and this vision is an important part of their consciousness and sometimes of their collective life abroad. Thus one man in London, asked how far it was from Charing Cross to Hyderabad, said, placing his hand on his heart, 'Hyderabad is here, *Janaab* (sir).' Another London Hyderabadi sent a story titled '*Jism London me, Dil Hyderabad me*', or 'the body is in London, the heart in Hyderabad' to Hyderabad's leading Urdu newspaper, *Siyasat*, in 1991.[4]

A second assumption is that the concept of a diaspora is useful in the study of Hyderabadis abroad. The Hyderabadis have become a good example of transnationalism in many ways. They are moving from their homeland to other societies and linking at least two societies as they do so. They are extending their social fields, their knowledge and their networks, across national frontiers. Yet they are not the proletariat envisioned by many scholars of transnational migrants,[5] since most are highly educated professional people (save for many working in the Gulf), and they do not quite fit the definition of a diaspora community. Some scholars who move beyond the historic and narrow restriction of the term diaspora to the Jewish diaspora have used a very broad definition—'that segment of a people living outside the homeland'—and this the Hyderabadis fit. But a more meaningful definition has been proposed, citing six characteristics, at least several of which should be shared by members of communities which are minorities in their new settings, and may be argued that Indians in general do not quite fit the definition of a diaspora community.[6] The characteristics are: that members or their ancestors should have been dispersed from a center to two or more other regions; that members retain a collective memory of the original homeland; that they believe that they are not and perhaps cannot be fully accepted by the host society; that they regard the homeland as the true home to which they or their descendants should eventually return; that they are committed to the maintenance or restoration of the homeland; and last that they continue to relate to that homeland and define their collective consciousness importantly by that relationship.

I argue that Hyderabadis fit this definition of a diaspora community better than other Indians in some respects. Migrants from India (including Hyderabadis) have not 'been dispersed' but are leaving voluntarily. Yet the disproportionately Muslim participation in emigration from Hyderabad, while not the result of forcible expulsion, did and does stem to some extent from a loss of power and status in Hindu-majority India. Certainly Hyderabadi Muslims might have a smaller stake in the homeland than some other Indians, a feeling probably increased by the 1992 demolition of the Babri Masjid in Ayodhya and the general escalation of Hindu nationalism which has led to more frequent and serious communal riots in Hyderabad. Further, one can argue that those Hyderabadi Muslims who migrated to Pakistan and envisioned it as a homeland now feel less stake in Pakistan because of the continued treatment of migrants from India as refugees (Muhajirs) there, so from Pakistan too their emigration can be viewed as a diaspora. Certainly Hyderabadi emigrants retain a collective memory of the homeland, and most continue to relate to it and to define themselves with respect to that relationship. And for some Hyderabadi migrants there may be a conviction of non-acceptance by the host societies. But there is not really a myth of return among Hyderabadis. Despite the continued existence of Hyderabad city and at least some elements of Hyderabadi culture there, many Hyderabadis claim that they no longer have a homeland. Related to this is the fact that few Hyderabadis feel the homeland can be maintained or restored.

Because Hyderabadis do demonstrate several of the characteristics of a diaspora community, the descriptive and theoretical literature on that subject is useful in the comparative analysis. The empirical investigation of transnational immigrant networks[7] in this case contributes to the growing number of comparative migration, family, and community studies. I have been investigating changing patterns of household composition, education, occupation, and property-holding in Hyderabad and their extensions abroad. Marriage patterns are another focus: marriages are still almost universally arranged among emigrant Hyderabadis, and they are now spanning national boundaries to continue family, caste or religious preferences. These are all issues of contested authority with respect to generation and gender; they are all issues of great concern to the immigrant families in every place they are settling.

The new nations of settlement are significantly shaping Hyderabadi emigrant perceptions of their personal and national identity. Such perceptions are moulded by the historical constitution of personhood, through learning and social practice, as well as one's sense of personhood, of collectivity or community, and of struggle.[8] Emigrant definitions of the homeland and of 'Hyderabadi culture' are being transformed and diversified in ways that facilitate participation in the 'new homeland' societies, at least from the migrant's point of view. These diverging personal and national identities will be particularly noticeable for members of the second generation. Even for the immigrant first generation, many of those most nostalgic about Hyderabad have not lived or visited there for some time, and their images of it have been largely constructed 'in exile'. Thus we have the problem of 'invented' or 'imagined communities', of homelands reconstructed from afar.[9] In addition to the laws and cultures of the new homelands, factors like class, gender, religion, caste and ethnicity are determining how Hyderabadi culture is defined, practised, and transformed outside its native place.

The exploration of immigrant formulations of a cultural identity based on a lost homeland contributes to developing theories about cultural flexibility and the relationship between culture and nation.[10] Some Hyderabadis in Los Angeles, for example, express a commitment to a multi-ethnic/multi-cultural society, like that of old Hyderabad, they say, and this serves them well in the United States. Others, some among the Muslims, reject the old Hyderabadi culture, saying it privileged culture over religion. These immigrants go on to say that they are becoming real Muslims here, in the United States, that it gives them an opportunity to start over! The politics of exile[11] and of ethnic pluralism[12] are thus raised as emigrant views of their 'fit' with Pakistan, India, Great Britain, the United States, Australia, Saudi Arabia, Kuwait, and the UAE are compared and contrasted.

The research method is chiefly that of interviews, particularly the collection of oral 'experience narratives'[13] emphasizing family and individual migration experiences. I make limited use of questionnaires to help establish and evaluate the characteristics of the emigrants,[14] but the study relies on observations and interviews conducted at each place of settlement. At the time of writing this, I had interviewed persons in Hyderabad, London, the US (Chicago, Washington, Los Angeles, San Jose, New York, Houston, and Dallas), and Pakistan (Islamabad, Lahore, and Karachi). Pakistan has the first and perhaps still the largest emigrant community of Hyderabadis, and the Pakistani Hyderabadis are quite important since they are becoming 'twice migrants'.[15] They chose to leave Hyderabad in or shortly after 1948 but many are now choosing, they or their children, to leave Pakistan for the Western, secular democracies. Their identity is problematic as they have rejected Pakistan but find it difficult to lay claim to Hyderabad and India again.

PRELIMINARY FINDINGS

Even though emigration is now common, Hyderabad remains home to many relatives of these emigrants and constitutes a baseline for the research. I began by going to Hyderabad to see how the emigration looked from there and to confirm how much the city and its region have changed since 1948. The 'homeland' was broken up in 1956 into three newly-drawn 'linguistic states', causing major cultural discontinuities and re-orientations. Hyderabad city's new position as the capital of a Telugu-speaking state dominated by Hindu politicians from coastal Andhra has meant displacement of the old Urdu-based urban culture which linked members of the Nizam's ruling class and reflected the plural society of Hyderabad city. Tellingly, the celebration of the city's 400th birthday, the anniversary of its founding by the Qutb Shahis in the late sixteenth century, took place in Kuwait, Jiddah, London, Los Angeles, and other centers abroad, but really in Hyderabad.

Socio-political discontinuity has been great. The city's growth from 7,39,159 to 33,09,000 (from 1941 to 1991)[16] has meant the destruction of landmarks, the construction of new buildings and roads, and general chaos. The dramatic changes in Hyderabad occasion much lament among those who return for visits and justify non-return for others. Hyderabadi emigrants mention, most of all, the fact that in the old days the city was clean, and they go on to speak of the easy civility and gentle courtesy with which people treated each other. This view is tinged with some elitism: the face to face recognition and mutual respect of the families in the socio-political elite was a striking characteristic of the old urban culture. Even the children were known: one man told how, as a small child, he tried to give some coins to a street beggar but was rebuked because the amount was too small for one of his family! Such anecdotes testify to the small ruling class in the days of the Nizams.

People returning to visit Hyderabad also talk about the buildings, the fine old *devrhis* or palaces which have been torn down or become dilapidated, perhaps even divided into portions and rented out to unrelated families or government offices. Those who sold hurriedly after the Police Action to go to Pakistan tell of the changes in their former houses; having sold most often to Hindus from Andhra, they find striking changes in decoration when they return to visit. Everyone mentions the crowded streets and the pain of hearing Telugu instead of Urdu everywhere. Muslim young people in Hyderabad now speak Telugu readily and go to Telugu movies. Beloved institutions, such as St. George's Grammar School, Mahbubiyah Girls School, Nizam College, and Osmania University, have suffered from crowding and inadequate maintenance. A woman from Karachi regretted taking her daughter to see the Mahḇuḇiyah school buildings—her daughter simply does not believe her account of the school's former beauty, and her own happy memories have been displaced.

Second generation Hyderabadis abroad cheerfully told me that they had not liked Hyderabad at all when they visited it and saw no resemblance to the place described by their parents. Some who had not visited Hyderabad said they had the Taj at Agra and the historic buildings in Delhi on their list of places to visit ahead of Hyderabad. One organized visit of second generation youngsters from the United States was in some ways a disaster, filled with disappointed expectations and cultural misunderstandings: many of these youngsters said in the end that they preferred Bangalore.[17] The homeland has in effect disappeared, so transformed that it is unrecognizable.

With respect to immigration and emigrations, historic patterns have been reversed with a vengeance. The flow of emigrants from Hyderabad is increasingly steadily, although the preferred destinations have changed over time. Pakistan has been replaced by Great Britain, then by Canada and the United States, and most recently, perhaps, by Australia. These preferences have been conditioned by both political and economic factors: the earliest migrants to Pakistan were primarily middle class Muslims reacting to Indian incorporation of a state in which they had been part of the ruling class. These migrants expected to play (and did play) important political and economic roles in the newly-created Islamic and Urdu-using state of Pakistan, but later, dissatisfaction with opportunities in Pakistan sent them on. From India, too, highly-educated Hyderabadi emigrants began to leave for Great Britain and Canada, and, as immigration laws changed in the 1960s and 1970s, for the United States and Australia. (Australia is also receptive to working class migrants.)

The Gulf States have attracted both professional and working class Hyderabadis, chiefly but not entirely Muslims, but only on a short-term contract basis. While these migrants cannot settle there permanently, their remittances have produced a dramatic effect on the largely Muslim and impoverished old city of Hyderabad, reversing the socio-economic status of families in locality after locality and stimulating communal feelings against Muslims as well.[18]

The impact of emigration on families in Hyderabad has been disruptive. Almost every adult over fifty whom I encountered in 1991 had relatives, sometimes *all* children and grandchildren, overseas, and in more than one place too. Maintenance of ancestral property has become a problem: many fine old places are being replaced by condos, modern smaller units which can be rented out and reclaimed for brief visits by the young people residing overseas. In these condos, grandchildren being raised abroad can be protected from the inconveniences of the older houses; food can be prepared to suit their tastes and avoid illnesses allegedly caused by grandma's kitchen. Worse, maintenance of physical health and personal morale has become a major problem for the ageing parents left behind. Many lamented that they had never dreamed children sent abroad for education would stay there. Other parents were reluctant to admit that their children were not coming back, that they were in fact emigrants, but this reality underlay conversations about the absent sons and daughters. These adult children typically besieged their parents with phone calls and written requests to join them overseas, but such a move seemed difficult or undesirable to many oldsters. One painted a graphic picture of his son's lifestyle in the US: shower the night before, arise at 6 a.m., get into the car at 6:30 with a cup of coffee stashed by the gear shift, drive 45 miles through heavy freeway traffic to work—to the father, this was clearly not a desirable lifestyle. But even widows living alone with their servants in Hyderabad stated that in view of the greater opportunities for their children abroad they could hardly blame them for staying away.[19]

In London, preliminary findings stressed general concerns about the second generation which were shared by immigrants elsewhere. People feared their loss of the Urdu language and Hyderabadi culture and their acquisition of unwanted features of Western culture such as dating, lack of respect for elders and relatives, and 'extreme individualism'. But more particularly, those Hyderabadis settled in the UK shared a consciousness of ancestry and status, and a sense that Britain's class society was congenial to them. People commented that the British, like them, valued privacy, courtesy, and literary pursuits. Numerous descendants of the old Hyderabadi ruling class, both Muslim and Hindu, are settled in the United Kingdom (this includes the younger of the last Nizam's two grandsons, Prince Muffakham Jah, although he lives half the year in Hyderabad). These men dominate the national Hyderabad association. They had a strong sense of regret and responsibility that they, as culture-bearers of the former state of the Nizam, by leaving Hyderabad were destroying its distinctive culture. A poignant Urdu poem was recited to me by a Hyderabadi gentleman while we had tea at Selfridges. The last two lines, roughly translated, read: 'now the remaining remnants of the culture are few, we are the scattered history of the Deccan'.[20]

Many Hyderabadis in London contrasted themselves with the more recent and less well-born emigrants to the United States and elsewhere. But they were aware that those emigrants were doing quite well, not only economically but socially. There was some resentment that, while the class structure of Britain had failed to fully admit *them* at the level they deserved, less deserving immigrants in the newer destinations were benefitting from more open (or less knowledgeable) social structures. Yet among those who fiercely defended their own move to Britain, some were planning to send their own children to the newer destinations and perhaps would join them later on. Educational and marriage strategies for the children reflected those plans.

Australia, probably represents the greatest contrast to the United Kingdom as a Western destination, and interviews in London and Hyderabad provided some clues as to why this is so. Those going are both white collar and working class, and they are from all religious groups. Anglo-Indians in London and Hyderabad indicated that most of the Hyderabadi Anglo-Indians have finally ended up in Australia. The same consciousness of ancestry and class in the United Kingdom appreciated by other Hyderabadis worked against the Anglo-Indians when they went there. In Australia they have the freedom to be what they can. A letter from an Anglo-Indian in Australia featured a letterhead which read 'Jerry and Susie White (pseudonym), "Purani Haveli", followed by a street address . . .' Purani Haveli is one of the Nizam's royal palaces back in Hyderabad. In Hyderabad, I interviewed a migrant to Australia who was visiting his ageing parents. Wearing Bermuda shorts and thongs, he used words like mate, bloke, and bloody as he told me of the Deccan Blues cricket team on which he played. Reincarnated in Sydney, that famous Hyderabadi cricket team continues to bring together Anglo-Indians, Muslims, and Hindus for convivial gatherings featuring Hyderabadi food. The cricket network extends to parties, apparently, as my friend mentioned a twenty-first birthday party he had attended, complete with disco band, for the daughter of a Muslim doctor and fellow cricketer.

In the United States, most Hyderabadis are in Chicago and east coast cities like New York and Washington, DC, and Hyderabad associations have sprung up in several places.[21] There are some 3,000 Hyderabadis in Los Angeles, and the Hyderabad Deccan Association of southern California celebrated the 400th anniversary of Hyderabad in November 1990 with a dinner. The entertainment emphasized old Hyderabad's famed multi-cultural society and was attended by about a thousand Hyderabadis. In the areas of major settlement, there is a continuous round of Hyderabadi events, weddings, birthday parties, and *mushairas* (Urdu poetry recitations). Enjoyment of Urdu poetry is a major marker of Hyderabadi identity, and Hyderabadis clearly play a major role in sponsorship of *mushairas* in US cities. Urdu can also be a bridge to others from South Asia.[22] The Los Angeles branch of 'Urdu Markaz International', run by Hyderabadis, for its 1990 international *mushaira* brought poets not only from India and Pakistan, but from Great Britain, Sweden, and Canada Poets living in the United States performed as well. In Chicago, Urdu *mushairas* seem to be run through old Aligarhian networks, albeit dominated by Hyderabadis, and a recent one with the Bosnia crisis as theme added poems written in English, Arabic, Croatian and Bosnian.

In contrast to events and organizations which emphasize the culture and spirit of old Hyderabad, the Osmania Medical Graduates Association, dominated by Telugu-speakers but with significant participation by Urdu-speakers and/or Muslims, is undertaking a project which emphasizes the 'American' culture and spirit from which they have benefitted after immigration. SHARE (Science Health Allied Research Education) Medical Care, founded in 1982, is establishing a new teaching hospital just outside Secunderabad, one which will exemplify not just the technology but the energy and productivity typical of immigrants to the US.[23] Yet another tack has been taken by Indian Muslims based in Chicago, who have formed an organization to invest in the elementary school education of rural Muslims throughout India. The majority of its leaders are Hyderabadi (and old Aligarhian) and represent an alternative to the tendency of the Chicago Hyderabad Foundation to support elite college level institutions back in Hyderabad.[24]

Although Hyderabad society was quite secular and prided itself upon friendships across religious and linguistic lines, religious identity has clearly become more exclusive and more significant in the diaspora. Many Hyderabadis in the United States have become quite active in Islamic institutions and activities, and their salutation is not the familiar *adab arz* of Hyderabad but *salam aleikum*. Some Muslims in the US have rejected 'Hyderabadi culture' and talk about reforming their lifestyle to root out eclectic, non-Islamic customs. For example, at weddings, they have cut out some of the joking rituals involving women, terming them 'Hindu' and superstitious. (Although, as one husband told me this, another slant on this reform emerged as his wife amplified, 'yes, we used to do that because we women got together so seldom; now we can see each other more, we all drive, we just get in the car and go'.) The same husband and wife told me that they were quite prepared to give up the Urdu literary heritage, because the religious heritage was more important and English was quite adequate for the transmission of Islam. They voice the view expressed by many Muslims that Islam is a universal religion, opposed to regional cultures and not based in any one soil; it is to be understood and taught only in its ideal form (according to the Koran and *Hadith*, or traditions).

The culture versus religion issue is present in many Hyderabad associations, since Muslim dominance of the membership leads to confusion of the secular and religious elements in Hyderabadi culture. This is especially true in those associations which began informally when families gathered together to commemorate Id. Some secular Muslims and non-Muslim Hyderabadis claim that the associations are too Islamic, and do not have enough non-Muslim members. National origin is yet another factor creating divisiveness: some Los Angeles Hyderabadi Hindus say that the association there is dominated by Pakistani Hyderabadis and therefore they do not join it.

The generational factor is also very important in the various Hyderabad associations. Everywhere the associations are eager to attract the second generation, but despite 'youth awards' and much rhetoric, they have not been very successful. Sometimes the second generation of Hyderabadi Muslims has become more orthodox overseas (both in the UK and the US) and is more attracted to Muslim organizations. Perhaps this is because of a loss of competence in Urdu language and literature, the core of Hyderabadi culture as it has been defined in the past and a predominantly secular tradition. However, the young people can and do read about Islam in English, and reading about religion and culture, rather than experiencing it firsthand in the homeland, is how the second generation is learning about its heritage. Also, Muslims constitute a clearly identifiable and important minority group in the UK and the US. Islam is or will soon be the second largest religion in the United States,[25] and the term 'Muslim American' has been coined to bridge differences of national origin for political coalitions. For Muslim members of the second generation, Islam bridges the gulf between India and Pakistan still felt keenly by the parental generation, representing an alternative and/or reinforcement to the pan-ethnic Asian American identification being forged on many American campuses.

Ironically, while Hyderabadi Muslims from India may be becoming more Muslim in the Diaspora, those who went to Pakistan, people presumably motivated by a strong commitment to Islam, are viewed by the Hyderabadis from India as highly materialistic, no longer representative of the finest of Indian Muslim culture. Pakistani Hyderabadis themselves feel that they have changed in Pakistan. They had to shed their gentle unassertive ways to compete for opportunities in the new nation, and more of them are in business than was true back in Hyderabad. But some experienced downward mobility as a result of their migration, and a few openly regretted leaving Hyderabad and India. These migrants experienced major disruptions in relationships with family and friends, disruptions for which they were responsible and which they find hard to heal. While at first Pakistani Hyderabadis found it easy to revisit their homeland, the 1965 and 1971 wars between India and Pakistan produced tighter regulations, and even correspondence between relatives in the two countries ceased in some instances.

When Hyderabadis from India and Pakistan did encounter each other, when Pakistani relatives visited Hyderabad or, more typically, people met in a third country, many of the anecdotes about these encounters graphically expressed distance and a sense of loss. One Pakistani Hyderabadi told of visiting Hyderabadi relatives who had migrated to Toronto: there he met sixteen members of his family of whose existence he had been totally unaware, since they had been born in Hyderabad after he stopped writing to relatives there. An Indian Hyderabadi in California said that there was really no term such as 'Pakistani Hyderabadi', one politely called them 'our cousins from Hyderabad', since one did not know about or want to refer to their life in Pakistan. Hyderabadis from Pakistan coming back to Hyderabad for visits were often resented for their critical perspective. They were said to see through 'Western eyes', overlooking the human warmth which still distinguishes Hyderabad, to judge it as economically deprived. A Hyderabadi in Pakistan told of the pleasure with which he received Hindu friends from Hyderabad who made a point of visiting Pakistan; Indians apparently feel freer to travel in that direction than Pakistanis to go the other, though there are plenty of visitors in both directions. Another Pakistani Hyderabadi said he would never return to Hyderabad, he felt ashamed to show his face there because Muslim friends who had stayed had done quite well and everybody, Muslim and Hindu alike, asked him why he had left, why he had felt he had to leave. He had no answer for them.[26]

The extent to which old school and work bonds between Hyderabadis over the age of sixty have continued to command loyalties and friendships across national boundaries is striking, bringing Muslims, Kayasths, Gujaratis, Reddys, and Goswamis together in India or Pakistan or third countries for visits or the marriages of their children. These networks are misleadingly referred to as 'family' ties by those who participate in them, but it is doubtful that they will be continued by members of the next generation, who are no longer socialized in local educational institutions or work settings with others of Hyderabadi ancestry. What will replace them remains to be seen in each location; while some immigrants are revisioning Hyderabadi culture as a 'backpack culture', a portable culture which can be taken anywhere,[27] the infrequent Hyderabad association meetings are probably not enough to bind the members of the second generation to Hyderabadi culture and to each other. The older people, recognizing that the second generation is losing command of that language, hopefully say that Hyderabadi culture may not even depend upon continuing knowledge of Urdu. But it will certainly depend upon continuing ties of friendship and marriage, and therefore marriages being made across national boundaries and in the new homelands take on heightened significance.

HYDERABADI MARRIAGES IN CROSS-NATIONAL CONTEXTS

A Hyderabadi Hindu immigrant to California told me that, brought up in old Hyderabad as he was, in the Hyderabadi culture of the Nizam's days before the 1948 incorporation of the state into India, his boyhood dreams were always of a Mughal princess. It is likely that, when they came to the *jalwa* part of the Hyderabadi Muslim marriage ceremony—this is when, after the *nikah* or official part of the ceremony, the bride and groom sit side by side holding an open Koran with a mirror on one page, and, after reading a verse, look in the mirror and see each other[28]—many young men from old Hyderabad hoped to see a Mughal princess. But today, the dreams of Hyderabadi young people and the actual brides and grooms they confront in what has become a transnational marriage market are less easily imagined. Who stands in the place of the Mughal princess or prince for young members of the diaspora communities today?

A review of the marriages made by Hyderabadi emigrants themselves shows that while some of the earliest first generation migrants married non-Hyderabadis, by and large the marriages of the first generation of migrants were arranged in India or Pakistan and these migrants would like to arrange the marriages of their children in the traditional way, regardless of national context.

The first Hyderabadis to go abroad went to Pakistan and Britain. Whole families migrated to Pakistan, but many young single men went too, especially those who had been politically active in the militantly Muslim Ittehad ul Muslimen/Razakars just before the Police Action and who felt they had no future in India. Some of these young men returned to Hyderabad for brides in the years before the 1965 war, but there was some inter-marriage with other Pakistanis from the start. This happened partly because some families were badly split over the issue of Pakistan; the relatives who stayed in Hyderabad no longer felt obligated to those who left, obligated to supply a cousin or otherwise assist them in finding a spouse. These inter-marriages were seldom with Sindhis (the majority group in the Karachi area, where most Hyderabadis were settling) but were with other Urdu-speakers, often other migrants from India: Pathan, UP, Kashmiri, and Punjabi Muslims. Yet the Hyderabadis did not think of themselves as Muhajirs or refugees—'how could we be refugees, coming to our homeland', one said—and they identified themselves primarily as Muslims and Pakistanis.[29] There are such large numbers of ex-Hyderabadis in Pakistan that more than half of the second generation marriages are being arranged within that community, but other marriages are acceptable and increasingly common. The real issue seems to be whether or not to settle one's children in Pakistan.

Young Hyderabadi men, Muslim and non-Muslim, also went to the UK, not as immigrants initially but to study,[30] and some were already married. In the 1950s many stayed on to work and sent for their wives; others married English or European women and stayed on. As the bachelor society changed to a family one, an informal Hyderabad association was formed, sometimes debating whether or not to admit non-Hyderabadi spouses; as the size of the Hyderabadi community in England grew, attention shifted to the second generation and the importance of socializing its members to be Hyderabadis and arranging their marriages.

Those Hyderabadis first to go to the US, in the 1950s and 60s, went as single men, students. There was a strong tendency to marry out, with other Indians or Christian Americans, and their children did not trouble much about religion and are also marrying out. There are many such instances among both Hindus and Muslims, but this early pattern is being swamped by the large numbers of post-1965 South Asian immigrants who are trying hard to maintain their community identities and endogamous marriage networks.

In Pakistan, the UK, and the US, most parents are arranging the second generation marriages, bridging national boundaries to continue family, caste, or religious preferences. Sometimes endogamy is being redefined, by occupation (there are so many couples where both man and wife are doctors) or by 'ethnicity' (by which Hyderabadi [Indian] or Pakistani Hyderabadi is meant). These arranged marriages are still *family* strategies, emphasizing the parents' dominance and wisdom and the malleability and dependence of members of the second generation. Parents may arrange their children's marriages according to where they themselves want to reside in old age, taking into consideration immigration and citizenship laws and the various health systems, particularly with respect to geriatric care, in the different nations.[31] While there are sufficient numbers of Hyderabadi immigrants in all three countries for marriages to be arranged entirely within each immigrant community, all three continue to arrange marriages with partners from India; since there has been a sizeable secondary migration of Hyderabadis from Pakistan to both the UK and the US, these 'twice migrants' (Bhachu's phrase) marry back to Pakistan rather than India.

Making transnational marriages does present problems. People are quite conscious of the different contexts in which second generation Hyderabadis are being raised, of the differently con-textualized identities of the young people. Cousin marriages (practised primarily by Muslims), marriages essentially within family cultures,[32] could perhaps overcome these differences, it was felt, and perhaps girls raised in Hyderabad or Pakistan could adjust themselves across cultures. Brides brought up and educated in Hyderabad are especially desired. 'American-raised wives are a disaster, they won't sacrifice to those Hyderabad men the way an Indian-brought-up woman will do', I was told, and, 'girls brought up in Pakistan in a modern way will adjust themselves anywhere.' One man referred to the sending of US-raised girls back to Hyderabad as 'not a relocation, but a rehabilitation' of them! When Hyderabad boys have married girls raised in the UK or the US, sometimes divorces have resulted, and parents considering such marriages are warned against them by well-meaning friends.

In fact, few Hyderabadis have brought brides back to South Asia from the Western democracies; the trend is overwhelmingly the other way. Given the demand, young women in Hyderabad have been able to set some conditions. 'Girls in the market' in Hyderabad fall into two different age groups: girls between twenty-two and twenty-four,[33] and twenty-seven and twenty-eight. The latter are, at their own insistence, getting higher degrees and sometimes putting in some career years before marriage; this new trend pertains to both Hindus and Muslims. Among the younger women, the degrees most in demand (by their parents and the parents of bride-seekers) are Computer Science, English, and, among Muslims, Islamic Studies.

Hyderabadi young women worry about marrying boys raised in the Western countries. Boys raised in the US, particularly, may already have girl friends.[34] Friends exist who married, migrated, and then found they were in second place. In one case, the young woman divorced and came home to Hyderabad; another friend divorced and stayed there, unwilling to burden her parents and confident of making a life for herself. To guard against the possibility of divorce, relatives are relied upon, if not as potential spouses at least as go-betweens who have the family interest at heart; even this does not prevent tragedies.[35]

Migration abroad can result in striking upward mobility, and marriages made subsequently seek to confirm the new status. One thinks of the nearly impossible task of a Muslim artisan family in the old city of Hyderabad with a talented son, a boy who took an advanced science degree at a prestigeous US university and now works in a well-paid US government job. Ready to marry, he wants an educated girl. But the gulf between him and his parents is wide—they do not speak or read English, and they live in their workshop in a crowded area near the Char Minar. They anxiously distribute a xerox of their son's resume to their wealthy women clients and are looking for a nice house in the suburbs to rent and pass off as their residence, should a suitable prospect turn up.

The case above also illustrates another point about perceived social distance in the transnational marriage networks. Hyderabadis say it is easier to make marriages between Hyderabad and the UK than between Hyderabad and the US, because the standard of life in the UK is lower and South Asians are more segregated there; in the US the higher standard of life and greater integration with Americans means a wider gulf between the ways of life.[36] The former colonial relationship, the demographic profile (residential clustering and a higher proportion of working class immigrants), and the recent impact of the Salman Rushdie affair have clearly produced greater social distance, a worsening of race relations, in Britain, which has affected Hyderabadis along with many others from the Middle East and South Asia. The second generation in the US is said to be Americanizing rapidly, much faster than the second generation in Britain is becoming British, so marriages between Hyderabad and Britain have a better chance of success.

But in both Britain and the US, the children are losing their identity as Hyderabadis, according to their parents. One must take one's children 'back to Hyderabad and stay in relatives' homes, not in a hotel, immersing them in the life of Hyderabad', one London father said, 'or they won't be Hyderabadi at all.' A Hindu Hyderabadi woman, asked if her Texas grandchildren were Hyderabadi in any respect, said in despair, 'Hyderabadi, they aren't even Indian!' And a short story in the British Urdu Society journal *Hayat-i-Nau* expresses the worst parental fear: the father is waiting up for his adolescent daughter, having kept his family in Britain despite his wife's worries about Western culture leading the children astray. When the daughter finally comes home in the wee hours, dazed, drunk, with her blouse torn, she is annoyed to see him waiting up and announces that she wants her own apartment.[37]

But sending one's daughter back to Hyderabad as a bride is not necessarily a wise strategy. One woman raised in the UK talked at length about her problems when at twenty she married into Hyderabad. Her parents originally meant to retire to Hyderabad in their later years; now, they are less certain, concerned about the law and order situation there. But their daughter is settled there, with three children, her hair grown long by order of her mother-in-law and her barely serviceable Urdu considerably improved.[38]

The positions of Hyderabadi women in the diaspora are pivotal and have often been strengthened significantly within and through marriages abroad.[39] Women play important economic roles in many of the immigrant families, typically working either at home or outside after the children become older. Women can also use the transnational migration pattern to further their educational goals, secure the spouse they want, or develop personal autonomy after a divorce or widowhood. Some Hyderabadi women sought degrees or jobs abroad and then carried through with a love marriage denied them at home; their partners also secured places abroad, in advance or simultaneously. And sometimes after divorce or early widowhood abroad, Hyderabadi women have chosen to stay overseas and become self-supporting. Far from the advice and control of family members, some have remarried partners of their own choosing. The possibilities for autonomy vary with community size and household circumstances, and as parents and parents-in-law and other relatives become more frequent visitors to the immigrants these possibilities decrease.

But the first generation is still in charge in the immigrant communities, and its task has become easier over the decades. The family reunification features of immigration laws have brought reinforcements, and visiting back and forth has also become easier. India now gives a five-year visa to Non-Resident Indians and has liberalized its tax laws; first generation immigrants routinely send their parents tickets and money for visits to the UK, Canada, the US, and other places. The family is still the focus of activities.[40] An American married to a Hyderabadi reportedly said to her husband, 'I live in America, but you have more relatives here than I have!' Weddings are an oft-mentioned reason for international travel, and family members travel far and frequently to attend them.

While marriage networks have expanded worldwide—one Hyderabadi daughter has been married into a family settled in Singapore—parents still want to keep the networks narrow with respect to potential partners.[41] Nothing sharpens the Hyderabadi sense of collective identity like children approaching adolescence. The nearby Hyderabad association, or perhaps an Islamic, Hindu, or vernacular language organization, assumes new relevance. Few parents acknowledged that their children just might make their own choices, and fewer still thought that that would be all right. There are Hyderabad associations in many of the overseas settlements, with memberships always designated as family memberships, and great efforts are made to involve the youth.[42] But first generation men dominate association activities, and since they are also mainly Muslims, semi-purdah characterizes these activities. Dancing is not acceptable, for example. Thus hierarchies of age and gender bar any significant participation by young people.

According to some of the young people, Hyderabadis are more conservative than other emigrants from India, at least in the US, and perhaps they are more conservative than Hyderabadis in Hyderabad.

One US daughter sees her American girlfriends living with boys, her Indian girlfriends marrying partners of their own choice, and the Hyderabadi immigrant parents pushing for Hyderabadi partners. She thinks that almost all her Hyderabadi second generation friends are marrying within the community, in traditional five, seven, or eight day marriage ceremonies, while her cousins and girlfriends in Hyderabad are being allowed to date! Certainly the twice-migrants, those Hyderabadis who have moved on from Pakistan, also feel that recent Hyderabadi immigrants have a 'fossilized' culture in many ways. Yet recently in Hyderabad, a Muslim girl announced to her parents that she planned a marry a local Sikh, and it was their fault: they had not gone to Karachi, and there were no good Muslim boys left for her in Hyderabad.

While among both working class and professional Hyderabadi families everywhere, daughters are gladly given to men working at lucrative jobs in the Middle East,[43] there are few marriages between Pakistani and Indian Hyderabadis, either in South Asia or abroad (those between close relatives excepted). Pakistan seems to be a relatively isolated marriage market, possibly also a market for those who have failed to secure proposals elsewhere. One scenario was given: boys come to Pakistan from the US, spend one month looking, and want a fast wedding; the Pakistani parents worry, there is no time to check them out well enough. This can also be a problem with men from the Middle East: they are earning big money but may be only labourers. Girls marry them, go with them, spend a few days and then come back and get a divorce. Marriages within the Karachi Hyderabadi community, where families are *known*, are far less risky.[44] But typically big dowries are asked in Pakistan,[45] and there are limited economic opportunities and some fear of the political future.

People elsewhere do seem reluctant to marry sons or daughters into Pakistan. It is usually the boy's family which initiates marriage proposals, and when proposals from non-Hyderabadis in Pakistan come to Karachi they find no strong reasons for rejecting them and generally accept after sometime. But Pakistani Hyderabadis are sending sons out for education and marriage, and daughters out for marriage.[46] Thus marriages reflect more general migration strategies.

In Karachi there is no Hyderabad Association, no public proclamation of a collective identity within Pakistan.[47] Hyderabadis did have a strong sense of personal identity as Hyderabadis, and they had formed many old boy/old girl associations (Osmania, Mehbubiyah) and a Bahadur Yar Jung Academy (after the charismatic political leader who contributed to the growth of communal feelings and Muslim organizations in Hyderabad. He also contributed, by his influence on Jinnah, to the birth of Pakistan itself.). To organize as Hyderabadis would be to publicize their outsider status, and thus Hyderabadis have also generally refused to be conspicuous in the struggle of the Mujahirs, those who came from UP in India at Partition, for political power in Pakistan. They insist that they are Muslim first, Pakistani second, and Hyderabadi last.[48] Many Pakistani Hyderabadis have in fact been very much cut off from relatives and developments in Hyderabad. After the wars of 1965 and 1971, visits with family and friends have tended to take place in airports and in third countries. People from London, Toronto, or Phoenix on their way to weddings in Hyderabad may drop in to see old friends in Karachi, but the Pakistani friends usually have not been invited to those weddings.

Transnational marriages have brought about changes in Hyderabadi weddings, most obviously in the location of the weddings themselves. Until quite recently, Hyderabad and Karachi have been the preferred locations, not only because they are major sources of brides for the two transnational marriage networks and the residences of many relatives, but because of the availability of the necessary supplies and the relative inexpensiveness of holding weddings in the two South Asian cities. Hyderabad is better than Karachi in terms of cheapness and the availability of jewellery, saris, and other such items, but 'real' Hyderabadi weddings are proudly mounted in both places. Dowries in Pakistan range from Rs. 2 thousand to Rs. 2 lakh; they are said to be both less and more (for young men who are doctors) in Hyderabad. In both places, the bride's family is responsible for the *jhora/ghora*, the dress and the horse (on which the groom rides, often now a decorated car), and sometimes land and/or apartments are given to the bride as well.

In Pakistan, Hyderabadi weddings have influenced Pakistani culture more generally. No matter that one spouse is not Hyderabadi, the wedding itself must be, down to the last detail if possible. The sheer beauty and lavishness of the Hyderabadi bride's dress, the *khara dupatta,* and the complexity of the ceremonies inspire emulation. The Pakistani elite took up showy and expensive Hyderabadi wedding fashions and customs in the late 1960s (there is some movement away from them now because of their costliness). Some changes are being made, particularly by those Muslims who are becoming more Muslim in the diaspora by stripping away 'Hindu superstitutions',[49] but the putting on of the *kaliput*, the beaded necklace of the Hyderabadi married woman (associated with South Indian Hindus), was still part of a ceremony I saw in Pakistan.[50]

Although it is more costly and difficult to hold Hyderabadi weddings outside Hyderabad or Karachi, the balance is now tipping towards the countries where the young couples or their families are residing. Hyderabadis are flexible people, and, mastering national regulations about visas for fiancees, spouses, and wedding guests, they are scheduling weddings all over the world. A young man settled in Phoenix wanted to marry in Kuwait, where the bride and her family were living, but it was too difficult to secure visas for all the guests, so the wedding was held in Karachi. In another case, the bride and her family were in Hyderabad, but the groom's family wanted to hold the wedding in Ohio and New York, where most relatives on both sides are now residing. The US Immigration and Naturalization Service had to be persuaded to let the fiancee come in for her wedding.

There is a high level of commitment to weddings, as numerous instances of travel from California to Toronto, from Hyderabad to New Jersey, from Florida to Chicago, from London to Karachi, and so forth, attest. Childhood friends from Hyderabad are, in their later years, bridging religious and national boundaries for the sake of weddings, making numerous visits to relatives and friends around the world en route. Indian Hindus are travelling to Pakistan and Pakistani Muslims back to Hyderabad to attend the weddings of each others' children, although they appear to meet more often in New Jersey. If the parents are rich, they will fly guests over from Hyderabad and put them up in a hotel;[51] if their circumstances are more modest, they may settle for a reception back in Hyderabad, sending the bride and groom there to accomodate the Indian relatives and friends.

A South Asian wedding economy has developed recently in North America, so that weddings can be carried out in Chicago, Los Angeles, or Toronto more or less adequately.[52] The families in the diaspora try to reproduce Hyderabadi wedding dinners in every particular. In Los Angeles, there are two or three Hyderabadi cooks who are called upon for private parties and weddings, and *pukka*

Hyderabadi food is served with great pride. Sit-down dinners are the ideal, and serving trays and platters are brought over or copied as closely as possible. But in Karachi, buffet dinners prevail, and one wedding dinner featured Chinese food; in Hyderabad too the food can be eclectic.

Some of the desired wedding paraphernalia is much more expensive in the UK or the US or available only with great effort. For a California wedding family members went to great trouble to supply the jasmine garlands, flying the flowers in from the Philippines, having needles sent from Hyderabad, and spending hours making the garlands themselves. A well-to-do doctor allegedly spent $10,000 on flowers flown in from Hawaii, and one woman in the American midwest found local American craftsmen to make wooden tray covers typical of Hyderabad, painting the traditional designs on them herself.

Overseas weddings are held in hotels, community halls, or other hired meeting places, places less specialized than the 'function halls' of Hyderabad or the outdoor pavilions of Karachi, with their built-in *purdah* arrangements. In the US and London *purdah* has to be enforced by those attending, and men try to manage the space. In South Asia, women had their own spaces and their own ceremonies, but they are making new spaces for themselves at weddings in the West. At a Hyderabadi wedding in Los Angeles, men designated a rear section of the large room, a raised area with a railing around it, as the women's place to sit, but women were not satisfied to be seated so far from the platform where the *nikah* was to take place and immediately filtered down into the general seating area, taking over the front rows. Later the guests entered the dining room, where Mexican waiters had clearly been ordered to seat all the women on one side of the room and all the men on the other. One party, however, led by a young wife brought up in the US, insisted on sitting at a central table 'as a family', and this example was followed by many of the other guests. In another deviation from Hyderabadi custom which attracted comment, a *valima* (the dinner hosted by the groom's parents the night after the *nikah*) featured *bhangra* dancing initiated by Pakistani and/or Punjabi guests.

Guests at the Hyderabadi weddings range from 300 to 1,200 people, almost all of them other Hyderabadis. Since the parents have arranged the marriages, it is their friends who are the desired guests. At one wedding in Canada, when the bride was Canadian, the only

Canadian guests were the bride's parents. The young people have non-Hyderabadi friends, attend other types of weddings, and have a different sense of who might be invited, but they are not often able to influence the guest lists for their own weddings. A London conversation between a Muslim father and son showed me that, for the father, inclusion of the son's non-Hyderabadi friends was a startling new idea and one which probably could not be carried out, since the 300 guests they could afford to invite still would not include all the Hyderabadis who felt they should be invited![53]

Although the children are learning and practising new contextualized identities and are very different from their parents in many ways, most of them are not contesting the arrangement of their marriages. Their views about the spouse's country of origin and the country of their own future residence *are* being taken into account, however, and most often the preferences expressed are for their country of current residence. This means that the image of the Mughal princess is changing, as national markers become important to the young people and thus to their parents. Hyderabadi wedding customs and Hyderabadi Urdu serve everywhere as markers of a collective identity, but members of the second generation are less able to appreciate those things.[54] When they cannot share delightedly in Hyderabadi Urdu sayings at weddings, the image of the Mughal princess will recede further into the shadows—the images replacing her are still being formed.

NOTES

1. Karen Leonard, 'The Deccani Synthesis in Old Hyderabad: An Historiographic Essay', *Journal of the Pakistan Historical Society* (October 1973), 205-18; Syed Sirajuddin, 'Deccan-Hyderabadi Culture', unpublished mss., Hyderabad, 1990; Helen B. Butt, *The Composite Nature of Hyderabadi Culture*, Hyderabad: Intercultural Cooperation Hyderabad Chapter and Osmania University, 1990.
2. Some would restrict membership in the *mulki* category to those resident in the Deccan since the mid-eighteenth century (the Mughal conquest); others include immigrants to Hyderabad up to the late nineteenth century but bar those coming in after that. And some think that even people coming to Hyderabad today, after the demise of the state and its Urdu language Mughlai culture, can still become Hyderabadis through knowledge of Hyderabadi history and love of the city. For the pre-1948

period, see Karen Leonard, 'Mulki–non-Mulki Conflict in Hyderabad State', in *People, Princes and Paramount Power: Society and Politics in the Indian Princely States,* Robin Jeffrey (ed.), Oxford University Press, 1978.

3. Interviews in London, 1991 and 1993, with descendants of Anglo-Indian families long associated with the Nizam's military.
4. Aziz Ahmed, London, 1991, telling of the story he sent to *Siyasat* some years ago about the London Hyderabad organizations; Dr. Siddeshwar Raj Saxena, London, 1991 (he was then President of the Hyderabad Association there).
5. *Towards a Transnational Perspective on Migration: Race, Class, Ethnicity, and Nationalism Reconsidered,* Nina Glick Schiller, Linda Basch, and Cristina Blanc-Szanton (eds.), New York: The New York Academy of Sciences, 1992, especially the 'Introduction' by the editors.
6. William Safran, 'Diasporas in Modern Societies: Myths of Homeland and Return', *Diaspora* 1: 1 (Spring 1991), 83-99, especially the definition pp. 83-4 and 88-9.
7. Arjun Appadurai and Carol Breckenridge, 'Asian Indians in the United States: A Transnational Culture in the Making', paper presented in April, 1986, New York, Asia Society; Ulf Hannerz, 'The World in Creolisation', *Africa* 57: 4 (1987), 546-59.
8. Jean Lave, 'Historical Production of Persons in Practice', and Roger Rouse, 'Narrative, Social Space and Questions of Identity', both presented at the American Anthropological Association, Chicago, 1991.
9. *The Invention of Tradition,* Eric Hobsbawm and Terence Ranger (eds.), New York: Cambridge University Press, 1983; Benedict Anderson, *Imagined Communities: Reflections on the Origin and Spread of Nationalism,* London: Verso, 1983; Liisa Malkki, 'Context and Consciousness: Local Conditions for the Production of Historical and National Thought among Hutu Refugees in Tanzania', in *Nationalist Ideologies and the Production of National Cultures,* R. Fox (ed.), American Ethnological Society Monograph Series, 2, 1990.
10. See Gyan Prakash, 'Writing Post-Orientalist Histories of the Third World: Perspectives from Indian Historiography', *Comparative Studies in Society and History* 32: 2 (1990), 383-408; Renato Rosaldo, 'Ideology, Place, and People without Culture', *Cultural Anthropology* 3: 1 (February 1988), 77-87; and Dorothy Angell Rutherford, Bengalis in America: Relationship, Affect, Person, and Self, Ph.D. thesis, Anthropology, American University, 1984.
11. Zia Mohyeddin, 'Exile of a Non-Exile', in *Displaced Persons,* K.H. Peterson and A. Rutherford (eds.), Arhus, Denmark: SEKLOS, 1987.
12. Sally Falk Moore, 'The Production of Cultural Pluralism as a Process', *Public Culture* 1: 2 (1989), 26-48; James Ferguson and Akhil Gupta, 'Beyond 'Culture': Space, Identity, and the Politics of Difference',

Cultural Anthropology 7: 1 (February 1992), 6-23; John Higham, *Send These to Me: Immigrants in Urban America* (Baltimore: John Hopkins University Press, 1984, 2nd edition).

13. Samuel Schrager, 'What is Social in Oral History?' *International Journal of Oral History* 4: 2 (June 1983), 76-98; Virginia Yans-McLaughlin, 'Metaphors of Self in History: Subjectivity, Oral Narrative, and Immigration Studies', in *Immigration Reconsidered: History, Sociology, and Politics*, Virginia Yans-McLaughlin (ed.), New York: Oxford University Press, 1990, and Phyllis Pease Chock, 'The Irony of Stereotypes: Toward an Anthropology of Ethnicity', *Cultural Anthropology* 2: 3 (1987), 347-68.
14. I am working on questionnaires in collaboration with Prof. M.A. Muttalib, a retired Osmania University professor based in Red Hills, Hyderabad, where he works for MUAVIN (Mutual Assistance for Voluntary Organizations in India), and Los Angeles, California, where his three sons have settled.
15. Parminder Bhachu, *Twice Migrants*, New York: Tavistock, 1985.
16. D.G. Rama Rau, 'Urbanisation and Slums', in Helen B. Butt, *The Composite Nature of Hyderabadi-Culture*, Hyderabad: Intercultural Cooperation Hyderabad Chapter and Osmania University, 1990.
17. Interviews in Pakistan 1992, London and Chicago 1991.
18. Afzal Sharief, Socio-economic Transformation of the Kuwaiti Repatriates—a Case Study of Hyderabad, Ph.D. in Geography, Osmania University, 1994.
19. Interviews in Hydcrabad, 1991.
20. '*Baqi hai tamuddun ke namunee ab chand; bikree huii tarikh i Deccan bad, ham loog.*' Recited by Prince Mohsin Ali Khan, London, 1991.
21. There are Hyderabad associations in Chicago, Dallas/Fort Worth, Houston, Los Angeles, Washington DC, San Jose, Virginia, and Florida.
22. Thus in Britain, many Punjabis take part in Urdu activities, and Urdu is said to be the common language for Punjabis, Gujaratis, and other Indians in both the UK and the US.
23. About SHARE, Dr. Madhu Mohan, 1992 interview, Washington, DC.
24. About IIFA, Indo-Islamic Foundation of America, Dr. M.M. Farooqui 1993 interview, Chicago.
25. Raymond Williams, 'Asian Indian Muslims in the United States', in *Indian Muslims in North America*, Omar Khalidi (ed.), Watertown, Ma.: South Asia Press, 1991.
26. Ways of measuring the distance expressed between Indian and Pakistani Hyderabadis today include gathering quantitative data about participat-ion in marriage networks, association activities, and the like, and I am trying to make quantitative as well as qualitative statements about the diverging communities of Hyderabadis abroad.
27. This phrase was used by a young Hyderabadi and quoted by a leading

spokesperson, the last Nizam's grandson, Prince Muffakham Jah of Hyderabad and London: 11 October 1992, at the Los Angeles Hyderabad Association annual dinner, and in London, 20 December 1992, interview. The Prince, convenor of several Hyderabad associations in the US and Canada, occasionally attends functions as chief guest.

28. The *jalwa* is not included in the detailed discussion of Muslim wedding customs in Book Six of the Bihishti Zewar: Barbara Daly Metcalf, *Perfecting Women: Maulana Ashraf 'Ali Thanawi's Bihishti Zewar*, Berkeley: University of California Press, 1990. On the other hand, Peter Gaeffke points out that *jalwa* (the unveiling of the bride) has been part of the Deccani Muslim marriage ceremony since the seventeenth century: 'Muslim Marriage Rites in the 17th and in the 19th Century', in *Devotion Divine: Bhakti Traditions from the Regions of India,* Diana L. Eck and Francoise Mallison (eds.), Paris: Egbert Forsten/Groningen, 1991. Muslims in many other parts of India observe this too, terming it *arsi masaf* (conversation via a mirror); yet many Hyderabadis believe it is a feature special to them.
29. Interviews in Pakistan, Fall 1992.
30. The Nizam gave scholarships to young people for further education abroad.
31. While many emigrants urge their parents to settle with them overseas, the older people are often reluctant to do so; also, some of the migrants would really prefer to have their parents well cared for, by a sibling or responsible nursing personnel, in Hyderabad.
32. Sylvia Vatuk, 'The Cultural Construction of Shared Identity: A South Indian Muslim Family History', *Social Analysis* 28 (1990), 114-31.
33. In the UK, people mentioned only the 22-4 year old age group.
34. Note the lyrics by Apache Indian, a British Punjabi, for 'Arranged Marriage' on the album *No Reservation* (1992) where one of the last lines raises the question of how to treat the girl friend.
35. A Hyderabadi girl married a boy working in the US, thinking that because he had been born and educated in Hyderabad and because relatives made the arrangement, it would work out. But it did not, and she had to come home, divorce, and lose the *mehr*. After this disastrous 'foreign' marriage, however, a cousin in Hyderabad married her (re-marriage is easier for Muslim women).
36. There are some specific reasons for marriages to England too, as St. Georgians aver that they prefer to send their daughters there because of their own Anglophile leanings; many Hyderabadis feel that the British were allies, not enemies. St. George's Grammar School and the Nizam College Old Boys associations are strong in the UK.
37. Jitender Bilu, 'Bechatri Dhuup', *Hayat i-Nau* (May 1989), 162-9.
38. She was raised in Kent with few Hyderabadis nearby. All of her girl

friends were English, and she married first of all of them, after a visit back to Pakistan and Hyderabad, when a Hyderabadi family asked for her. When she married, she did not read Urdu at all. She loves her husband, but most of the Hyderabad girls she knew in the UK are happy to be married in the UK.

39. Karen Leonard, 'Ethnic Identity and Gender: South Asians in the United States', in *Ethnicity, Identity, and Migration,* Milton Israel and N.K. Wagle (eds.), Toronto: Center for South Asian Studies, University of Toronto, 1993.
40. One non-Indian wife of a Hyderabadi contrasted India to her country of birth (Turkey), saying that one's identity in India was based on family, not, as in Turkey, on the country. She remarked on how often Hyderabadis and other Indians took off to attend family events.
41. Thus some of the problems with the Associations, that they are dominated by Muslims and Sunni Muslims at that, are not problems at all when it comes to encouraging youth to meet potential mates.
42. The continuance of marriages with close relatives, among Muslims, is one way of avoiding risks. Among Anglo-Indian Hyderabadis also there seems to be a tendency to marry cousins. Members of Anglo-Indian families back in Hyderabad intermarried closely but this is breaking down with the second and third generations outside of Hyderabad.
43. Typically, such short term jobholders have ancestral property and/or the bulk of their relatives in Hyderabad. This produces a dilemma for the parents after some time, because the same families which have placed daughters in the Middle East have placed sons in the Western democracies, where they are settling and asking the parents to join them. But their daughters are tied to the husbands' families, to Hyderabad, forcing parents to choose between their sons and daughters (they are traditionally enjoined to live with their sons, yet there is often a tension with the daughter-in-law in the son's home).
44. Some are at a disadvantage in this Karachi marriage pool, those men who came alone and married non-Hyderabadi women or who have few or no other relatives in Pakistan. Women are needed to make the marriage arrangements, and if one's wife is a non-Hyderabadi or dead, or one has no relatives or has fought with the few in Pakistan, there can be problems. A son can be sent abroad and told to marry there.
45. The dowry situation is not helped by the fact that Punjabis also demand big dowries, and Punjabis are the most frequent marriage partners after other Hyderabadis.
46. One grandmother in Clifton, Karachi, happily entertains her three daughters and their children every autumn, daughters settled in Dubai, Los Angeles, and Istanbul. The daughters coordinate their visits home so that they and their children can be together. These young mothers

expressed some resentment at their ever-marginal status: in Pakistan they were Hyderabadis, and now overseas they are Pakistanis, in settings where those from India dominate.

47. I found that non-Hyderabadis in Pakistan were not always right about who was a Hyderabadi, mistaking people from Lucknow or Delhi for them, and even other Hyderabadis were not always certain. In Islamabad and Lahore, there were some cross-class marriages between members of the few Hyderabadi families there, and a reported early and short-lived Hyderabad Association in Lahore died when its founder moved to Karachi (where he did not activate it). Someone is now forming a Karachi Hyderabad Association. There was of course the Hyderabad Trust, holding certain resources, and at present best known for its renovated hospital in Karachi.
48. Interviews in Pakistan, 1992.
49. They try to adhere to the seven to eight-day ceremony, featuring the *mehndi, palki, naubat/shehnai*, the *chauthi*, and the *jalwa*, down to hiding the groom's shoes. However, at the *chauthi*, the dinner at the groom's home, more women go, taking candles at the *mehndi/* garlanding, a UP custom; they have given up the pelting of both sides with flowers. In the bride's trousseau, a *pandan* is necessary; Punjabis also have *pandans*, but not such fine ones, and not always in the trousseau.
50. A story about the *kaliput* reminds us of the part servants played in maintaining Hyderabadi culture—few servants came along to Pakistan from Hyderabad, and Pakistani servants do not *know*. One older woman, a first generation migrant from Hyderabad, broke her *kaliput*, and in great distress gave it to a servant for immediate repair, sitting down on a white sheet to abstain from food until its return. That, unfortunately, was not until the next day, because the servant forgot to do it until a day later, when she found her mistress still sitting on the sheet, not eating. (A similar problem exists back in Hyderabad, where Muslim servants from Kurnool, an Andhra district, do not know about Hyderabadi food and customs).
51. See Karen Leonard and Chandra Sekhar Tibrewal, 'Asian Indians in Southern California: Occupations and Ethnicity', in *Comparative Immigration and Entrepreneurship: Culture, Capital and Ethnic Networks*, Parminder Bhachu and Ivan Light (eds.), New Brunswick, N.J.: Transaction, 1993.
52. At a 1990 wedding in San Jose, some fifty guests from Hyderabad were put up at a hotel.
53. How different was the attitude of an Anglo-Indian father, himself a second generation immigrant to the UK who had married another second generation Anglo-Indian from the Punjab. Their daughter and her fiancee work for an airline and plan to be married at the Florida

Disney World theme park with some best friends in attendance; the parents are unlikely to go, much less family friends.

54. A good example of this came from graduates in Karachi of Mahbubiyah Women's College back in Hyderabad, giggling as they recounted the startled reaction of Pathan and Punjabi grooms in Pakistan when the order was given to *salaam* to older relatives with the words, *peet me mundi daloo*, 'shove your head/face in her stomach'.

Multiple-Migrants and Multiple Diasporas: Cultural Reproduction and Transformations among British Punjabi Women

PARMINDER BHACHU

The complexity of migration histories is emphasized in this paper to point to the multiple movements of direct, twice, and thrice migrant South Asian women. They possess different levels of 'migration skills' and command over the bureaucratic and economic processes required of them in order to operate successfully in their destination economies. This variation determines their cultural patterns, which are explored here through an examination of the wedding economy and the dowry system, especially in Britain. I argue for a complex conceptualization of the cultural locations of these multiply-migrant women, beyond the understanding of them as passive recipients of 'oppressive' cultures. I will also explore the construction and reconstruction of their ethnicity and diasporic identities to show that they are the products of their time and space in the migration process. Their marriage and dowry patterns are, like their identities, continuously negotiated and determined not by their migration histories but powerfully filtered through by the codes of their local and national cultures and also by their class positions. Equally important are the international forces which have a strong impact on their engagement with global economies and on their cultural patterns that are negotiated in these contexts. I want to point to the elastic and plastic nature of their ethnicities in the diaspora.

DIRECT, TWICE AND THRICE MIGRANT WOMEN

In previous work (Bhachu 1985, 1988, 1992) on the *twice migrant* British Asians who migrated from the Indian subcontinent to East Africa, thence to Britain in the late 1960s, I demonstrated that migrants and settlers have differential skills and experiences which are ultimately reflected in their destination economies in cultural reproduction, in economic participation rates, and in the varying speeds with which the infrastructures of their communities are established.

Experienced settlers, two- and three-times migrant women (in the British and US contexts respectively) possess considerable expertise in the management of their minority status, in the reconstruction of their ethnicities, and in the negotiation of their cultural systems. Their communities migrated from rural India in the latter part of the nineteenth century to East Africa where they established defined urban East African Asian identities. From Africa, they migrated to metropolitan Britain in the late 1960s, after their jobs were Africanized. Many of them moved on again to the US, Australia, and other European countries in the 1980s and 1990s. As relatively prosperous twice migrants in Britain with great command over mainstream skills, in comparison with the less experienced migrants, they also occupy separate class as well as caste positions and maintain exclusive marriage and community circuits. These are precisely some of the people who migrated a third time, to the US. They were able to enhance their already considerable migration skills initiated and developed in Africa, established and refined in Britain, and further reproduced very efficiently in the US and elsewhere.

Those who have emigrated more than once possess very powerful communications networks which have been greatly facilitated and enhanced by global communications. Their command over Western bureaucratic skills and the English language has given them considerable expertise at reproducing their cultural bases and community infrastructures in a range of countries. Such a scenario is in complete contrast to that of the less 'culturally and ethnically skilled' direct migrants, who are often characterized by home-orientation and 'a myth of return'. An important consequence of the latter characteristic is that the resources they generate in their new residences are frequently remitted to a country of origin where their positive (or for that matter negative) reference groups and status hierarchies lie. Unlike direct migrants, for whom migration especially in the initial stages is frequently a temporary economically-orientated move, for these people migration is not a sojourn but a move to settle. They aim to stay and keep their capital and resources with them. For these multiple migrants, the phases of settlement, from initial bachelor all-male households to the later reconstitution of their communities through family unification, often many years later, are greatly telescoped. They move as three-generational family units, or are united with their families within a year or two of settlement. Their communities possess a balanced age profile unlike younger, first-time migrants.

This pattern of migration involving a series of moves is widely applicable to a whole range of groups in the US, for example the Vietnamese, Armenians and Iranians. It also applies to migrants in Canada, Australia, New Zealand, Europe and Japan. Such migrants become transnational people with established international, national, and local connections. These features are critical to the reproduction of their cultural bases and ethnicities and to their engagement with the economies and polities of their countries of settlement. In all these processes migrant women are the key actors.

FEMALE ECONOMIC ACTIVITY AND THE RECENT LABOUR MARKET

The new cultural forms are analysed here by examining the consumption patterns, as viewed through the wedding economy in which the women play a much more significant economic and cultural role as a result of migration. This wedding gift exchange system has been elaborated since migration especially as a result of women's entry into the wage labour market in Britain. Their earnings go into it. There is greater control over cash by young Asians than ever before, due to their more active engagement with the British economy as wage earners. This is obvious from some of the recent labour figures. It has existed as long as the Indian presence in Britain (Bhachu 1988, 1991, 1993, 1994).

Contrary to the stereotype, many Asian women actively engage with the British economy. In certain cases they have higher economic activity rates than locally born, indigenous white women. The consequences of this for ethnic entrepreneurship are explored elsewhere (Westwood and Bhachu 1988), though they are also critical to the elaboration of the wedding economy.

For example, a higher proportion of Afro-Caribbean and non-Muslim women, including Sikh women, are in the labour market in full time employment than white women born in the UK who are economically active. Of women between 25-44, 66 per cent of white, indigenous origin are economically active as are 77 per cent of West Indian origin, 62 per cent of Indian origin, and only 17 per cent of Pakistani/Bangladeshi origin. (These latter categories constitute mostly first time migrant women from the subcontinent.) The rather low officially recorded figure for Pakistani/Bangladeshi women does not capture the paid homework/home sewing done by Muslim women (Brah 1987: 41). The reasons for the considerably lower rates of entry into wage labour by Pakistani and Bangladeshi women are not clear and need further research. In the case of Bangladeshi women, they are certainly amongst the last group of South Asians to reconstitute their families by joining their husbands in Britain in the 1970s, a number of whom had migrated twenty or thirty years ago. They have come mostly from rural areas and occupy a different class position from that of the experienced and highly metropolitan East African Asian women.

However, the class position of Pakistani Muslim women is really complex. There are many women from metropolitan Pakistan who occupy a range of class groups and whose engagement in the wage labour market is likely to differ from rural direct migrants. It is also possible that they have labour histories of much less involvement in the market than the twice and thrice migrant women, though Muslim women of the latter category (and there are many of them) may have shared labour participation rates. However, there are many queries to be made of the low officially recorded figure of Pakistani/Bangladeshi economic activity. Islamic religious idealogies, especially, as played out in the 1980s also must have a considerable impact on the construction of what are considered to be 'masculine' and 'feminine' roles.

Twice migrant East African Asian women have higher rates at 69 per cent than both indigenous white women and the directly migrant Indian and Pakistani women (Employment Gazette 1987). This is a product of their urban experiences in formal employment sectors in Africa, in comparison to the mainly rural background of the majority of the directly migrant women from the subcontinent, and also to the continuation of the employment trends established prior to migration from metropolitan Africa to metropolitan Britain. For example, the number of Asian women employees in Kenya had risen from 600 in 1948, to 3,750 in 1962, then comprising 10 per cent of the total Asian labour force in that country (Ghai 1965: 95). By 1967, this had risen to 18 per cent (Ghai 1970). This period coincides with the most intense Asian migration to Britain from Africa after the Africanization. This was very different from the directly migrant women's experiences, most of whom came either from rural areas or from places where there were fewer opportunities for female waged employment, or from traditions in which salaried work for women was discouraged.

The differences between white and Asian women in managerial and professional groups are slight, in fact proportionately the same in the case of the twice and thrice migrant East African Asian women: 7 per cent for white women, 7 per cent for African Asian women and 1 per cent for West Indian women (Brown-Policy Studies Institute Survey 1984: 198). As Sheila Allen (1987: 182) points out, 'The difference in types of jobs and earnings found among black and white women are much less than those found among men. There are proportionately almost as many Asian women in professional, employer to management sectors (6 per cent) as white women (7 per cent) and the percentage of white women in unskilled jobs at 11 per cent is higher than either West Indian (7 per cent) or Asian women (2 per cent).' The implications of this greater overlap between women's earnings and jobs, is that their expenditure and consumption patterns are also more likely to share a common ground—regardless of ethnicity and class—than that of men, who are much more unequally distributed.

There are significant regional differences in the economic participation rates of Asian women depending on the opportunity structures. Until the recent recession which has hit the South East of Britain particularly badly, this region was characterized by very high rates of economic activity and lower unemployment rates, a situation applicable to whites and blacks alike. Over half the Indian population and three-fifths of the East African Asian population is based in the South East of Britain (especially in London), in comparison to 31 per cent of white people. Thus, there are considerable differences in the number of economically active women (and men) in the South East in full time employment and elsewhere in Britain (Employment Gazette 1988). Also in the South East, there are many more Asian women in white collar/clerical and managerial/professional jobs than anywhere else. There was an increasing amount of salaried employment for Indian women in the Midlands in the late 1980s filling in the jobs created by the mushrooming 'anorak industry', the rapid growth of the clothing manufacturing sectors. There are significant regional differences in the economic niches and employment opportunities of British Asian women.

It should by now be clear that the labour market profile is much more complex than presented in most literature on Asian women. They are more widely distributed in a range of economic niches and employment structures than I have actually outlined here. Their occupational profile is, therefore, determined by local economies and the opportunity structures in them. However, I want to reiterate that this should not detract from their predominantly working class locations. It should equally be emphasized that they also occupy a number of non-working class sectors, that they have had different histories of participation in the labour market prior to settlement in Britain and also since settlement in different regional economies in Britain. These varied economic histories are further played out in the reinterpretation and reproduction of the wedding gift exchange system in the diaspora.

MIGRANT AND DIASPORA DOWRIES

It is to this important role of cultural reproduction by British Punjabi Sikh women that I will focus, in particular, on the impact of the economic on the cultural, and on the formulation of identities which are responsive to the local cultures in which they are situated. I want to explore this variation through an examination of one facet of culture which reflects British consumption styles and class locations and encodes reflections of their identities. Dowries—*daajs*—which represent the legitimate and recognized property rights of women and have been elaborated since migration to Britain, as a result of women having begun to take jobs. Young Punjabi women play a central role. Dowry is a cultural idiom that has always been relevant to them and has seen significant inflation. Its commoditization is determined by the specificities of class and sub-cultural consumption styles, especially in the 1980s and 1990s, when most of the brides and younger Punjabi women are either locally born or have arrived as youngsters, and are therefore educated and socialized to regional and local British cultures.

There is a close similarity between Punjabi Sikh notions of dowries—*daajs*—and those of high status north Indians. The high caste status north Indian ideology of *kanyadaan*, the pure gift of a maiden for which no return is expected and the accompanying *stridhanam*—exclusive female property—in the form of movable goods, presented as pre-mortem inheritance from the patrimony (Goody 1975: 1), applies to Punjabi Sikhs regardless of their place within the migration chain and the diaspora. The four components of the *daaj*: clothes and gold for the bride, household goods including utensils, furniture, linen, quilts, kitchen gadgets, crockery, and consumer items, and gifts for the in-laws are always presented.

These four major components, constituting the external framework of *daajs,* have remained stable with migration and diasporic cultural reproduction, though there have been internal content changes in the gifts presented. The designation of wedding gifts has also shifted according to the various phases of migration and in response to structural changes in the household and power relations within families. For example, the *daaj* presented in India and Africa in the early days was designated for the mother-in-law, the most powerful and senior female decision-maker of expenditure and consumption choices within the domestic domain. She could redistribute it, often using it for further gift-giving. The brides of this period had direct control only of their *muklawa* received from their parents at the consummation of the marriage, years after the wedding ceremony and the presentation of the original *daaj.* It was after this rite-de-passage that thc bridc took up permanent residence in her affinal home.

By now, among the twice and thrice migrant women in Britain and the US, *daaj* has acquired a different meaning. Affinal gifts had been separated so that the mother-in-law had little control over bridal clothing items and gold, though household goods in the 1950s and 1960s were often absorbed into extended family households which were then quite prevalent. By this stage, bridal control over her sectors of the *daaj* increased, undermining the redistributive authority of the mother-in-law. This development coincides with the early *daaj* of brides whose marriages had taken place in India where the joint family system was stronger, and families were less fragmented by migration. None of these Indian-married brides had their own households, though an increasing number were establishing nuclear residences in urban Africa, a trend reproduced by the vast majority of twice and thrice migrant brides in the since 1970 in Britain and in the US.

By the 1970s, the *daaj* in Britain, though not in Africa or India, contained fewer heavier household goods (like bedroom, dining, and sitting room furniture), because there has been an increase in expensive easily movable consumer items. There was around this time, a total separation of the affinal goods from those reserved for the bride. This trend began in the 1950s in Africa, and was the norm by the 1970s among twice migrant brides in Britain. This separation of affinal and bridal gifts partly reflected household changes but were also a consequence of changing residential patterns, which facilitated the establishment of a separate residence immediately after marriage. The quite dramatic increase in the earning powers of brides in Britain catalyzed this process, being contributors to house mortgage payments and sometimes initiators of house purchases. Also, since they helped to make the *daaj*, they also expected to control it. Few before 1970 could exercise such options. Their command over resources, if any, was considerably lower.

Thus, changes in the structure and control of the *daaj* is a product of the migration process. Of course, some of these trends are also obvious among urban households in India and are a consequence of changing female employment patterns and residential patterns. In East Africa, these processes had already begun, although they have become more firmly established in Britain, as families have separated into nuclear units and as women have become cash contributors to family incomes. Also, the erosion of control by the affine over the redistribution of bridal gifts and of the residential choices of couples, is a result of the increased couple-orientation as opposed to kinship group-orientation of earlier times. Spouse-selection criteria have also shifted to take more account of suitability and personal demands rather than extended family expectations (see Bhachu 1985).

To summarize: Dowries which consisted of minimal items both for the bride and her affinal kin in the earlier phases have escalated since the 1970s. The three components of the *daaj*—the elaborate traditional garments and some 'western' clothes, household goods including luxury consumer items and gold ornaments in the form of 'sets'—that are designated specifically for the bride, and the fourth component of gifts for the groom and his close kin are always adhered to rigidly for caste endogamous East African Asian marriages. Hence, the structure of the *daaj* has not changed over time, even though there have been internal changes in the items presented reflecting the move to urban Britain. The designation of the *daaj* has also shifted reflecting structural changes in the organization of the household and the various power relations within it. Migration, changing residential patterns and more working women in the diaspora have favoured the brides.

COMMODITIZED WEDDING ECONOMIES

The varied economic profile of British Asian women is reflected in their different positions in the class hierarchy and their various cultural and regional locations in Britain in the last decade, a period which has the most number of British-born or British-raised women. This regionality is reflected in the consumption and cultural styles that they adopt, even though patterns that emerge from London are the most influential because they are products dominant minority community. The wealth generated through their own relationship with the labour market is deployed and expended in accordance with their sub-class styles and related consumption values. These specificities are reflected in their marriages and dowries.

I present a brief summary of the escalation of the dowry system since migration to Britain, not so much to detail the process of elaboration within it (Bhachu 1985, 1986 and 1988), but to point to the significant inflation within it of those spheres that directly concern the brides. This elaboration of the dowry system is just one facet of the cultural and religious effervescence that has taken place amongst the Sikhs in Britain. I have discussed these processes elsewhere (Bhachu 1988 and 1991), in relation to the various phases of settlement in Britain, to highlight the important role of women as agents and catalyzers of cultural reproduction and as generators of symbolic capital (Andizan 1986: 265) for their communities.

The spheres within the wedding economy that have been most significantly inflated in Britain, especially since the late 1970s, concern the brides themselves. The wedding economy has been greatly elaborated. Inflation applies both to the ritual/wedding procedure and to the dowry, to which young brides are significant contributors. A consequence of their direct engagement with the wage economy is that they save for their own dowries even as the content of the *daaj* has remained highly conservative throughout the various migrations (Bhachu 1988, 1991).

For example, as mentioned above, dowries have increased from 11-21 clothing items in Africa, to anything from 21-51 items since 1970 in Britain and the US. Some of these are very high quality silk saris and prestigious designer clothes, and are accompanied by expensive Gucci and Bally shoes and bags, especially in the case of high-earning professional brides. The 'standard' East African Punjabi Sikh dowry of 21 clothing items and a whole range accompanying accessories and prestigious consumer items for the bride are always presented in Britain. This norm persists regardless of the standing of the families involved and has been further reproduced in Britain and the US. Twenty-one clothing items are commonly presented in the Indian subcontinent and Pakistan and among the diaspora Indians.

However, even though, a 21-item *daaj* constitutes the 'British/ American/East African Sikh' pattern, there are major qualitative differences in its content, according to the earning powers of the brides themselves. A bride who has not earned in her own right before marriage, invariably has a basic 21-item *daaj*, in comparison to the earning brides whose *daajs* are much more elaborate and voluminous. The latter *daajs* are characterized by the inclusion not only of higher quality garments and personal accessories but also a more vast range of consumer durables like china sets, silver cutlery, electronic music equipment and exclusive linen that the brides have themselves purchased from their own earnings and which they themselves are likely to utilize and also control.

In the late 1980s and early 1990s, British sub-cultural/regional styles have become are influential in the interpretation of not only the 'traditional' garments/goods/gifts but also of their class-encoded consumption patterns. There are *daajs* that are Sloane Rangerish in their interpretation reflecting the 'London S.W.1,3,5,/ Knightsbridge/ Sloane Square' consumption patterns of some of the high earning and professional brides, just as there are prestigious 'Designer Ethnic/European' *daajs*, the Middle/Lower Middle Class 'Oxford St. Marks and Spencerish/Mass Produced-Departmental Store' types, Working Class 'East Ender' types, provincial 'Liverpudlian Sikh' and 'Mancunian types'. Different regional styles are discernible. For example, a Midlands *daaj* is interpreted differently form those of London brides of an equivalent class group, despite the similarity in content and the persistence of the external framework. These regional patterns are also obvious from the marriage circuits—an informal metropolitan hypergamy—which operates in Britain. London girls tend not to marry outside London and the South East. If they are married out, in a majority of cases they move back to London to set up a nuclear family within a couple of years of marriage.

I have simplified a complex procedure mainly to point to the elaborations in the bridal spheres which have seen the most significant inflation. Punjabi Sikh women's increased command over productive resources and the translation of their wages into a cultural idiom which has existed for centuries and survived their two migrations from India to Africa and to Britain, and then to North America. Traditional structures have not only been reproduced, but also enhanced in the changed circumstances since their entry into the British labour market as wage earners.

Dowries in the last two decades are particularly reflective of the British sub-cultural/regional styles, especially in the interpretation of their 'traditional' ethnic garments. Dowries that are 'very London' emerge from the various areas and sub-cultures of the capital and according to the class positions occupied by the brides and their kin. Dowries reflect the various regional styles and cultures and dominant consumption choices of the areas in which the brides have been brought up as also the local cultures to which women have been socialized. They are, therefore, class- and region-coded consumption patterns of particular phases of settlement and migration and this is asserted in the content of the dowries. All this also applies to the identities and ethnicities negotiated and generated by these diaspora Asian women. They too have their specificities and activated differently according to the various contexts.

CONCLUSION: CULTURAL REPRODUCTION AND MULTIPLE MIGRATIONS

Twice and thrice migrant, indeed transnational women, interpret and reinterpret their cultural systems in the context of their local and national localities being the *cultural entrepreneurs* that they are in the multiple diasporas they occupy, internationally. By engaging with their cultural frameworks in the context of their local and national codes and the international forces that impact on women internationally, they transform them to manufacture *new cultural forms and diasporic spaces* which take from their ethnic traditions and which are continuously formulated in the context of their class and local cultures. Yet, there is little perception of these migrant women as active agents and as negotiators of their cultural values, which are frequently presented as non-negotiable entities enforced on them as passive victims by patriarchies and capitalist producers. Indeed, the latter agencies are powerful in determining their cultural patterns and cultural reproduction. However, these women also have agency which plays an important role in their choice of lifestyles, their role as innovators and originators of new cultural forms and new diasporic spaces. Their agency as actors in multiple migrations is one that is largely absent in the literature.

The assumptions in the literature are that the crucial determinants of identity and cultural base, especially in the context of migration and settlement, are the nurturing forces of a homeland culture (which at least in the early stages of migration and settlement provides cultural reinforcement), the maintenance of ethnic boundaries through the exclusionary forces of racism, confrontations that are said to lead to identities of resistance and defiance, and the desire of migrants/settlers/diaspora Asians to emulate and aspire to particular 'white' class cultures and their symbols. There is a great deal of emphasis on boundary maintenance and on the perpetuation of what are presented as clearly worked out, homogeneous and fixed cultural values. Importance is attached to the impact of rejection, racism and discrimination as the *fundamental forces* in structuring their identities and cultural locations in diaspora. In all this, ethnicity is presented as a thing that has fixed components and symbols and is considered to be the primary agent controlling and generating their various identities and migrant cultures. Indeed, all these are important social mechanisms in structuring their lives and in determining their life chances. However, my concern is that there are a number of other forces that are equally important in framing their experiences and for diasporic cultural reproduction.

These include international forces which have a strong impact on their engagement with global economies and on the cultural patterns they negotiate in local and international economies. Thus, particular ethnicities and identities are not stable, despite a common core of key fundamental religious and cultural values that constitute their cultural roots. They shift according to the forces that operate on them. In the case of direct, twice and thrice migrant women, these are not just products of confrontation and rejection, or wholesale transference of homeland culture, but emerge out of vibrant and changing cultures in which Asian women are situated in Europe and in international contexts over which they have *genuine unself-conscious command.*

REFERENCES

Allen, S., 1987. 'Gender, race and class in the 1980s', in *'Race' in Britain: Continuity and Change,* Charles Husband (ed.), London: Hutchinson.

Andizian, S., 1986. 'Women's Roles in Organizing Symbolic Life: Algerian Female Immigrants in France', in *International Migration: Female Experience*. New Jersey: Rowman and Allanheld.

Ballahatchet, K.A., 1980. *Race, Sex and Class Under the Raj: Imperial Attitudes and Policies and their Critics, 1793-1905,* London: Weidenfeld and Nicolson.

Bhachu, Parminder, 1985. *Twice Migrants: East African Sikh Settlers in Britain,* London and New York: Tavistock.

———, 1986. 'Work, Marriage and Dowry among East African Sikh Women in United Kingdom', in *International Migration: The Female Experience,* New Jersey: Rowman and Allanheld Publishers.

———, 1988. 'Home and work: Sikh women in Britain', in *Enterprising Women: Ethnicity, Economy and Gender Relations,* London and New York: Routledge.

———, 1988. 'Ethnicity and School Performance: A Comparative Study of Sikhs in Britain and the United States', in *Ethnic and Racial Studies,* 11.3: 239-62.

———, 1989. 'Ethnicity Constructed and Reconstructed: The Role of Sikh Women in Cultural Elaboration and Educational Processes in Britain', *Gender and Education* 3: 147-62.

———, 1991. 'The Dynamics of Educational Decision Making: A Comparative Study of Sikhs in Britain and the United States', in *Minority Status and Schooling.* New York: Garland Publishing, Inc.

———, 1991. 'Culture, Ethnicity and Class among Punjabi Sikh Women in 1990's Britain', *New Community* 17.3: 401-12.

———, 1993. 'Identities Constructed and Reconstructed: Representations of Asian Women in Britain', in *Migrant Women: Crossing Boundaries and Changing Identities,* Britain: Berg Publishers.

———, 1994. 'New Cultural Forms and Transnational South Asian Women: Culture, Class and Consumption among British Asian Women in the Diaspora', *Nation and Migration: The Politics of Space in the South Asian Diaspora,* Pennsylvania: University of Pennsylvania Press.

Brah, Avtar, 1987. 'Women of South Asian Origin in Britain: Issues and Concerns', *South Asia* 7.1: 39-53.

Brown, Colin, 1984. *Black and White Britain: The Third PSI Survey,* London: Heinemann.

———, 1987. *Ethnic Origin and Economic Status,* January, 18-29.

———, 1988. *Ethnic Origin and the Labor Market,* March, 164-77.

Ghai, Yash, 1965. *Portrait of a Minority: Asians In East Africa,* Nairobi: Oxford University Press.

Gilroy, Paul, 1987. *There Ain't No Black in The Union Jack: The Cultural Politics of Race and Nation,* London: Hutchinson.

Goody, J., 1985. 'Bridewealth and Dowry in Africa and Eurasia', *Bridewealth and Dowry,* Cambridge: Cambridge University Press.

Hall, Stuart, 1989. 'Minimal Selves', *Identity Documents*: ICA: 44-8.

Parmar, Pratibha, 1984. 'Gender, Race and Class: Asian Women in Resistance', in *The Empire Strikes Back: Race and Racism in '70's Britain,* London: Hutchinson.

Westwood, Sallie, 1988. 'Workers and Wives: Continuities and Discontinuities in the Lives of Gujarati Women', in *Enterprising Women.*

Hindu Gods in an American Landscape: The Sri Siva-Vishnu Temple in Suburban Washington, DC

JOANNE PUNZO WAGHORNE

A wooden 'country' mailbox, metal encased in wood, stands on the road in front of an archetypical suburban split-level house. Wrought iron letters read 'SSV Temple'. Behind this erstwhile symbol of American family life rise the ornate *vimanas* or spires of what devotees claim is the largest Hindu temple in the United States. The temple stands on fourteen acres of former Maryland farmland at the edge of the sprawling suburbs of the nation's capital. Its congregation comprises the first generation of a new wave of immigrants. Neither tired nor poor nor huddled masses, the technological and scientific elite of India began coming to the United States in the late 1960s and early 1970s when changes in the immigration laws removed odious restrictions against Asians. Unlike immigrants from the past who began their life in America far lower on the occupational hierarchy, these educated newcomers quickly prospered and chose to settle in the suburbs among their colleagues from major technological corporations, hospitals and universities. Thus the Sri Siva-Vishnu Temple is located on Cipriano Road, the local route to the NASA Goddard Space Center less than a mile away. It shares that same road with two churches. Just next door is another split-level used by a gospel study group. Another house, now used as a Hindu temple for those devoted more exclusively to Murugan, is in the vicinity. On Saturday mornings, East Asians, African-Americans, and Euro-Americans can be seen mowing their lawns. Lanham, Maryland thus remains a multi-ethnic and multi-racial area united only, it seems, by its middle-class ethos marked by good fences, good houses, and the good jobs that make home ownership a reality.

It is precisely this lack of an Indian neighbourhood—this seeming utter incongruity of the temple with its surroundings—that is so interesting. Indians around Washington have not settled in any one neighbourhood although Arlington and Silver Springs do have a larger proportion of South Asians than other areas. Very few Indian immigrants chose to live in 'the district' which seems reserved for the African and Hispanic American poor, or young professional European-Americans. For unlike earlier European immigrants, many of these recent arrivals left middle-class homes in the suburbs of larger Indian cities and chose to take up residence in areas with an already familiar middle-class ethos in the United States (Bhardwaj 1990). Many of their parents belonged to the English-speaking civil service or business community and were already mobile within India. The traditional ties that bound persons to places in India had been severed a generation earlier in the families of many of the new Indian-Americans. Many members of the Sri Siva-Vishnu Temple are, then, used to maintaining a sense of community and extended family without actual close physical proximity. Thus the community of devotees of the Sri Siva-Vishnu Temple stretches over the Washington area into regions within a day's driving distance, and includes members from as far away as the Research Triangle Park in North Carolina. The devotees also maintain contacts and share resources with members of other temples throughout the United States and with certain circles of temple priests and temple architects in India.

In many ways, the Sri Siva-Vishnu Temple is part of a network that creates a Hindu space defined neither by the old American ethnic neighbourhood model, nor by the pattern of very close community characteristic of traditional Indian villages and even Indian cities at the turn of the century. The model of little villages within a larger urban corporation characterized Indian cities until the mid-nineteenth century, when British residents of colonial port cities like Madras began to move their personal residences from the trading-cum-governmental centres to new garden suburbs. The rising middle-class Indians in Madras city, for example, began to build new neighbourhoods like their British overlords, but they always recreated an older Indian sense of space: a central temple surrounded by a combination of houses and shops. The Mylapore area of Madras is a perfect example of this older urban model that continues even today. Ironically, only after Independence in 1947 have Madrasis created purely residential suburbs in the American sense of bedroom communities. In the Indian context, the often quoted maxim—do not live where there is no temple—is taken seriously in the new suburbs which have seen the rise of small temples built by new multi-caste and multi-ethnic constituencies that are within residential neighbourhoods but no longer at their literal centre.

In the new American context, devotees of the Sri Siva-Vishnu Temple have built and now maintain a multi-million dollar temple complex that is even less the centre of a new neighbourhood than its Indian counterparts. They have moved one step beyond the Indian urban middle class. Their temple is not even contiguous to their residential neighborhood. The temple takes on even greater importance, then, as the only concrete embodiment of the community. Ironically, situated in a non-Hindu neighbourhood it nevertheless remains the focal point for a Hindu community with no clear edges except its own sprawling middle-class suburbanness.

Suburban areas such as Lanham, Maryland must not be ignored as an important environment for the definitions of a new sub/urban pluralism. New Hindu temples in Boston, Los Angeles, Pittsburgh, Chicago, and Nashville also rise up at the very edge of urban centres in the same way that new temples now complete the suburban landscape of Bangalore (Lutgendorf forthcoming), New Delhi, London (Knott 1987; Jackson 1981; Vertovec 1992; Nowikowski and Ward 1978/9), Singapore (Clothey 1992), and Durban (Mikula, Kearney and Harber 1982). Indeed, the same English-speaking and highly articulate architects, trained at government-sponsored schools of religious architecture in Mamallapuram outside of Madras city and in the famous temple city, Tirupati, in Andhra Pradesh, have provided designs and guided the construction of new temples in suburban India and the United States. Thus, the sacred homes built for these Hindu Gods of the American city are at the same time a part of what could be called global Hinduism, which in turn may be part of a larger emerging global culture. Recently termed 'diaspora' in a new journal of the same name, this 'world of crisscrossed economies, intersecting systems of meanings, and fragmented identities' is the great third force in the suburban world of the nation's capital.

Amid all this complexity stands the new Hindu temple as a symbol of what John Fenton (1988: 171) calls 'the process of becoming at home (having a *desh*, or place where one belongs) on the foreign soil of America'. Other scholars of contemporary temple-building in America verify the almost literal sense of the 'transplantation' of Hinduism on to the American soil (Clothey 1983) and of the process that makes God 'immediate; this land, holy' (Narayanan 1992: 18).

But amid this process of implantation—the ceremony to consecrate a Hindu temple creates strong analogies between planting a seed and 'planting' a temple—remain the shifting borders of modern life—the transfers and new assignments and career advances that necessitate continued mobility. The Hindu temple in America, then, remains the embodiment of a Hindu community and a mark of acceptance of the American soil; at the same time, this holy house cannot be so easily associated with a new stable group of people permanently tied to the land.

In *Space and Place*, Yi-Fu Tuan reminds his readers that 'the original inspiration for building a city was to consort with the gods'. There are few cities in India, no matter how industrialized, that do not have a plethora of temples, and the Hindu temple in many ways remains the best contemporary example of the ancient housing of the gods in those first Mesopotamian temple-cities. The Gods live in Hindu temples quite literally, embodied in iconic form and firmly fixed in a specific locality. The most common words for temple in classic Sanskrit texts, according to Stella Kramrisch, are *vimana* (measured out), and *prasada* (seat). Both words emphasize the fixing, seating, settling of the divine in a constructed abode (1976: 131-44). The most familiar contemporary words for 'temple' in both Sanskrit and vernacular languages translate as palace, house of God, place of God, abode of God. As S.S. Janaki puts it, 'synonyms like *alayam, mandiram* and *grha* are in a general way applicable to the dwelling place of both human beings and divinities' (1988: 122). The Indian city, then, continues as a place where humans and divine inhabitants share the same space—each in their own respective houses. Stella Kramrisch, in her now classic study of the Hindu temple, quotes texts which state that the installation of divine icons in temples should be made 'in forts; in auspicious cities, at the head of shop-lined streets' (1976: 5). And indeed in many of the still living temple cities of South India, the best shops are located on the four streets that surround the urban temple complex, the *mada* streets. Here the finest silk weaving, the best brass ware, and jewellery can be found.

That Hindus in America should begin to build temples near their home cities should not be surprising. Such temples would have the immediate effect of giving a jumble of shops, industrial sites, parks, and human homes the status of a *devasthanam*, a place of God. The temple-building activity of the particular group of diaspora Hindus in Lanham presents a paradox, however. Because temples 'fix' (literally the word *pratistha*) a divine image in one locality, temple building is associated with 'religion that binds people firmly to place' as Yi-Fu Tuan puts it. Tuan here invokes the axiom that 'Religion could either bind a people to a place or free them from it.' Tuan contrasts 'universal' religions with an 'omnipotent and omniscient' Gods with 'earthbound' deities that require permanent houses (1977: 152) and so sets up the association temples = rooted = bounded on the one hand, and placelessness = universality on the other. From this perspective, the temple-building activities of the highly mobile Hindu diaspora of suburban Washington seems quite unexpected. Here is a case of what can only be named by an oxymoron—shifting concreteness, unbounded finitude, universal particularity. The 'space' of the Sri Siva-Vishnu Temple exists somewhere between the concreteness of the traditional Hindu temple and the shifting space of the everywhere/nowhere/ everybody's/nobody's split-level world of the migrating international middle-class. Without acknowledging and understanding that conundrum, the *place*—defined both as space and as status—of the temple among Hindu Americans would be lost.

INSIDE/OUTSIDE: THE MODERN HINDU TEMPLE IN A SUBURBAN WORLD

The Sri Siva-Vishnu Temple sits at the very edge of the metropolis—literally, for the chain link fences in the backyards of an older development form its northern boundary. A strip of green separates this fence from the temple's parking lot with its present reminders of American car culture. On the temple's southern border is more of its own land backing on the yard of a neighbouring split-level which houses a Christian organization. The temple faces east, looking towards its virgin fourteen-acre plot, with Cipriano Road forming its western border. Across this road is an apartment complex that could be seen as it appeared on the weekend of 4 July 1991 when the second of a three-year cycle of consecration rituals occurred. The apartments formed an incongruous backdrop for several open crates, marked with an address in Tamilnadu, that held the sacred stone sculptures of the temple's major deities transported from the hands of their *silpis* (sculptors) to their new guardians in America. Several *silpis* had arrived from Madras to complete their installation in the temple as part of the five-day *mahakumbhabhishekam* rituals which would fully consecrate the images.

The temple on this 4 July 1991 weekend still lacked its exterior decoration, thus exposing the basic form of its architecture. The base unit is the traditional square, in this case 90 x 90 feet. The two stories, however, are very untraditional. The upper floor, which reaches ground level at the rear, houses the divine images; the lower story, which opens from the side to the parking lot in the front, contains a large auditorium for cultural performances, the dance and music that have long been part of Hindu temple activities. This central auditorium is ringed by a modern kitchen, rest rooms, classrooms, library, office and meeting rooms. On this day, families gathered in the auditorium, eating lunch while keeping an eye on the video monitor which carried every moment of the ongoing, five-day ritual in progress upstairs.

The Board of Trustees of this impressive religious institution takes great pride that this temple was designed by one of India's leading temple architects, Sri Ganapathi Sthapati. 'Sthapati' is a title borne by certain families who know and control a special set of sacred texts which give careful guidelines for the proper forms and methods of their work. Within these formal parameters, however, there is always latitude for change, provided the architect himself commands respect for his own knowledge and personal religiosity. Thus, because of its architect, devotees can rightly claim that this temple is thoroughly 'authentic' in spite of the considerable innovation that is apparent.

The most striking distinctions between this modern American temple and its older urban counterparts in India are its use of levels and its manner of enclosing space. The Kapaleeswara Temple, for example, in the Mylapore section of Madras not twenty miles from Mamallapuram, where Sri Ganapathi Sthapati works, has no basement. The idea of a basement would normally be unthinkable because the deities should always be in unbroken contact with the ground. During the consecration rituals, the stone images are literally glued to their base and the base firmly fixed into the temple floor and thus to the earth. When I asked Ganapathi Sthapati about this seeming unorthodox practice in building the temple in Lanham, he explained that under each of the images is a separate hollow pillar that is filled with dirt. From the basement level it looks like a supporting pillar but, in fact, theses hollow pillars permit each image the requisite contact with earth. The columns allow the temple to remain a pillar of orthodoxy and also have a basement!

In the Kapaleeswara Temple in Mylapore all functions occur at one ground level but not under one roof, as in the temple in Lanham. The Madras temple is actually a walled courtyard enclosing many smaller structures. Under the *mandapam*, the pillared pavilions, musicians often perform. There is no auditorium with a stage, but musicians perform close to the Gods in their holy sanctums. Musicians direct their music to the Gods which devotees only rightly overhear. Built onto the inner walls of the temple, the kitchens and the business offices carry on the temple's daily routine. Outside, the four surrounding streets are lined with shops but on festival days become the Gods' royal roads down which divine images proceed. Thus the Kapaleeswara Temple, like the Sri Siva-Vishnu Temple, provides space for music, daily office-keeping chores, and preparing the *prashad*. However, while the Sri Siva-Vishnu Temple divides these functions from the actual seats of the Gods in one two-storied building, the Kapaleeswara Temple remains a single-level complex.

Climatic differences alone cannot account for this change in architecture from walled compound to single structure. The design of the Sri Siva-Vishnu Temple openly articulates theological changes that have occurred in the transplanting of Indian gods to America. The community of devotees in the Washington area chose to construct a temple that would unite the two major Hindu traditions, Vaishnavism and Shaivism, 'under one roof' as one member of the board of trustees put it. Thus Siva and Vishnu, are each housed in their own shrines but within this single building. Other deities associated with each tradition have smaller shrines along the sides and the back of the first floor. A large shrine of Murugan is at the centre of the temple. The *vimana* (cupola) over his image seems to blossom out of the temple's roof. The *vimana* of other shrines are confined to the interior of the building. A member of the Board of Trustees explained that the temple was carefully designed to balance the two cosmic forces embodied in Siva and Vishnu. Thus, while the divine image of the powerful Durga rests on the north wall next to the Siva shrine, an image of the powerful Rama was to balance her power on the east next to Vishnu's shrine in the original plans. Now Hanuman stands in this place as a deity of dimensions expansive enough to balance the Goddess's own staggering force. These stone images of Durga and Hanuman were the first to be consecrated on 27-30 September 1990.

The choice of the divine occupants for these shrines were the result of much discussion by the trustees and the community of devotees here, and still remains in flux. I recently received notice of a proposal to raise $3,00,000 to construct a shrine to Ayyappa as 'an extension of the existing structure with the traditional eighteen steps'. Now the Board of Trustees announced that 'in response to the overwhelming desire of the devotees', it had decided to build a Sri Venkateeswara shrine as another extension to the present temple at the cost of $2,40,000. That addition was consecrated over Memorial Day weekend of 1993. These decisions to include certain images reflects the creation of what could be called a new American Hindu pantheon. This particular combination of deities would simply not have occurred previously in India (although such new eclectic temples are under construction in Madras). If this trend spreads in India, then it will be American Hindus who have created a new model for the mother country. The point is crucial. In suburban America all gods live in the same house.

The curious feature, however, of this great effort at unity within the diversity of Hinduism is the concomitant separation of sacred from secular in the use of two levels. Music, eating, office work, education are now 'downstairs' functions. Upstairs is reserved for the holy rituals and ceremonies. Further, no festival actually spills out into the streets of this quiet suburban neighbourhood. The Gods were carried in procession inside, around the first floor. During important rituals, like the recent consecration rites, the priests carry holy water in sacred pots around an outer promenade which forms a railed porch around the entire first floor, and opens out onto a grand staircase now leading down to the lower parking lot. Processions around this outer promenade are the only public display of Hindu rituals that Lanham, Maryland will normally see. The only God whose eyes turn to Cipriano Road is Ganesa, who can be seen looking out from his niche in the exterior wall. Ganesa, as the divine guardian of doors, is by his very nature a border-ward and thus looks out to the world. The other deities will live their lives, on the upper level, within these cinderblock walls. Dance and education will not be conducted in front of the very eye of the Gods as is the case in India; Hindu deities in America truly live in a split-level suburban world with its inside/outside, upstairs/downstairs dichotomies.

The transplantation of Hinduism to America in the case of the Sri Siva-Vishnu Temple is not just a matter of finding a home and feeling at home, as John Fenton so well describes it; it is a matter of building and maintaining a house. The crucial clue revealed in the design of the temple and its place on Cipriano Road is that ultimate marker of the American dream, home-ownership. In India, ancient temples were built and maintained by kings. During the colonial period, this royal function passed to the new British Government which created a system of temple trusts both independent of and yet part of the state governments—a system, much like the US federal reserve, which remains today. In modern India the very wealthy build temples and the state still has a hand in their maintenance and construction. Here the devotees own the temple in the form of a joint trust. Several members of the Board of Trustees pointed out that the model of administration by elected and appointed trustees supported by hundreds of individual contributions is new. They would agree with the way the chairman of the Board of a Hindu temple in Nashville described the situation: 'We found ourselves, a bunch of amateurs, trying to manage the complexities of a religious institution.' Through their Trustees, devotees pay the mortgage each month and all the other problems of home-ownership must be met without fail. But this house belongs to the whole community and marks the true rise of the middle-class Indian. For in owning a temple, the middle class has thrown down the rights of kings, the rights of the British Raj, and the rights of the state over such structures. Is it not a rare coincidence that as the fireworks blasted above Washington on 4 July 1991, the Sri Siva-Vishnu Temple was installing its gods!

But what does this phenomenon of home-ownership have to do with the issues of the universality and particularity of this Hindu temple? The point can be stated simply: The mobile middle class in the world now goes from house to house, not place to place! The temple stands amid other houses but is not in any serious way related to them except in one important fact—this suburban world allows such a temple to exist as a house among houses. Even the zoning laws in such areas recognize such Houses of God as residential and not commercial property. In this sense only such neutral areas that are not bounded neighbourhoods could so easily tolerate such diversity. The Indian community at the temple takes great care not to disturb its close neighbours and those whose houses border the temple. Devotees have invited their neighbours to participate in important activities and a few of these folks did drop by as good, but somewhat bewildered, neighbours.

Suburban land on the borders of the metropolitan area remains segmented into plots. Like their neighbours, the devotees of the Sri Siva-Vishnu do not bring their now private religious life out into the streets. It is carried on within the confines of their own religious castle—in a very middle-class sense of that term. Here is one structure that is to hold the new Hindu family in America under one roof, separate but equal with the other religions of America. The gods of India have a new home, a foothold on the western shore, a life beyond the borders of India but yet a life confined to a house. Is this not the quintessential characteristic of the suburban home, a family on the inside facing out, a patchwork quilt, a cut and paste world of multiculturalism that is stitched together by neighbourliness and good fences? And yet ,within the walls of each square lives a private world, a blue heaven, as the American old song goes, 'with a plot of, not a lot of, land'.

Thus as a house, the Sri Siva-Vishnu Temple becomes a very particular and concrete entity, but as a place Lanham, Maryland remains seemingly neutral—the location a plot on a surveyor's chart of streets and houses. But this America Hindu holy house also contains two levels. What are the upstairs and downstairs of this world? Certainly the downstairs is not in Lanham, Maryland, but it is also not in the orthodox upstairs where the priests imported from India do their holy work. Ultimately, the split-level world of suburban Washington provides an apt image for the cultural world of the affluent Indo-American community here. The Hindu–Indian cosmos in America is not a little India inside a very big America. In America, Indians live in a split-level universe that is at once 'traditional' above, but with a lower floor that is the space of the world wide modern middle-class family life—from which Indians originated but which is now enhanced by their move to America.

UPSTAIRS/DOWNSTAIRS—NEGOTIATING GENDER AND GENERATIONS

In an attractive folder introducing the temple to prospective donors, the temple lists its services as 'religious', 'cultural' and 'philosophical'. The category of religious is confined to the celebration of festivals, group-worship, the performance of weddings and other life-cycle rites and classes on 'Sanskrit, Vedas, and Hindu rituals'. In essence, the term 'religious' now belongs only to the ritual performances of the priests. These are the upstairs activities. Philosophical talks and discussions—the preaching activities of Hinduism—now belong downstairs with teaching activities such as summer camps for youth and adults, and even yoga classes, dance classes, and lessons in the various vernacular languages of India. Although such an upstairs/downstairs division of the temple reserving the word 'religion' for the upstairs is quite out of step with much Hindu tradition, the division makes sense in America. Sacred is not really divided from secular here, but middle-class family life has actually invaded what were once professional and priestly realms. The family is now on the lower floor of the temple. The middle-class world has been reconstructed within the temple as it has been within the house. These are not sanctuaries from America, because the suburban outside has been integrated into both floors of the temple as an Indo-American, not a Euro-American, phenomenon.

Take the case of dance. Until the early part of this century, dancers in India were temple servants who worked alongside the priests to provide ultimate comfort and pleasure to the gods embodied in the temple. A rigorous reform movement accused these *devadasis* of being nothing more than glorified prostitutes and corrupting the temple. They were soon expelled. But within two decades, Indians realized that they had thrown out part of their cultural heritage in the name of moral purity. Dance was revived outside the temple as an art to be cultivated by the daughters of the rising upper middle class. Dance still remains in performance halls in India but now in America once again it has returned to the temple. However, now it has taken on much the same place that ballet lessons have in the Euro-American home—a matter of family pride in their daughter's accomplishments which none the less are rarely encouraged beyond high-school and college.

In the American context, pride in the 'culture' of the homeland frequently marks the middle-class first and second generation's most permanent tie to the mother country. For the secular Indian, just as for the educated Italian-American, the categories of 'culture' and 'philosophy' have become neutral terms with little religious overtones. A great Karnatak vocal recital in the common room is like the Ave Maria sung in a concert hall. Similarly, discussions of the meaning of religious texts are 'philosophy' and fully part of the modern rational world, whereas the same text chanted in ritual might seem an embarrassing incantation. There are many in the Indian American community who are not sanguine about ritual, but they do want to keep up family values and keep Hinduism as a moral and aesthetic category in their life. The lower floor auditorium is for them. It is a family affair.

The lower floor is also for the second generation for whom the activities upstairs often seem as confusing as for any American youth. John Fenton summarizes the dilemma for the generation who pledged much of their lives, and even their fortune, to help build this temple: 'The irony of Hindu temple-building activity in America is that it emphasizes that aspect of Hindu religion that so far has the least meaning and that is the most opaque to second generation Indian immigrants' (1988: 179). 'We have built this for the sake of our children,' said one older devotee while pointing to this grand edifice in the nation's capital, 'Are we building it for nothing?' A telling scene in the movie *Mississippi Masala* shows two young second-generation children playing cowboys and Indians (the native American variety) in the midst of the celebration of the holy Hindu wedding rites in a small town in Mississippi. Several young boys with baseball bat in hand ready to 'play ball' could be spotted outside the holy *yagyasala*, the tent constructed to build the sacred fires needed to awaken the Gods during the great installation rituals in July. A sight I will never forget is looking up during one of the crucial rituals to spot a teenage girl walking down the temple steps wearing a sweat shirt with an enormous Mickey Mouse.

Such 'youths', quite at a loss on the upper floor, are more at home in the classrooms below. Those families who chose to watch the ritual on video downstairs sat in congenial groups, as mother-father-children, while upstairs the south Indian proprieties were tacitly observed and husbands sat with the men, wives with other women. In Hindu ritual the family that prays together does not stay together—such gatherings are for that lower floor. During this *mahakumbhabhishekam* ritual, an active group of young people who were trying to get into the spirit of things none the less did not remain upstairs for the rituals but sold 'Om Shanti' T-shirts on the lower floor, while their mothers cooked a phenomenal amount of food, which they sold downstairs at nominal cost to raise money for the temple.

Women in the kitchen downstairs and men carrying out priestly, now defined as 'religious', functions upstairs is the source of low level—but palpable—tension in the temple. This gender dichotomy in part reflects traditional Indian society but also is created by this upstairs/downstairs spatial division. There are some real ironies here. For American feminists, women in the kitchen stands for gender segregation and subordination. But these women work in the temple kitchens, a task in India reserved for Brahmin men whose ritual purity was a prerequisite for handling the holy food which was always first served to God. When women now make this *prashad* they are assuming a former priestly role. Their domestic task has expanded in America into temple service. In essence, the downstairs of the temple now has become truly a home where the housewife cooks and serves the larger family of devotees. Women share this home-space with the youth, they are at once enlarged by their greater role but oddly diminished because that role is no longer on a level with the other ritual functions of the temple. In very American fashion, food, now only vaguely sacralized as the *prashad*, is served as 'lunch' in styrofoam plates by the exhausted volunteers—and eaten with plastic spoons.

Women are grumbling about this aspect of the new split-level world. Many of these women work and succeed in America, as do their spouses. Yet here in this space the division could be seen as even more segregated than in the 'control' temple, Kapaleeswara in Madras, where the cooking is left to the Brahmins and women are not behind kitchen walls. I heard grumbles in the American temple; women mentioned to me that they have no real say in serious decision-making. Yet women were forceful and very active not only with the cooking but also in decorating the temple upstairs, in organizing fund-raising, and I also heard a number of women chanting in Sanskrit along with the priest as they sat 'listening'. I suspected a desire for an increased ritual role and my suspicions were realized late on the holy night of the installation rituals that July. After a long, quite beautiful, marriage ritual for the God Murugan and his wives while the congregation chanted the wedding vows for the divine couples, the lovely palanquins with the bronze images of the deities inside were lifted by male devotees for the ride around the borders of the interior of the temple. Apparently as the palanquin reached the shrine of the Goddesses Sarada and Parvati, the women took the palanquin—for when the procession came out the other side of the temple some joyous women were carrying the two palanquins. I asked one female palanquin-bearer if it was usual in India for women to do this. Quickly came the reply, 'In India they are male chauvinists, but this is America.' As the palanquin turned the corner, one middle-aged woman grumbled about seeing women behave in this manner, but the faces of these hijackers revealed the gleeful expressions of women taking their first steps toward a new role for their ritual and managerial position in the temple.

Upstairs/downstairs may be solid architectural space but it is not stable social space. The more domesticated the temple becomes, the more its overarching model becomes the family, the more the tensions in middle-class family life will explode through the seemingly solid floors. This temple is far from an oasis from middle-class life in America. By adopting the suburbs as its locale, by opting for the suburban split of domestic life from public life, the temple seeks to create a Hindu family within the American world of family life and family values. American life has not been factored out, it has been invited in to rest right under the Hindu holy sanctums. But as the women here have already shown, the space between the floors is not airtight.

BETWEEN UPSTAIRS/DOWNSTAIRS: TECHNOLOGY AS THE THIRD STREAM

At the moment when priests awakened the Gods to their new life in America, pouring the holy waters, the *abhishekam,* over the stone images, many devotees viewed this on video monitors carefully placed alongside of each sanctum. In the *pranapratistha* ceremonies (September 1990) which awakened Durga, Hanuman and Ganesa, the *abhishekam* for each deity was performed in rapid sequence in each sanctum. Devotees sat facing the deity whose rituals they had sponsored though donation. The video monitors allowed devotees to get the closest view of the ritual in front of them but also to witness each of the consecutive consecrations. The chief engineer for this the complex system of technology switched like a T.V. director from camera to camera to catch the crucial moments at each shrine. A telling moment in this conflation of authentic ritual with advanced technology occurred when I was seated with a large group of devotees in front of Hanuman with another group of devotees at our rear, facing the Durga shrine in the opposite direction. At the moment when the holy waters awakened Durga, my Hanuman group raised their folded hands in the sign of the devotion to the image on the video monitor in front, when a simple twist of the head would have revealed Durga in the flesh just behind. The image on the video monitor was an acceptable double for the image to the rear.

In the consecration ritual this video system, operated by an African-American crew and director, became an ever-present symbol of the utter modernity of these ancient rituals. Although few non-Indians participated in the rituals, the video crew was afforded the clearest vision of the holiest of sights by virtue of their skills in the new medium of imaging. This use of the video camera in temples is by no means new to the Hindu temple. The video cameras now have the first sight of the holiest of rituals in the sanctums of major temples in India during times when there is no other way to accommodate the desire of all of the vast crowd of devotees to share in these holy sights. But what is new in America was the choice to put these cameras in non-Hindu hands. The crew remained patient and respectful through the long days of these rituals. The remark of one tired 'group' showed how well the presence of the video cameras had made the translation of this temple ritual to a very American idiom. 'This is the longest church service I ever attended', he sighed on the fifth straight day of the rituals.

Again, the non-Hindu community was directly incorporated into the ritual at the point of another technical skill. The African-American mason who carefully cut and fixed the marble on the walls of the interior of the sanctum, the very place where the divine images would reside, became an important participant in the consecration ritual. On the first day of the rituals in July, this mason found himself standing with his shirt and shoes removed in front of the sacred fire. Minutes later with a turban on his head, this obviously serious but delighted mason, pulled a burning straw man through each of the interiors of the new sanctums in the temple. His was the final act of purification to make the sanctums ready for their divine residents. His work as mason had taken on its full ritual significance.

The Sri Siva-Vishnu Temple lives with its doors open to its neighbours. No one is excluded and indeed an announcement of the consecration rituals in July invited 'all Hindus and non-Hindus alike to join in this unique event'. Some non-Hindu Indians, some non-Hindu Americans and some Hindu Euro-Americans indeed came. But they were not more openly representative of the greater American community than the mason who was seen to personify the many non-Hindus who had a hand in constructing the temple and the video crew whose presence was hard to miss.

Also present with these technological people were many little things from the American manufacturing world. Rows and rows of the family grocery store plastic gallon milk jugs were poured into the many pots which were then used to bathe the Gods. *Dannon* yogurt cartons, paper towels and paper plates all took their place near the divine sanctums and the holy fire pits to play their part in the ritual. The most delightful integration of the American department store world occurred when the stone and the bronze images of the Ganesa could be seen in a magenta, child-size swimming pool as priests began the rituals to awaken him to his first morning in America. The cartoon characters seem to pay their homage to this God whose own playful spirit is said to tease and yet to bless his devotees. Deep at its centre, the world of manufacturing and technology has entered and been integrated into the temple. A telling expression of this third stream of technology appeared in a recent report sent out to devotees from the temple, which announced that 'the civil construction of the temple building that began in 1989 is now complete. The "Indianization" was a team of seventeen *silpis* [which] has since made significant progress'. In its technological skeleton, the temple can be stamped 'Made in America', while its outer surface which looks out on the world of Lanham, Maryland, will wear an Indian face.

REFERENCES

Agarwal, Priya, 1991. *Passage from India: Post 1965 Indian Immigrants and their Children,* Palos Verdes, CA., Yuvati Publications.

Ashby, Philip, 1974. *Modern Trends in Hinduism,* New York and London: Colombia University Press.

Babb, Lawrence Alan, 1986. *Redemptive Encounters: Three Modern Styles in Hindu Religion,* University of California Press.

Bachelard, Gaston, 1969. *The Poetics of Space,* Translated by Maria Jolas, Boston: Beacon Press.

Bhardwaj, Surinder M., 1990. 'Asian Indians in the United States: A Geographic Appraisal', in *South Asians Overseas: Migration and Ethnicity,* Colin Clark (ed.), Cambridge: Cambridge University Press.

Clothey, Fred W., 1983. 'The Construction of a Temple in an American City and the Acculturation Process', in *Rhythm and Intent: Ritual Studies from South India,* Madras: Blackie & Son.

———, 1992. 'Rituals and Reinterpretations: South Indians in Southeast Asia', in *A Sacred Thread: Modern Transmission of Hindu Traditions in India and Abroad,* Raymond Brady Williams (ed.), New York: Columbia University Press.

Fenton, John Y., 1988. *Transplanting Religious Traditions: Asian Indians in America,* New York: Praeger.

Ganapathi Sthapati, V., 1988. 'Symbolism of *Vimana* and *Gopura*', in *Siva Temple and Temple Rituals,* S.S. Janaki (ed.), Madras: The Kuppuswami Sastri Research Institute, 112-21.

Jackson, Robert, 1981. 'The Shree Krishna Temple and the Gujarati Hindu Community in Coventry', in *Hinduism in England,* David G. Bowen (ed.), Bradford, West Yorkshire: Bradford College.

Janaki, S.S., 1988. '*Dhvaja-Stambha*: Critical Account of its Structural and Ritualistic Details', in *Siva Temple and Temple Rituals,* S.S. Janaki (ed.), Madras.

Knott, Kim, 1987. 'Hindu Temple Rituals in Britain: The Reinterpretation of Tradition', in *Hinduism in Great Britain,* Richard Burkhart (ed.), London and New York: Tavistock Publications.

Kramrisch, Stella, 1976 [1946]. *The Hindu Temples,* Varanasi: Motilal Banarsidass.

Lewandowski, Susan, 1974. 'Changing Form and Function in the Ceremonial and the Colonial Port City in India: An Historical Analysis of and Madras', *Modern Asian Studies* 2: 183-212.

Lutgendorf, Philip, (forthcoming). 'My Hanuman is Bigger Than Yours', *History of Religions.*

Mikula, Paul Brian Kearney and Rodney Harber, 1982. *Traditional Hindu Temples in South Africa,* Durban: Hindu Temple Publications.

Narayanan, Vasudha, 1992. 'Creating South Indian Hindu Experience in the United States', in *A Sacred Thread: Modern Transmission of Hindu Traditions in India and Abroad,* Raymond Brady Williams (ed.), Chambersburg, PA.: Anima Press.

Nowikowski, Susan and Robin Ward, 1978/79. 'Middle Class and British? An Analysis of South Asians in Suburbia', *New Community* 8 (Winter 1978/79): 1-10.

Smith, H. Daniel, 1985. 'Pratistha', in *Agama and Silpa,* K.K.A. Venkatachari (ed.), Bombay: Ananthacharya Indological Research Institute, 1985.

Tuan, Yi-Fu, 1977. *Space and Place: The Perspective of Experience.* Minneapolis: University of Michigan Press.

Vertovec, Steven, 1992. 'Community and Congregation in London Hindu Temples: Divergent Trends', *New Community* 18 (January, 1992): 251-64.

Waghorne, Joanne Punzo, 1993. 'Mylapore', in *Temple Towns of Tamil Nadu,* George Michell (ed.), Bombay: Marg Publications, pp.114-28.

Williams, Raymond. B., 1984. *A New Face of Hinduism: The Swaminarayanan Religion,* Cambridge: Cambridge University Press.

———, 1988. *Religions of Immigrants from India,* Cambridge: Cambridge University Press.

Singing for the *Sadguru*: Tyagaraja Festivals in North America[1]

KATHRYN HANSEN

It is 9 a.m. and the beginning of what promises to be an extraordinary event. Speeches are to commence and the Governor of Ohio's proclamation will be read, declaring 18 and 19 April as St. Tyagaraja Days throughout the state. But now scores of musicians are coming up and sitting on the carpeted stage. Vocalists and instrumentalists, amateurs and professionals, women and men, old and young crowd together until there is room only in the wings. After a flute prelude, they launch into brisk unison singing, commencing with '*Jagadanandakaraka*', a Sanskrit composition enumerating the 108 names of Rama, composed in Raga Nattai. Immediately follow three equally wordy but lively, rhythmic pieces set to different *ghana* ('heavy') ragas. The chorus falters a bit on the multiple stanzas of composition number four (Raga Varali), the least familiar of the pieces, but the leaders at the front pull them along musically. '*Endaro mahanubhavalu*', a homage in Telugu to all the great souls who have gone before, brings the group singing triumphantly to an end. The *pancharatna kritis*—the five gems or masterworks—have been completed, and another Tyagaraja festival has officially begun.

Tyagaraja festivals, known as *aradhana utsavas* (or *jayantis,* when held on the birth rather than death anniversary of the poet-composer), are becoming increasingly popular in the North American diaspora. I estimate that at least a hundred such observances are held in the US and Canada each year. Festivals have been held for about fifteen years at Toronto, Cleveland, Chicago, Madison, Milwaukee, Atlanta, and Queens, and have spread to many other places, including the recently built south Indian-style temples. Their prototype is the annual festival in Tiruvaiyaru, Sri Tyagaraja's home village in Tanjore district, and there are similar festivals all over south India as well as in the north. On this continent, festivals take place in urban areas with significant concentrations of south Indians. Organized locally by small groups of volunteers, they receive their staunchest support from music-lovers, amateur musicians, and music teachers. Audiences are overwhelmingly of south Indian origin, with Tamil and Telugu-speaking high castes predominating. Many of these festivals originated as small-scale observances in private homes. Lately they have taken on a grander, more public character as community size and resources have expanded. Common venues are university or high school auditoriums, churches, and the multifunction halls within newly constructed Hindu temple complexes.

The attachment of south Indians to these festivals has a number of interesting dimensions. The figure of Tyagaraja (and Karnatak music in general) has served both as an instrument and an icon of group identity for some time, although the boundaries of the groups that appropriate Tyagaraja have shifted and are undergoing further change in the diaspora. Just as it does in India, the Tyagaraja festival in the diaspora provides structural and ideological unity to the community that identifies itself as south Indian. Vasudha Narayanan states, 'This festival is seen by many South Indians as the main event by which they maintain, preserve and transmit their culture.' (Narayanan 1992; Williams 1992: 322) Its overt function is to transmit musical tradition from one generation to the next, by honouring the historical figures and present-day leaders of Karnatak music, and by providing an opportunity for both amateurs and professionals to perform. Through its rituals and rhetoric, the festival additionally situates performance and learning within a matrix of Hindu devotionalism.

The Tyagaraja festival offers a prime example of the process of cultural 'reproduction' or 'transplantation', the relocation of distinctive cultural practices to new territory, so noticeable in the current spate of temple-building, classical dance instruction, language-learning and the like. Mapped against the north American landscape, the meanings of the festival are compounded for its participants. As well as constituting a celebration of cultural attainment, it becomes a statement of cultural difference, an emblem of resistance to engulfment within mainstream north America. Even as the festival forges a bond with the past through remembrance of a culture hero, it cements present ties with the artistic community in India, extending transnational flows of capital via cultural patronage. Of particular importance to those who maintain regular contact with the 'old country' (and many middle-class immigrants have the means and the desire to visit India frequently), participation in the festival, especially in the capacity of organizer, announces to those back home that Indianness is being preserved by those who have settled outside India. It legitimizes the act of migration and validates the status of the Non-Resident Indian (NRI) among 'resident Indians'.

It may seem grandiose to claim that one festival can serve so many purposes. I would argue that cultural performances in general offer their participants a superfluity of meanings or benefits. They operate on a number of levels, and individuals and sub-groups take from them what they need (and give what they have). That qualification aside, I find that the Tyagaraja festival is characterized by both a complexity of structure and a richness of symbolism that make it a particularly versatile medium for diasporic expression. I would like to begin by looking at the way in which diverse interests are incorporated within the festival's temporal order of events, an order that has remained fairly standard even after the shift to the north American environment. But first, a few words about Tyagaraja.

Tyagaraja (1767-1847) followed in a tradition of *vaggeyakars* who both composed poems of praise to the divine powers and musical compositions to frame those poems. While such a dual role was not uncommon, his contribution was to develop the *kriti,* a tripartite genre of composition that greatly enhanced the musical sophistication of devotional song. Considered pre-eminent among the Trinity of Composers (which includes his contemporaries Muthuswami Dikshitar and Syama Shastri), his importance in the history of Karnatak music stems from his large corpus of enduringly popular pieces. Yet this is never separated from his stature as an enlightened being. Tyagaraja's devotion to Rama and his selfless dedication to music are viewed as inseparable. His poetic utterances are treasured as a compendium of wisdom on philosophy, religion, and moral conduct. Called the patron saint of Karnatak music, Tyagaraja's hyphenated identity as saint-composer pervades the festival.

Not surprisingly, the festival begins with rituals of worship (*puja* or *abhishekam*) to both Tyagaraja and the God Rama. In the public ceremonies I have observed, the worship is always performed by a priestly specialist, officiating on behalf of a small congregation consisting of those closely involved with the festival. He makes offerings of various sanctified substances to two framed portraits. Tyagaraja's picture is below, typically an image of the seated composer playing a tanpura; directly above is an equal-sized picture of

Rama, who may be accompanied by Sita, Lakshman, and Hanuman. The priest lights incense, garlands the portraits, and concludes the ceremony with *arti,* circling a tray with a small wick lamp before the images and extending it to the devotees, who receive the flame's smoke as a blessing and prostrate themselves before the altar.

Little of the audience is present at this early hour, and those who are present are not required to participate; they may be visiting with one another, busying themselves with preparations, or minding children. After the ceremony, if the images have not already been moved to the side of the stage, this is done, and there they remain for the duration of the festival, where they are a visible but not dominating presence. I do not wish to read too much into the apparent lack of focus upon these rituals, given my limited observation of them (I usually don't make it on time either). None the less the minor degree of attention directed toward them suggests to me that they may function rather more like the preliminary rituals commonly enacted before a stage performance (the *purvaranga* described in Bharata's *Natyashastra*) than as a central event in the proceedings. The rituals are required to sanctify the event and honour the saint and his *ishta deva* (chosen deity). It is important to be able to say that 'the day began with pooja in the traditional manner' (Shanker 1990). None the less the principal medium for offering homage is to be music.

The next event is ordinarily the *pancharatna kritis,* although they may be preceded by a few simple *bhajans,* often performed by children. The hubbub in the hall increases, more people arrive, and as the participants assemble on the stage for the group singing, the festival finds its centre. Singing or playing the *pancharatna kritis* is a test of musical skill, requiring years of learning and practice. The musicians who participate in this segment of the festival are demonstrating a high degree of commitment to Karnatak music. Amateur singers may prepare specially for this event, rehearsing the pieces with a teacher or in a group of friends. In Cleveland, the mridangam player Ramnad R. Raghavan (who was formerly at Wesleyan University and now lives in Cleveland) has for many years trained a group of singers especially for participation in the festival. He leads the Cleveland group singing as conductor. Other music teachers in other cities play a similar role among the local enthusiasts who wish to join in this part of the festival. In spite of these rehearsals, it is a common sight at diaspora festivals to find the performers closely following the musical notations in their copy books or looking to others for guidance during the group singing.

The *pancharatna* performance is the first whole-hearted manifestation of *bhakti* at the festival. To sing these elaborate works is an act of devotion, an offering of musical service (*sangitopasana*) made by those who revere Tyagaraja. It is a means of showing honour and loyalty to the composer as the *sadguru,* the supreme teacher of Karnatak music, and through Tyagaraja's saintly mediation to exalt his chosen deity Rama. The collective performance of the *pancharatna kritis* however is something more than a demonstration of knowledge and obeisance. It is an enactment of community, and more specifically, a representation *for the community itself* of their special relationship with their culture hero. By singing *together* for the *sadguru,* members of the group annually affirm their connections with each other. Placed at the start of a celebration that brings into the present the words, music, and faith of a powerful figure from the past, the act re-establishes the collective identity of those assembled. It further links them with other groups who celebrate similarly in other places, as it connects them with those who have done so in the past.

Singing the *pancharatna kritis* normally takes one hour. What follows and lasts throughout the middle portion of the day is the most democratic and participatory event of the festival, the offering of musical tribute by individuals. This is essentially an open mike, with certain ground rules: all compositions must be *kritis* by Tyagaraja, each person's performance time is limited to five minutes, no *alapana,* elaboration, or improvization is to be done (just the fixed parts of the composition, its *pallavi, anupallavi* and *charanam*), no percussion accompaniment is provided, and as much as possible *kritis* should not be repeated. Every skill level is welcomed, and in actuality one gets to hear the young and the old, the beginner and the advanced, the talented and the not so tuneful. Sometimes the participants are grouped by age or by vocal/instrumental categories, and participants are usually asked to register in advance as places are limited; depending on the festival, these limits still allow thirty-five to sixty individual performers access to the stage during this section.

In the diaspora, this part of the festival has increasingly been given over to children who are studying Karnatak music. Many parents who came to north America within the last twenty years are concerned that their offspring may be losing their Indian values and identity. Conscious efforts are under way to provide instruction to children in religion, arts, languages, and other subjects. Among south Indians, many students are learning Karnatak music, and for them participation in Tyagaraja festivals is a focal point. Some children have a flair for performance from a young age, and take eagerly to the stage. Child prodigies seem to hold a particular fascination for south Indians, as for music fans generally. Family and friends—but mostly mothers—provide a great deal of encouragement by bringing their children to these festivals, having them perform, and praising them for their efforts. The children get support from their peers and the challenge may move them to excel. In some festivals, part of this programme is explicitly organized as a competition, with trophies awarded to the best student performance in each age group. The North Jersey Music Lovers, for example, organize their Tyagaraja Aradhana by holding two sessions, first a music competition for children, and then individual participation by children and adults on a non-competitive basis. In other festivals competition is eschewed, partly under the influence of a *bhakti*-oriented ideology that stresses the equality of all music that is offered sincerely and humbly.

The unadorned, unaccompanied singing of Tyagaraja's compositions offers a rare opportunity to glimpse the clarity of melodic lines, the beauty of ragas, and the emotional power that some singers can draw from within. When a singer, especially a professional, sits on the bare stage and opens her or his heart to sing without the support of accompanying instruments, the expression of humility can be moving indeed. Here again is witnessed the re-enactment of community, the representation of the musical self as a member of a group emulating the simple and selfless *sadguru*. Occasionally some adults use this part of the festival to compete or exhibit their knowledge. Those who are mature artists, however, may call forth exquisite expressions of emotion, making their tribute a gift for the audience as well as the saint.

While the musical mood deepens inside the concert hall, outside the festivities are becoming merrier. Friends meet after a long time, family members are introduced, children run about and play, and smells emanate from the kitchen. About halfway through the individual performances the music is interrupted by the collective partaking of a south Indian feast. The meal is provided free and is served from large pots on to styrofoam lunch trays. This is firmly in the hands of a committee of women who have planned, shopped, cooked, and transported large quantities of rice, sambar, vegetables, sweets, savories, and pickles. Knowing that their participation is essential to the success of the festival, they can now enjoy the satisfaction and power that comes with feeding large numbers of people. The Cleveland Festival particularly prides itself on the abundance and excellence of its meals. In 1992, the Festival mobilized 130 cooks, all volunteers, each of whom prepared one dish of ten quarts. A *Sruti* magazine reviewer commented on the 'steady flow of food and music at the Cleveland *aradhana*' (Sundaram Sankaran 1991). The commensal dining replicates the festive atmosphere at a large Indian wedding. Once more a sense of community is established, through the most persistent marker of ethnic identity: food.

The final item of the day, for which the maximum number of people congregate, is the concert by professional musicians late in the afternoon or evening. The concert is conducted like a regular *katcheri*, beginning with short compositions and proceeding to the exposition of a longer raga with the introductory *alapana*, various kinds of rhythmic improvization (*niraval, kalpana swara*), and percussion solo (*tani avartanam*), finishing with lighter pieces. It is not necessary to perform only compositions of Tyagaraja.

The number of artists and their prestige depends upon the financial resources and scale of the festival. Smaller festivals invite artists from the locality, whereas larger festivals contract top-ranking performers from India. At north America's largest Tyagaraja festival to date, in Cleveland in 1992, five artists were flown in from India: two soloists (U. Srinivas on the mandolin and N. Ramani on the flute), two percussionists (Guruvayur Dorai on the mridangam and Zakir Hussain on the tabla) and a violinist (Kanyakumari). This format facilitated *jugalbandi* not only between the two principals but also between the percussionists. It also introduced a Hindustani musician (and that too, one of megastar stature) into the Karnatak realm, breaking new ground.

Whereas the musical tributes demonstrate the internalization of knowledge, performance skills, and a devotional attitude among those who train in Karnatak music, the concert represents the height of artistic achievement produced by the tradition. It stresses not only mastery of rhythm and melody, but the extraordinary capacity of great musicians to reach beyond, to tap their originality and spontaneously create pleasing new patterns. In the best of performances, the multifaceted genius of the musical system itself is on display. The music communicates a superior level of civilizational accomplishment, giving those who identify with it a sense of deep pride and elation. Of longer duration perhaps is their renewed belief in the sophistication—even superiority—of south Indian culture, which may assist them in deflecting the demeaning stereotypes of themselves as 'Third World' people, so often encountered in the north American media, educational system, and society at large.

In addition to these events, the festival includes speeches of welcome and introduction and an awards ceremonies to honour veteran musicians. The inclusion of elected officials on the dais, or their messages published in the annual souvenir, point to the growing political influence of the professional class of South Asians and their participation in local, state, and national electoral politics. Other features include educational lectures and singing of simple devotional hymns such as *bhajans* and *nama sankirtanas*. Festivals that emphasize children's participation, such as that organized by the North Jersey Music Lovers, often include an essay-writing competition that tests students' factual knowledge of Tyagaraja's life and his place in Karnatak music.

Certain features of Tyagaraja festivals in India have not been widely adopted in the north American diaspora, probably because of difficulties in executing their performance or a shift of emphasis. For example, the enactment of *unchavritti,* wherein an individual impersonating Tyagaraja leads a group of devotees and goes out begging for alms, is rare. Another neglected practice is the *akhanda ganam*, or continuous singing for twenty-four to forty-eight hours, without pause. Usually understood as representing a superlative degree of devotion, *akhanda* recitation of sacred texts such as the *Adi Granth* and the *Ramcharitmanas* is found among diaspora Sikhs and north Indian Hindus, but seems to be rarely associated with Tyagaraja. Another ritual in the Indian context is the *anjaneya utsavam* or dedication to Hanuman, to close the festival; I have been unable to observe this so far.

It seems clear that the structure of the festival is inclusive. It is designed to maximize contact between its symbols, rituals, and practices and the individuals who make up the community. Participation is encouraged by individuals of various ages, genders, or skill levels, and there is space for everyone to contribute and get involved, whether in a musical or organizational capacity. Beyond this, there is another way of looking at participation that brings in the ideology of *bhakti*. *Bhakti* as a non-ritualistic, non-hierarchical mode of approaching the divine has historically placed great emphasis on the use of the expressive arts (music, dance, theatre) as vehicles for mystical realization. Singing the names of the divine, enacting the stories of gods and goddesses, and even hearing the praise of god through music or poetry are acknowledged as powerful methods of gaining grace. In this understanding, participation is immersion. It is significant that one of the meanings of *bhakti*, from the root *bhaj*, is to participate, to share intimately. Even without volition, participation through singing and hearing can lead to transformation, to intuitive recognition of the transcendent.

Like many collective activities within the *bhakti* tradition, the Tyagaraja festival articulates the value of voluntary service. No coercion is brought to bear on those who do not wish to participate, no fees are charged for admission even to the high-profile concerts. Instead, small groups of friends assume responsibility for the most active roles in planning and financing. Every act of assistance is interpreted as service to a higher being or cause. Thus the audience is asked to make donations for the support of the festival, but the spirit in which they should do so, with open hearts filled with the warm sentiments of the occasion, is emphasized at least as much as the financial needs of the organization. Not only monetary gifts but time and labour are required, but they must be offered freely. Again the conceptual framework of *bhakti* supplies the underlying notion of *seva* or service. *Seva*, like hearing or singing, is an avenue for realization that bypasses the mind and its constant striving. Performing tasks for others, ideally in a disinterested, selfless way, is an active kind of engagement that promotes the welfare of all. The organizers who tirelessly work to produce these festivals take strength from such beliefs. The concept of *seva* thus is a sort of recruitment strategy, serving to harness the talents and energies of a large number of people towards a common goal.

Organizers generally assert that they are 'following tradition' when asked about the different kinds of activities that make up their festivals or the particular arrangement of events in the festival day. The tradition that is most often cited is that of the Tyagaraja Aradhana Utsava at Tiruvaiyaru. In Tiruvaiyaru, for example, the emphasis on group singing of the *pancharatna kritis* and individual offering of musical tribute was established (Srinivasan 1991). Discontinuities between Tiruvaiyaru and the diaspora festivals are also numerous, the most obvious being the shifting of its date. North American festivals are frequently *not* held on Bahula Panchami, the death anniversary of Tyagaraja, which ordinarily falls in the first week of January. Residents of the north-east US argue that the weather at that time of year is prohibitive, and they routinely shift the *aradhana* date closer to spring and Tyagaraja's birthday, which occurs in May. In Florida, one group held the festival on Thanksgiving day, another celebrated it on the actual day in January, and two other cities observed it a few months later (Narayanan 1992). These alterations have led to uncertainty among participants as to whether it is Tyagaraja's birth or death that is being commemorated.

None the less, the massive festival at Tiruvaiyaru is invoked as the model for Tyagaraja observances all over the world. Tiruvaiyaru was the village in which Tyagaraja resided for most of his life, and its festival occurs at his *samadhi,* the memorial site near the Kaveri river. Although commemorative rites are said to have started immediately after the composer's demise in 1847 (and therefore 1992 marked the 145th *aradhana*), the Tiruvaiyaru festival in its present form dates only to 1941; its golden jubilee was observed in 1991 (Srinivasan 1991). In the course of its history, the Tiruvaiyaru festival has witnessed numerous splits, clashes and factions. Each year in India it draws harsh criticism, and modifications in its order of events are being made constantly. Hence Tiruvaiyaru, although it has enjoyed the position of authorizing festival and source of legitimacy, is itself none other than the ubiquitous site of contestation, where competing groups and ideologies collide and no one tradition represents everyone.

William Jackson, in his attempt to locate Tyagaraja within his own time, discovered that the composer was not nearly as well known as one Alkondar, a local saint of Tiruvaiyaru who performed exotic yogic feats. Tyagaraja earned mention in Sourendra Mohan Tagore's list of ten 'renowned musicians of the present century in Southern India' in his *Universal History of Music,* published in Calcutta in 1896. The *Tanjore District Gazetteer* of 1906 devoted half a sentence to him (Jackson 1991: 93-4). From this, Jackson tentatively deduces that outside of a limited circle of disciples and cogniscenti, Tyagaraja was not well known and his *aradhana* was not widely observed in the nineteenth century.

The change in his popularity occurred when Tyagaraja became 'a hero to Indian nationalists'.

> What was known of Alkondar was unbelievable and unpresentable; he represented an unusable past. Tyagaraja became a 'native son' all could be proud of—within the nation-to-be of India with its regional singer-saints of times past (like Mira Bai, Purandaradasa, and so on), and within the international context of present and future: Tyagaraja the creative genius who brought the old traditions to a new fruition was celebrated as 'the Beethoven of South India,' respectable, and exemplary. Thus, nationalists of the Indian *risorgimento* gravitated towards him as symbolic of essential Indian values. (Jackson 1991: 95)

It was presumably during the first decades of the twentieth century that the celebration of Tyagaraja's *aradhana* attracted more notice and grew in scope.

By some point in the early 1900s, rival organizations emerged in Tiruvaiyaru and held separate annual functions to honour Tyagaraja. These were known as the 'large' and 'small' factions (*periya* and *chinna katchi*). Neither faction permitted women to appear on the concert stage during the *aradhana utsava*. This, despite the fact that women like Veena Dhanammal, M.S. Subbulakshmi, and others had already achieved prominence. It was left then to Bangalore Nagaratnammal, 'a patron of the arts, a learned woman, a musician, and a distinguished courtesan' (Tharu and Lalita 1991: 3) to undertake to provide access for female performers by establishing a third Tyagaraja festival at a different venue, in Tiruvaiyaru. Finally the three factions came together in 1941 under the leadership of S.Y. Krishnaswami, Musiri Subrahmania Iyer and Kumbakonam Rajamanickam Pillai (Srinivasan 1991). A united committee, the Sri Tyagabrahma Mahotsava Sabha, was formed under whose auspices the festival in Tiruvaiyaru has been held ever since. Despite the unified banner, each group preserved the right to conduct its own religious rites. There continues to be disagreement over whether the *sraddha* ritual should be performed, with one group claiming it is compulsory for Brahmins, and another contending that insofar as Tyagaraja had joined an ascetic order shortly before he died, he had entered into the state of *sannyas*, for which *sraddha* is not enjoined.

There are other ways in which the Tyagaraja legacy became contested. In a not unfamiliar pattern, Tyagaraja's disciples separated into three branches, identified by the place-names Umayalapuram, Tillaisthanam and Walajapet, and it is to representatives of these that is owed the propagation of Tyagaraja's compositions (Raghavan

1981: 15). Another source of contention developed when Tyagaraja's lineage terminated within two generations. One line of succession is observed through Tyagaraja's elder brother, Jalpesan, with whom the composer had grave disagreements, resulting in the partition of the family property. A rival line based on matrilineal succession is maintained by the descendants of Tyagaraja's wife's brother. Tyagaraja's grand niece and great grand nephews inherited his Rama *vigraha* (idol), and it now forms the central focus for their own *aradhana* festival in Tanjore every year, which they consider to be the 'only such celebration' (Tuttle 1992).

Another natural division exists between the two small towns with which Tyagaraja's life history is linked. On the one hand there is Tiruvarur, his birthplace, an ancient *kshetra* or cultural and religious centre (Raghavan 1981: 8). It was at Tiruvarur that the great temple dedicated to Tyagaraja stood, the manifestation of Siva for whom Tyagaraja was named. Tiruvarur, perhaps not coincidentally, was the birthplace of the other two members of the Karnatak music Trinity, Dikshitar and Syama Shastri. Twenty miles away is Tiruvaiyaru, the place where Tyagaraja spent most of his life, wrote his compositions, and died. Here too stood a famous temple, dedicated to Panchanadisvara, whose praise is found in the poems of the Tamil Nayanmars, although Tiruvaiyaru derived its sanctity fundamentally from the proximity of the Kaveri river with its rich delta. Competition between the two places, one the seat of the deity Tyagaraja enshrined in the temple, the other the seat of the musician Tyagaraja at the *samadhi,* threads through the legends and emerges in the festivals celebrated today.

Tiruvaiyaru has enjoyed hegemony in this unequal rivalry for some time. Its enormous festival attracts pilgrims from all over south and north India, and live coverage of its events is broadcast by Doordarshan throughout the country. Inevitably perhaps, Tiruvaiyaru has also come to represent the evils of corruption, sycophancy, and publicity-seeking that beset the Karnatak music scene. A case study is provided by back-to-back reports in *Sruti* of *jayanti* celebrations held in Tiruvarur and Tiruvaiyaru in 1986. In Tiruvarur, home of the Trinity, the Kanchi Sankara Mutt (a Hindu religious body) renovated the houses that had belonged to the musicians' families and then organized a festival attracting very large crowds and coverage on All India Radio and Doordarshan. Meanwhile in Tiruvaiyaru, a much smaller observance of Tyagaraja's birthday was carried out by fifty musicians from Madras. They took a procession through the streets to several temples, singing en route, and then started a twenty-four-hour non-stop performance that concluded after 253 *kritis* had been rendered. *Sruti* praised the group highly for its endurance in the scorching heat of May, while lamenting the lack of participation by the local people who had no idea that it was the saint's *jayanti*. The neglected *jayanti* observance in Tiruvaiyaru formed a 'ridiculous' contrast to the fame of its annual *aradhana* festival, even as the dedication and sincerity of its participants marked the event as 'sublime' in the eyes of the reporter; the bigger Tiruvarur function amounted to a display of 'pomp and show' (*Sruti* Staff 1986; Thyagu 1986).

In this example, festivals and places are connected in a circular logic. Significantly, in neither case were the celebrations held by the inhabitants of the sacred locality; the organizers and main participants in both instances can be seen as 'pilgrims'. None the less, the proceedings are interpreted as though they present a 'true picture' of the nature of the place and those who live there: the place's prestige rises or falls according to the success of the festival. Conversely, the festival's success depends upon its location at a reputed, sanctified site. If a festival succeeds, its success is credited to the auspiciousness of its locale. If it fails, perhaps there was a temporary defect in the bounty of the natural environment. Lamenting the lacklustre performance of the *pancharatna kritis* at the Tiruvaiyaru festival in 1991, N. Srinivasan named a long list of musicial giants who used to grace the occasion. Then he remarked:

> Perhaps the flourish is also related to the flow of water in the Kaveri on whose banks the event is held. The greater emotional attachment and commitment to the *aradhana* shown by the earlier generation vidwans possibly parallelled the copiousness of the river's flow in those years; the river was practically dry this year. (Srinivasan 1991)

Temples and festivals have played a major role in the territorialization of south India since early times. Kings, Brahmins, and other powerful groups have cemented their relationships to localities by constructing and endowing temples and sponsoring festivals. The establishment of a temple or festival sanctifies the local territory, transforming it into a sacred place, a *kshetra*.[2] The *kshetra* not only links the locality with transcendent sacrality; it also inscribes the locality in a wider geographic system. Only those sacred places that attract others from outside the locality, that draw pilgrims, retain their stature as *kshetras*. Rivalry between parallel sites develops as they compete to fulfil their requirements for pilgrims, resources, patronage, and fame.

A similar constellation of beliefs about locality, sacrality, and prestige is apparent in the practice of musicians being named after their native places. Examples such as Madurai Seshagopalan, Palghat Mani Iyer, Mysore T. Chowdiah, the Bombay Sisters, Hyderabad Brothers and so on abound in Karnatak music. By attaching their place of origin before their personal and caste names, artists not only distinguish themselves from others with similar names, they give credit to the communities that nurtured their talent. They further communicate the complex histories of their regions, including sacred associations due to the presence of temples, pilgrimage sites, or famous personages, and the musical lineages attached to those places. Taken in the aggregate, the assemblage of place-names signifies the extent of the domain of Karnatak music; as the list grows, its glory is magnified. It is notable that in the diaspora, this practice is being continued. One of the organizers of the Cleveland festival, who is also a *kanjira* (tambourine) player, has become known as 'Cleveland Balasubramaniam'. In an ironic forecast of the future, a *Sruti* staffer predicts that at the annual music season in Madras in the year 2027, the chief item will be an appearance of the Baltimore Brothers, with special accompaniment provided by Melbourne Mahadevan and Toronto Tanga Vel (Sundaram Sankaran 1991).

Summing up, the connections between music festivals, sacred sites, and personages illustrate the principle of 'localization of the universal' (Clothey 1983: 195). The transplantation of Tyagaraja festivals to the diaspora can be understood as part of a process of re-territorialization, following the displacement ensuing upon migration. Through the reproduction of territorially specific rituals and festivals, the new locality is invested with the properties of sacrality and prestige. Symbols tied to localities—forms that might otherwise be called parochial—are in this instance highly effective in connecting groups to new places and re-rooting people's cultural lives.[3]

As the celebration of a festival for Tyagaraja becomes localized in new territory, the process of segmentation also sets in. Rival localities and organizations vie with each other to claim audiences, artists, and recognition. Tiruvarur and Tiruvaiyaru are matched by pairs like

Cleveland and Chicago, or Dayton and Columbus, jockeying for position. What is remarkable is the choice of forum through which these new rivalries are expressed. Person-to-person communication still serves as the principal medium of exchange, enhanced now by the ease of long-distance telephone communication. High-tech modes are also widely employed: computer bulletin boards link Karnatak music lovers, fax and e-mail assist organizers in quickly putting concerts together, and videotaping provides an instant archive for every cultural performance. But old-fashioned magazine columns and letters to the editor still serve in the playing out of local contests. Curiously, opinions about events in north America are channeled through the capital of Karnatak music, thousands of miles away, the most popular print medium for these debates being *Sruti*, the music and dance magazine published in Madras.

As an illustration, in the August 1990 issue an author from Westerville, Ohio, published an article called 'Aradhanas Abroad', in which she recounted details of the Cleveland Tyagaraja *aradhana* and a combined Tyagaraja-Purandaradasa function held in Dayton. Seven issues and months later, the magazine published a letter from a reader from Columbus, who was annoyed because although the author of the previous article lived in a suburb of Columbus, she failed to mention the annual festival for Tyagaraja and Purandaradasa held in that city. In its favour, she stressed that it was the only programme in that area that brought together people from the whole Indian community, and that people attended from all over Ohio as well as out of state. Six months after that, the author of the original article responded, pointing out that the Columbus event had no invited artists performing (that being the alleged focus of her article); its evening concert featured its own organizer, a local resident. She admonished her critic: 'in an attempt to vie with one another in celebrating the aradhana, one should not forget the spirit of Tyagaraja or that of his compositions' (Shanker 1991; Shanker 1990; 'A Carnatic Music-Lover' 1991).

What is unprecedented in this diasporic altercation is that rivals resort to the pages of a journal that is published miles away and reaches them only after a considerable duration. The dispute occurs publicly and in India, and once set in print it acquires a permanent character that makes mediation difficult. If Tiruvarur and Tiruvaiyaru engaged in mutual recrimination through the pages of a New Delhi newspaper, one would perhaps have a parallel situation. Yet such an occurrence is not unimaginable, especially if one group were suddenly to be awarded a large subsidy by the Indian Government. In the NRI case, the benefits are not material; they are in the realm of reputation, recognition, and respectability. These reports and complaints make appeals for acknowledgement of the new locales that patronize Karnatak music. They attempt to establish place-name recognition in India for one's new *kshetra.*

Moreover, debates revolve around a broader issue: are Indians in north America genuinely interested in and devoted to Karnatak music? Is NRI attachment to Tyagaraja and his festival up to the standard found in India? Could it even be superior? In competing with each other for recognition in India, NRIs are demonstrating their accomplishments and rivaling India itself. According to T. Temple Tuttle, a musicologist intimately involved in the organization of the Cleveland festival since its inception, the biggest challenge for the Indian community in north America is to preserve tradition here *better* than is being done in India (Conversation, 20 April 1992).

At one level, this desire to outdo the homeland betrays an insecurity about the lack of cultural pedigree among many NRIs. Many who organize festivals, establish music societies, teach their children, and otherwise engage with the Indian arts, had little training in such areas growing up. Their families were not generally the ones who produced concert performers or led sabhas, and even attendance at recitals was something they became interested in only after settling abroad. There is also the attitude that given the uncertain future of their cultural traditions in their new environment and the ease with which their children are becoming 'mainstreamed', they must work even harder to strengthen their community organizations and promote the Indian arts. A sense of urgency energizes them, and they feel slighted and misunderstood when their considerable efforts are not given credit. At another level, some organizers feel that only in the diaspora can the Indian arts escape the pressures towards commercialism, nepotism, declining taste, and other problems that are perceived as rampant within India. Theirs is a mission to restore sobriety and high standards to the concert scene both in terms of production values and aesthetics. These aspirations trigger anxieties back in India that run through the pages of *Sruti*. Will the banner of Karnatak music ultimately pass outside the subcontinent? What would that mean for the sacred connection between the music and its home territory? Can the relationship between art and the transcendent so powerfully symbolized in Tyagaraja be preserved in the godless, materialistic West? The negotiation of space for the diaspora within the segmented transnational arts scene is at the heart of this conversation.

In closing, I do not see north American Tyagaraja festivals as part of the ideological construction of 'national' culture in the diaspora. As Anannya Bhattacharjee describes it, a national cultural essence or 'ideal of Indian unity' offers the Indian immigrant bourgeoisie a place of refuge from the 'threat of losing its power to stay un-named', which following Barthes she terms the 'habit of ex-nomination' (Bhattacharjee 1992: 25). The coalition groups she mentions, such as the National Federation of Indian American Associations (NFIAA) and the Association of Asian Indians in America (AAIA), although engaged in cultural representations, are informed by somewhat different purposes and politics than Karnatak music festivals. Karnatak music remains a profoundly sub-national musical culture, limited to the four southern states of India. Whereas Hindustani music is known and admired in the south, the converse is not true. Bharata Natyam, Karnatak music's sister art, which developed in almost identical regional circumstances, has assumed a wider role in diasporic constructions of identity, partly through its relevance to a nationalist discourse of the arts.[4] But Karnatak music remains restricted in its circulation and appeal. None the less with respect to the disparate languages, histories, and cultural traditions of the southern states, it plays a unifying role, eliding difference and constructing a sub-national identity that serves many of the same functions as all-India organizations and festivals.

Unlike celebrations like the Divali festival at South Street Seaport in New York City, Tyagaraja *aradhanas* are not demonstrations of 'unity in diversity', smorgasbords of regional customs, costumes, and foods. They are not intended to represent Indian 'otherness' to those outside, and thus do not cater to the tendency to convert multiculturalism into a fetish. As representations of identity for insiders, Tyagaraja festivals tacitly avoid the dominant culture's concerns and principles. They form part of the ongoing process through which diasporans, in the words of Keya Ganguly, shield 'their cultural anxieties and investments [from] those whom they view as "others", while they 'attempt to negotiate links and gaps between "mother culture" and diaspora' (Ganguly 1992: 29).

NOTES

1. This research forms part of a larger project, 'Text, Performance, and Ideology: South Asian Arts and the Diaspora', funded by the Social Sciences and Humanities Research Council of Canada (1992-5), for whose assistance I am extremely grateful. I also wish to thank the American Institute of Indian Studies for a senior fellowship in performing arts, which enabled me to study Karnatak music in South India in 1990-1. This paper draws heavily on my observations while attending the Cleveland Tyagaraja festival in 1992 and 1987. I also attended a number of Tyagaraja festivals in the New York/New Jersey area during 1992-3. I visited the Tiruvaiyaru festival in 1978 and performed on veena and sitar at the Tyagaraja *aradhana* at the Lakshmi Sundaram Hall in Madurai in 1991.
2. These ideas have been elaborated by many scholars, but particularly relevant for diaspora studies is Fred W. Clothey's discussion (Clothey 1983: 194-200). It is noteworthy that since 1977 and the founding of the Sri Venkateswara Temple at Penn Hills near Pittsburgh, as many as fifty new temples have been established in the US ('United States' 1992).
3. William Jackson, in trying to understand how Tyagaraja and performances of his music became a symbol for Indian nationalism, notes Ashis Nandy's insight into the relevance of the parochial, which 'could protect some forms of universalism more successfully than does conventional universalism' (Jackson 1991: 106).
4. See my unpublished paper, 'Indian Dance in the Diaspora', presented at the International Dance Conference on 'New Directions in Indian Dance', Toronto, 11 February 1993.

REFERENCES

A Carnatic Music-Lover, 1991. 'Aradhanas Abroad', *Sruti* 78 (March): 8.

Bhattacharjee, Anannya. 1992, 'The Habit of Ex-Nomination: Nation, Woman, and the Indian Immigrant Bourgeoisie', *Public Culture* 5.1 (Fall): 19-44.

Clothey, Fred W., 1983. *Rhythm and Intent: Ritual Studies from South India*, Madras: Blackie & Son Publishers.

Ganguly, Keya, 1992. 'Migrant Identities: Personal Memory and the Construction of Selfhood', *Cultural Studies* 6.1 (January): 27-50.

Jackson, William, 1991. *Tyagaraja: Life and Lyrics*, Madras: Oxford University Press.

Narayanan, Vasudha, 1992. 'Creating the South Indian 'Hindu' Experience in the United States', in *Modern Transmission of Hindu Traditions in India and Abroad*, Raymond Brady Williams (ed.): 147-76.

n.a [no author]. 'United States of Little Indias: Hindu Revival in an Alien Land', 1992, in *Little India* (November): 14.

Raghavan, V., 1981. 'Saint Tyagaraja: Introductory Thesis', in C. Ramanujachari and V. Raghavan, *The Spiritual Heritage of Tyagaraja*, Madras: Sri Ramakrishna Math.

Sangeet Natak Academy Bulletin, 1967. Special Tyagaraja Number (October-December).

Sankaran, Sundaram, 1991. 'Carnatic Music & NRIs', *Sruti* 77 (February): 35.

Sankaran, T., 1988. 'Ariyakudi: Attitude Towards the Fair Sex', *Sruti* 42 (March): 34.

Shanker, Meenakshi, 1990. 'Aradhanas Abroad', *Sruti* 71 (August), 15.

Shanker, Meenakshi, 1991. 'Response to CM Lover', *Sruti* 84 (September), 6.

Srinivasan, N., 1991. 'Tyagaraja Aradhana in Tiruvaiyaru: Mahotsava Sabha's Golden Jubilee Programme', *Sruti* 77 (February): 7-8.

Sruti Staff, 1986. 'Tiruvarur Trinity Jayanti Festival', *Sruti* 23 (June-July) 13.

Tharu, Susie and K. Lalita (eds.), 1991. *Women Writing in India*, vol. 1, New York: The Feminist Press.

Thyagu, 1986. 'Jayanti in Tiruvaiyaru: Sublime plus Ridiculous', *Sruti* 23 (June-July): 13.

Tuttle, T. Temple, 1992. 'The Tyagaraja Aradhana in Historical Perspective', in Souvenir brochure for the 15th Year Celebration of Sri Tyagaraja Music Festival at Cleveland State University and Siva Vishnu Temple, n.p.

Williams, Raymond Brady (ed.), 1992. *Modern Transmission of Hindu Traditions in India and Abroad*, Chambersburg, PA: Anima Publications.

Inter-Ethnic Relations within the Ahmadiyya Muslim Community in the United States

LINDA S. WALBRIDGE
FATIMAH HANEEF

On 25 February 1920 Dr. Mufti Muhammad Sadiq arrived at Ellis Island. He had been sent to America by Mirza Bashiruddin Mahmoud Ahmad, recognized as the second *khalifa* of the Qadiyani faction of the Ahmadiyya Movement of Islam. Dr. Sadiq's mission was to propogate the message of Mirza Ghulam Ahmad, the founder of this Movement.

Mirza Ghulam Ahmad, born in 1835, is accepted by his followers as the promised messiah and *mahdi*. His movement officially began in 1889 in Ludhiana, India, with a ceremony in which those who believed his claim paid allegiance to him. Ahmad would, in turn, teach them the true belief and faith (Friedman 1989).

In his voluminous writings, Mirza Ghulam Ahmad stressed his role as the Messiah, maintaining that he received revelations from God, though he did not bring a new *shari'ah* to mankind. Ahmad claimed that his religion and the world in general were in desperate need of reformation. Ghulam Ahmad was quickly branded as a renegade and his form of Islam has been deemed heretical in the Islamic world ever since.

One factor that contributed to the antagonism expressed towards the Ahmadis in India was their pro-British stance. While anti-imperialistic feelings festered in India, Ahmad taught that the British were just and fair in their governance. *Jihad* against the British would not be carried on by his followers. This pro-government sentiment has become part of the general teachings of Ahmadi Islam: the believers abide by the rules of the land in which they reside. They believe that they are abiding by the Quranic injunction: 'O ye who believe! Obey Allah and obey His Messenger and those who are in authority among you . . .' (al-Nisa, Sura 4).

Appreciation for British government was not accompanied by a similar affection for Christian missionaries, whom Ahmad often challenged in open debates. While he was eager to show the truth of Islam, he appeared equally concerned to teach an unorthodox version (by both Muslim and Christian standards) of the death of Jesus Christ. The majority of Muslims believe that it was not Jesus who died on the cross, but another in his stead, yet Jesus nevertheless was bodily resurrected into heaven. Ghulam Ahmad also denies Christ's death on the cross, but this is where his and the standard Islamic version of the story part company. According to Ahmad, Christ truly was crucified but he did not die. Rather, when he was removed from the cross, he was found to have only sustained injuries. He was nursed back to health, then travelled eastward until reaching India, where he lived until the age of 120 years (Gualtieri 1989).

While this paper will not explore theological issues, it is important to emphasize this one point of doctrine because it is the one most central to mainstream Christianity. In sending its missionaries westward, the Ahmadis would be directly confronting the Christian world.

Upon Mirza Ghulam Ahmad's death in 1908 leadership passed into the hands of one of his earliest supporters, who had enough support of his own to be accepted as the first *khalifa* of the Movement. Since the membership was mostly drawn from the middle classes, even in the early years of the Movement, members were receiving advanced degrees in the sciences and professions. Under such circumstances, a religious community is very likely to find diversity of views on matter of doctrine and procedure. Of particular concern in these early years was the issue of Ahmad's claim to prophecy. While the split in the community was a drawn out, complicated affair, the ultimate result was that the son of Ghulam Ahmad, Bashiruddin Mahmoud Ahmad, became the second *khalifa* and leader of the majority of Ahmadis, known as the Qadiyanis [after the town of Qadiyan, where most lived]. The Qadiyanis believe that Mirza Ghulam Ahmad was a *nabi*, or prophet, while their opponents, known as the Lahoris, say that Ahmad was simply a *mujaddid*, a reformer (Lavan 1974).

HISTORY IN AMERICA

Drawn by its large Muslim community, Dr. Sadiq, a missionary of the Ahmadiyya Movement, began his propagation efforts in Detroit, Michigan. Detroit's Muslim population, though diverse, was and still is largely Arab. One of the first mosques in the United States was built in Detroit (Highland Park) for the Sunni and Shi'a Muslims residing there. At first, it appears that Dr. Sadiq's skills and knowledge were perceived as valuable assets to this fledgling community. It was he who started the first Islamic publication in America, *The Moslem Sunrise*. Within a few years, however, he moved his headquarters to Chicago, Illinois.

At first, Sadiq used *The Moslem Sunrise* to expound on what he believed to be theological fallacies in Christian teachings, such as the belief that Christ died on the cross. However, in the relatively short time that he was in the United States, his emphasis changed. Christianity, in his writings, became linked with oppression of people of color. Islam offered a viable alternative to 'racist' Christianity. Sadiq wrote, '. . . the African is slowly but surely realizing that under the Crescent he will be better able to reach the goal of his ambition than under the Cross'. He adds that 'a Negro may aspire to any position under Islam without discrimination'. In this same article he states that 'the White man lives in fear that El-Islam may become the religion of the Negro. And why should it not be? El-Islam would be a wonderful spiritual force in the life of the colored races, uniting us in a bond of common sympathy and interest.' Furthermore, Arabic could become the 'universal language of Negroes . . .'.

Sadiq was a seeker of souls for his dearly loved Islamic Movement. It is apparent that color had meant little to him until he realized the potency of the claim that Islam 'would be a wonderful spiritual force in the life of the colored races,' implying that he saw himself and his fellow Indians as members of these colored races.

There had been some whites among his early American converts. (In England the new Muslims were largely middle-class whites.) But it became apparent the middle-class American whites were not going to be very susceptible to Islam. Also, there was a growing antipathy in America for all non-white, non-western European immigrants. These sentiments were reflected in immigration laws. Rather than turn inward Sadiq found himself equal to the moment. He saw an opportunity when it presented itself.

Richard Turner (1988) states that at this stage of development the goals of Marcus Garvey's Universal Negro Improvement Association and the Ahmadiyya Movement intertwined. According to Turner, 'the success of the Ahmadiyya mission among Afro-Americans would not have been possible without the influence of Marcus Garvey. Furthermore, the Ahmadis were Indians—one of the "darker races of the world"—and the Garvey movement stressed the internationalist perspective which led Afro-Americans to think of themselves in concert with Africans and the "darker races of the world" over against White Europeans and Americans' (Turner 1988, 1990). Christianity came to be viewed as a ' "clan religion" for whites' and criticism from both groups directed towards Christianity became more strident. With the suppression of Garveyism, Turner argues, came a suppression of radical views in the Ahmadiyya Movement as well.

During the period between 1921-5 the Ahmadis claim that more than a thousand persons embraced Islam (*Ahmadiyyat in America*, 1992). Long-time members of the Movement confirm that African Americans continued to join the Ahmadiyya Movement. This fact is also evidenced in a publication from the mid-1970s (no exact date given) in which there are reprints of photographs from the 1940s showing groups of men and women (photographed together) in which African Americans are in the majority. Later pictures, apparently from the early 1970s, also include many African Americans. Of most interest is a picture of the '*Amirs* of the U.S. *Jamaats*'. In this picture are 16 men, well over half of whom are clearly African American. *Amirs* among the Ahmadi are administrators of mosques, who, in the absence of an *imam* (who is the missionary assigned to that mosque) may lead prayers and perform spiritual duties.

Today, under the guidance of Mirza Tahir Ahmad, Khalifatul Masih IV (the fourth *khalifa* of the Ahmadiyya Movement), the community boasts forty centers in twenty-three states in the US. Each of these centers, or *jamaats*, consists of men's local chapters (Ansars and Khuddam) and women's organizations (Lajna). There are co-ordinated with international men's and women's organizations. The growth in the community is not only reflected in numbers but also in the improved quality and sophistication of the literature being produced.

REVIEW OF THE LITERATURE

The subject of Islamic groups in North America has only recently begun to generate active scholarly research. Works such as Eric Lincoln's *Black Muslims in America* (1982) and Clifton are helpful in giving us historical background on the evolution of the Black Muslim community. Elkholy's early (1966) study of the comparison of the Detroit and Toledo Muslim communities serves some of the same purposes for the Arabic-speaking community in North America.

The various Arabic-speaking Muslim groups in the Detroit/Dearborn area have drawn the attention of other scholars, most notably Abraham, Abraham and Aswad (1983), and Aswad (1974, 1989 and 1990). One of the authors of this paper (Walbridge 1990) conducted research on the religious life of the Lebanese Shi'i population of Dearborn.

Haddad and Lummis (1987), with the assistance of a research team, explored the issue of Islamic values in this country. More recently, Haddad (1990) has compiled the research findings and essays of a number scholars writing on various Islamic communities, both indigenous and immigrant. Waugh et al. (1991) have directed their attention to the challenges and adaptations of Islamic families in Canada and the United States. In these three works there are contributions on the Pakistani community, one alluding to the Ahmadiyya Movement.

But the work that has been most beneficial in providing background for this research is Richard Turner's study (1988, 1990) of the history of the Ahmadiyya community and its relationship with the Garveyite Movement.

THE PURPOSE OF THIS STUDY

The Ahmadiyya Movement in North America presents certain unusual characteristics. First, it is among the most zealous Muslim groups in its missionary activity. Unlike other Muslim communities in the United States, the believers did not arrive first and then send for a cleric to guide them. Rather, the missionary came first and had to found a congregation to serve. It would be many years before a substantial population from the missionaries' homeland followed.

Most of the large Muslim immigrant communities in North America are preoccupied with their own needs. Certainly among the Arabic-speaking groups there is a general sense that Islam is a Middle Eastern religion alien to the West. Hence, an active outreach program is lacking. Some religious leaders have written about Islam for a Christian audience, but certainly not on the scale that the Ahmadis have done, nor with the same sense of conviction that converts will actually be made to Islam. Furthermore, the language of the literature and of the sermons in Ahmadi mosques is English, in accordance with the Movement's firm policy of using the language of the land in which Ahmadis find themselves.

Second, the Ahmadis, unlike most other groups, have an international religious leader, a *khalifa.* (The Shi'i have a *marji' taqlid* but he is a scholarly and not an administrative figure.) The Ahmadi *khalifa* is truly a recognized and revered figure among the followers. While he may not be officially considered infallible, this seems to be irrelevant, as so much moral authority is vested in his office. As such, he has a great deal of power to direct the development of his community.

Third, the Ahmadis, though generally looked upon as heretical, are actively ecumenical in their approach to other Muslims. When holding public meetings for propagation purposes, they regularly invite *imams* from other mosques to share the podium. Even groups actively opposed to them will seek out and purchase their general Islamic literature. However, the Ahmadis do not pray in the mosques of other Muslims. While the Ahmadis say this is because other Islamic groups have condemend them as heretics, it can also be argued that Ghulam Ahmad and his son, Mahmoud Ahmad, made the same accusation against their Islamic detractors.

Fourth, since the inception of the movement, the writings of Ghulam Ahmad, his successors and the missionaries have been defiant not only of the Church's refusal to accept Islam, but of Christian doctrine itself. While orthodox Islam denies the divinity of Christ and his death on the cross, it does not deny the resurrection of Christ. More important, other immigrant Muslim groups are not as vocal in their disagreement with Christian doctrine. Attempts to illustrate the superiority of Islam over Christianity, especially in the early Ahmadi literature, often took on a negative tone about Christianity in general.

Finally, the community consists of two major groups from significantly different cultural backgrounds: Pakistani/Indians and African Americans. There are many immigrant Muslim communities from the Middle East, South Asia and elsewhere and there are indigenous (mostly African American) Muslim communities, but to find a community dominated by two such different ethnic groups is most unusual. The fact that African Americans have such a strong religious heritage of their own makes this phenomenon that much more interesting.

This paper will focus on the last factor—the relations between the two ethnic groups. After 60 years of interaction, how have these two groups affected one another? What roles do the two groups play in the community? How do their perceptions of their religious life and commitment differ from one another, if at all? And how do the two groups perceive one another? While the issue of ethnic relations will be the central theme here, some of the other factors listed earlier have impinged upon this issue to some extent and will, therefore, be addressed.

METHODOLOGY

We mailed some 700 questionnaires to Ahmadis throughout the United States. Along with the questionnaire was a letter stating that the Ahmadi National Amir in Washington had given his blessing to this study. (He reviewed the questionnaire and no changes were made after his having seen it.) We felt it necessary to have his approval since the Ahmadis feel some reservation about being studied. They share a concern with many other Islamic groups that Americans are hostile to Islam and therefore cannot be trusted to write about them fairly. Furthermore, while the Ahmadis consider themselves Muslim, they are still a relatively young group and, as such, wish to control the image of themselves projected to the world at large. It is principally because one of the researchers in this project (F.H.) is a long-standing member of the Movement that we have had the cooperation of the community. Having said that, it should also be mentioned that the non-Ahmadi member of this research team (L.W.) has been treated with the utmost courtesy by individual Ahmadis.

At this writing 70 questionnaires have been returned. From the South Asians we received 32 responses from males and 16 from females. Eleven American-born men and eight American-born women returned completed questionnaires. We are still making efforts to have members complete the questionnaires and return them. With this relatively small number of responses, we cannot handle the data statistically. Still, trends are clear, and the statements made by the respondents will be referred to throughout the following discussion.

We have also developed an interview schedule so that first-hand interviews can be conducted. At this point, only three of these have been completed. We plan to visit centers throughout North America to make this study complete and thorough.

We also rely on information from knowledgable informants to discuss recent events in the community, and on published literature. Visits to mosques and public meetings which allow for observation and for informal conversations with the congregation helped in gleaning information about the community.

FINDINGS

Some of the questions asked of the believers concerned the relations between American-born and foreign-born Ahmadis. Most of the American-born respondents said that the relationship was weak. One said that the interactions were good, but occurred only in the mosque. The Pakistani-born men were also likely to refer to the need for stronger bonds between the two groups, while Pakistani-born women felt that the relationships were positive and strong.

To understand these responses it is necessary to look back over the past twenty years or so of developments in the community. While the Ahmadis have experienced persecution in their homeland (Pakistan) and elsewhere, they began facing their gravest problems in the 1970s and 1980s. The worst situation came when General Zia-ul Haq imposed the military ordinances of 1984 that were incorporated in the Pakistani Penal Code. These stated that the Ahmadis could not identify themselves as Muslims, refer to their house of prayer as a masjid (mosque) or utter the *kalimah*, the Muslim profession of faith (Gualtieri 1989). It was at this point that large numbers of Pakistani Ahmadis came to North America. Up until that time the Pakistani Ahmadis in the US were mostly single men who had come to study or work. Therefore, the majority of believers in US *jamaats* had been African Americans. While this pattern reportedly still exists in some areas of the US it is less prevalent today, particularly in the East Coast cities where so many Pakistanis have settled.

Part of the reason for the change in proportion of numbers of the two groups is simply the number of Pakistani immigrants to North America. But the other reason is that when the Pakistanis came in large numbers, some of the African Americans left the Movement.

The pattern of settlement is important to understanding the group and inter-group dynamics occurring here. Once entire families came from South Asia, the needs of these immigrants changed. Single men working on their studies were not necessarily motivated to become active members in the mosques. Furthermore, as some of the Ahmadis themselves have suggested, these men were not as deeply committed to their faith then as they would later become.

The appearance of women and children on the scene necessitated a number of changes. (This is certainly not a unique situation. In colonized countries relations between the colonized and the colonizers also underwent radical changes when the men began to bring their famlies abroad. See Schermerhorn [1970] for a discussion of this topic.) The women would need a safe haven where they could meet with others who would completely share their beliefs and customs, particularly regarding modesty and the segregation of the sexes. The children would require religious training in keeping with what they were accustomed to back home.

The Pakistani-born men therefore felt much more inclined to find active roles for themselves in the mosques. By doing so, they antagonized the African American men. The latter began to see Pakistani men not as men of color like themselves, but as substitutes for the American whites who had traditionally deprived them of power. The wife of one formerly active member of the community complained that the Pakistanis behaved like *nouveau riche*. Some of the American-born membership travelled to Rabwah, Pakistan where the center of the Movement had been before it felt compelled to move to London. They were quick to point out to their South Asian-born brethren that they had not been living the life of the middle classes prior to coming to North America. Obviously, social class issues were creating tensions, which were heightened by the fact that they were linked with race.

Another related factor that worked against the harmony of the two ethnic groups was the fact that the Pakistanis felt a great need to ensure that the mosques were in 'safe' neighborhoods. In 1974 a mosque had been opened in Brooklyn. It is reported that this mosque, seen as centrally located, was well attended. The Pakistanis, however, did not like the location: they perceived the neighborhood as being dangerous. The New York mosque and mission house is now located in a middle-class area in Queens. The participants in a recent Friday prayer service which we attended were almost exclusively of South Asian origin. On that occasion the subject of the sermon was the need to attend Friday prayers regularly. In New Jersey, the Center which was formerly in Newark is now located in Clifton, also a middle-class community, without a large black population.

Male/Female Diferences in Reaction to the Influx of Immigrants

The influx of Pakistani men seems to have had a more negative impact on African American men than on the women. The Pakistani men arriving in large numbers came with graduate and professional degrees. Conscious of their social status, they sought out others of their class. While African American Ahmadis have been influenced by the emphasis placed on education in their religion, by and large they have not yet attained the educational levels of their South Asian counterparts. They complained of being made to feel inferior and powerless once again.

African American women seem not to have been any happier than the men with the change in circumstances they experienced upon the arrival of the South Asians, yet they ultimately did not experience as much upheaval. It was at this point that the American-born women were admonished to follow the religious sanctions regarding dress and sexual segregation. This reportedly was a test for many of the women, yet they could understand these rules as being within the purview of Islam. Most conceded to the new enforcement of rules, at least to some degree. Concessions were not to be made in other areas, however. Observing the relations between Pakistani men and women, African American women were quick to label the perceived submissiveness of Pakistani women towards their men as being a cultural and not a religious matter. Some American-born women expressed a feeling of superiority over the Pakistani-born women, whom they saw as accepting an inferior position to men. One woman, very active in women's group activities, reports that there were expressions of pity from the American women for the Pakistani women, whom they saw as socially isolated and prevented by their husbands from becoming fully involved in the women's auxiliary organization.

Nevertheless, the Pakistani women were not seen by the African American women as a threat to their leadership roles in the mosques. The American-born women had brought with them from their churches the knowledge of how to run an organization. It is beyond the scope of this paper to trace the history of women in American churches, but it should be mentioned that churces have been excellent training grounds for both black and white American women in terms of developing organizational skills. This has been acknowledged by the South Asian women, who have quite consistently elected American-born women as presidents of the women's organization on local and national levels. The skills of the American women have not been lost on the leadership either. A committee of American women indexed a five-volume Quran in English translation. The names of these women appear on the front pages of the volumes. While inter-ethnic tensions did leave some African American women disaffected, the exodus from the community has not been as dramatic as that for the men.

A Comparison of the Two Groups Religiously

Since the questionnaires were distributed through the Ahmadi centers, it is obvious that the people whom we reached were active members of the Movement and regular attendees at the mosque. Reaching those who were less involved would be a far greater task. However, the questionnaires do serve a purpose in that they compare active members of the community of both major ethnic groups.

Certainly devotion to Islam is not a point on which one finds differences. The South Asians commonly reported feelings of renewed conviction now that they live in North America. The American-born Ahmadis express a new vision of and purpose for life. At least in the questionnaires, the Americans are more likely to speak about their personal relationship with Allah than are the South Asians, which would be expected considering the American propensity to have a personal relationship to Jesus (Bellah et al. 1985). However, this again is a very tentative finding. One informant did talk about the African Americans experiencing 'excitement' that takes on a physical demension at times, a phenomenon commonly found in American churches, and particularly the Black church. To what degree this is found is certainly an area that should be explored.

All respondents expressed concerns about trying to live an Islamic life in a materialistic and immoral society, but the South Asians expressed a degree of reproach for North American society that was not found in the responses of American-born participants. One man said that Americans 'lack respect for elders, were materialistic, selfish, disrespectful of religion, and casual regarding sex'. His comments were quite typical of both South Asian men and women. The Americans' responses were less stereotypical and were more likely to express racism as one of the ills of this society. The highly personal responses found among the Americans were lacking among the South Asians. One woman wrote, '[I am] an African-American Ahmadi Muslim female and that places me in a distinct minority. Sometimes [I] feel separate and isolated.' No such response came from any of the South Asians.

While almost all the South Asians were married and married to Muslims, there were far more unmarried American Ahmadis. In reading the questionnaires, it is apparent that most of these had once been married or in a relationship that produced children. Issues of marriage are of course paramount in most religious communities, but it would be of particular concern in this situation. Chastity in Islamic society carries a degree of importance that is difficult for most late-twentieth century Americans to comprehend. On the other hand, discussion of AIDS and the distribution of condoms on school grounds is probably even more incomprehensible to many South Asians. Few Americans have been untouched by the impact of the sexual revolution and there are many African American Ahmadis who have not escaped the legacy of the breakdown of family.

The vast majority of Ahmadis in our sample believe that Muslims should not marry outside of their faith. In this case, it means that Ahmadi women should only marry Ahmadi men. There was a slight tendency for the Americans to feel less inhibited by this restriction than the South Asians, but on this point both groups were largely in agreement.

For the most part, differences in the community are not about religious practice and theology. The differences that do exist are about cultural matters, often subtle behaviors that have nothing to do with religion. One woman from the Midwestern US wrote at length about her experiences and observations in the Movement. She wrote,

> Both groups are continually challenged to understand the others' mores, value system and habits. We must practice being accomodating, tolerant and patient. For example, Americans like to remain quiet when others are still praying. Pakistanis, when they complete the prayer, like to whisper while others are still praying. They find nothing disrespectful about it. In many areas what one side considers appropriate etiquette the other culture disdains. Another example [is that] Pakistani hospitality is developed to an art form. Americans' level of hospitality is far beneath the Pakistani comfort level.

The Role of the Khalifa in Intra-Community Problems

In 1989 Mirza Tahir Ahmad, the fourth *khalifa* of the Ahmadiyya Movement, visited this country to 'celebrate the Ahmadiyya Centennial Celebrations [*sic*] with the Ahmadi Muslims in the USA' ('Ahmadiyyat in America' 1992). According to one informant, however, the main object of his visit was to try to mend the rift between the two ethnic groups. She reports that when he was brought to a meeting in which only South Asians were present, he looked around and asked 'Where are my American brothers and sisters?' When told they were not present, he demanded to be taken to them immediately. He insisted on visiting the Americans in their homes and wherever they were assembled.

How much of an impact the *khalifa's* admonitions have had on the community is hard to assess, though there are indications that the two groups have become more conscious of attempting to be more understanding of each others' problems and outlooks. One very active African American woman stated, 'Since 1987 the internal cohesion and development of the Community has accelerated due primarily to a *khalifa* who absolutely will not tolerate overt nationalism and racism within the Ahmadiyya community. I have seen the *khalifa* catch a plane and come to America only to quell reported "incidents" (from both cultural groups).'

The problems outlined earlier are more prevalent in areas where there has been a large influx of South Asians. Where the proportions of numbers between the two groups is more in balance, the community seems to be able to cope with the differences. It is reported by one informant that 'in areas where there is still a significant American-born Ahmadi membership, Americans get assigned media and public relation duties while Indo-Pakistanis tend to be elected as Secretary of Education, moral training, and the like'.

Before leaving the issue of the role of the *khalifa*, there is an incident that (1) illustrates some of the challenges this community faces and (2) helps in understanding the limitations of the power of the *khalifa* in the American community.

There is little inter-marriage between South Asian Ahmadis and American-born Ahmadis. Indeed, Pakistanis are reported to frequently send home for spouses for their children, especially for brides for their sons (Waugh 1991). The American-born women, because so many of the African American men left the Movement, have found it difficult to find husbands. One of the 'sisters' wrote to the *khalifa* bewailing the plight of the American women believers. She said that they wanted to live by Islamic law, that they wanted Muslim husbands, but were having difficulty finding them. The *khalifa* apparently felt the urgency of the woman's appeal and began to take action. He wrote back to her saying that he had located men in Pakistan who were willing to marry the American sisters if they would agree to this arrangement. Not one of them accepted. The primary reason given for this rejection was that the American women, sensitive to the differences in culture between themselves and the Pakistanis, could not face the prospect of a cross-cultural marriage. They simply thought such a marriage would not work.

DISCUSSION

As Turner has shown, race was the overriding concern of the early African American converts, many of whom were also Garveyites. Other groups appealing to Blacks for their allegiance—most notably Black Muslims—emerged out of the Garveyite Movement and became competitors to the Ahmadis. Those who became alligned with the Black Muslims were individuals interest in racial separation. Eric Lincoln (1982) made an interesting observation when he said,

> To be identified with a movement that openly rejects the fundamental values of the powerful majority is to increase vastly one's self-esteem and one's stature among one's peers. This social incentive to defiance is not limited to the Muslims; among black intellectuals generally, a deviation from the white man's way of doing things has come to be called 'independent thinking' and reaps its rewards. The difference between the intellectual and the Muslims in this regard is simply one of degree: the intellectual's defiance is carefully calculated; the Muslim's is wholehearted and absolute. Thus the intellectual will not become a Muslim, but he will embrace Baha'i. Both men are repudiating an identity to which they are hypersensitive in the presence of the white man, and both are chiding Christianity for its racism. But the intellectual astutely remains within the orbit of the white man's culture, while the Muslims set themselves completely adrift. (p. 31)

The Ahmadis probably stand somewhere between the Black Muslims and the Baha'is. The early members were taught that there should be harmony among the races, but this ideology was not really put to the test until large numbers of South Asians joined their communities. And since the arrival of so many South Asians, the movement has been growing only slowly among African Americans. One knowledgeable African American member stated,

> For those Blacks interested in Ahmadiyya Islam, when they are exposed to our predominantly Asian membership they shy away from joining. [They] see that the leadership is Pakistani, and Blacks have a problem with that. For those who allow themselves a closer look they hear Urdu spoken, see curry served at dinner and a sharp separation between men and women in the mosque. Not allowing themselves to get quite close enough to be indoctrinated with the ideals of the *real* New World Order launched by the Promised Messiah . . . they turn away from us. She continues, 'If they find racial and class superiority overtones coming from a few members, they also run.

While many adherents of the Ahmadiyya Movement thus far have found its stance on racial issues and its emphasis on brotherhood to be particularly attractive, other points of doctrine will also have to be emphasized if teaching is to be successful in the future. The days of reaching large numbers of poor and perhaps even middle-class Blacks are over, particularly in areas where the South Asians dominate. The South Asians are by and large economically very successful. They tend to live in well-to-do suburbs and associate with people of their own rank. Where Islam is growing most rapidly in this country is in the prisons, the teaching being done by individuals who relate to the experience of being an American prisoner. The South Asian Ahmadi community would not bring such experience to bear in their propagation efforts. When asked where these efforts are being most emphasized, at least in the New York region, a prominent Pakistani-American Ahmadi explained that the youth are the focus of most of the efforts. Since their own youth tend to be seious students, either in college or college-bound, it may be presumed that it is among this class of people that most of the propagation will be done.

In order to reach this population, issues of racial harmony cannot be abandoned, but neither will they be sufficient to attract large numbers of Americans. Racial issues have become increasingly complex, and certainly Muslims, let alone Ahmadi Muslims, are not unique in promoting better understanding and equality among the races. However, there are other social issues that Muslims can address in this society, and the Ahmadi have shown some awareness of this fact. At public meetings they unabashedly discuss 'family values', and the problems brought about by the use of drugs and alcohol and other social evils.

They do exhibit flexibility and a desire to be sensitive to the specific needs and problems of the society. Yet, at least in the short run, this probably will not meet with huge success. At this writing, the Ahmadiyya Movement faces the following obstacles:

1. While Americans are reported to be taking a renewed interest in religion, this has meant returning to 'the church' and to the religious experiences of one's youth. The halcyon days of the 1960s and early 1970s are with us no longer. These were the days when individuals 'found' themselves through dramatically different religious ideologies than the ones from which they came.
2. The Ahmadiyya Movement will not be appealing so long as it is so closely identified with a foreign community. It matters not from which country they have originated; their customs, dress, speech style, etc., are alien to the large society. They might draw respect for having fine manners and for presenting no problems to society, but this is not enough to draw adherents. There are indications that the Ahmadi leadership in the US is aware of this.
3. As Muslims in America, they suffer from a particular obstacle as Islam takes on the role that communism held in this society until the demise of the Soviet Union. Muslim immigrant groups have to expend a great deal of energy just to convince Americans that they are not a threat to the well-being of their neighborhoods. These are not ideal circumstances under which to propagate one's faith.
4. While racial considerations may have overridden any theological considerations for African Americans, this probably would not be the case for white Americans. It is true that many denominations that have sprung up on American soil have been either short on creed or have had creeds that are contrary to ideas of mainstream Christianity. Yet to openly preach that Christ did not die on the cross and ascend into heaven has not been and probably will not be well-received by most church-going Americans. On the other hand, there are certainly other religious groups (within Christianity) in the US that do not ascribe to orthodox Christian dogma and yet have been very successful, the Mormons being one example. Prospects for reaching other Muslims, however, may be brighter. The Ahmadis stress a stong community life—with some communities being more successful than others. This would undoubtedly be attractive to young Muslims, particularly

those who find themselves alone and adrift in this society. Furthermore, the Ahmadis are a rejuvenated movement in Islam with a strong sense of fitting into modern society without being corrupted by it. Also, as people loyal to the government, Muslims who join this Movement do not need to experience the dissidence one might feel about living in a predominantly Christian land. Here in the US the Ahmadi have an opportunity to be influential in Muslim activities in general because they are well organized, have direction from a religious leader (the *khalifa*) who pays close attention to the developments of the community, and have an abundant, well-produced literature that is clear in its presentation of Islam and is often purchased by non-Ahmadi Muslims.

While it is not possible to predict the success of the Ahmadiyya Movement in the long run, it seems likely that the current period will be mostly devoted to consolidation of the existing community and will experience limited growth among Americans.

REFERENCES

Abraham, Samir, Nabeel Abraham and Barabara Aswad, 1983. 'The Southend: An Arab Muslim Working-Class community', in Sameer Y. Abraham and Nabeel Abraham, eds., *Arabs in the New World: Studies on Arab-American Communities*. Detroit: Wayne State University Center for Urban Studies, 163-84.

The Ahmadiyya Movement in Islam, 1992. *Ahmadiyyat in America*, Washington, D.C. (July).

Aswad, Barbara C., 1974. 'The Southeast Dearborn Arab Community Struggles for Survival against Urban "Renewal".' in Barbara C. Aswad, ed., *Arabic Speaking Communities in North American Cities*, Staten Island, NY: Center for Migration Studies, 53-84.

———, 1988. 'How the 'Rich Peasant Mentality' and Welfare Affect Immigrant Arab Women and Employment Patterns,' paper presented at Middle East Studies Association Meetings.

———, 1989. 'The Lebanese Muslim Community in Dearborn, Michigan,' paper presented at the Centre for Lebanese Studies' *Conference on Lebanese Emigration*, St. Hughes College, Oxford, England.

Bellah, Robert N., Richard Madsen, William T. Sullivan, Ann Swidler, and Steven M. Tipton, 1985. *Habits of the Heart*, NY: Harper and Row.

Elkholy, Abdo, 1966. *The Arab Muslims in the United States*, New Haven: College and University Press.

Friedman, Yohanan, 1989. *Prophecy Continuous: Aspects of Ahmadi Religious Thought and Its Medieval Background*, Berkeley: University of California Press.

Gualtieri, Antonio R., 1989. *Conscience and Coercion: Ahmadi Muslims and Orthodoxy in Pakistan*, Montreal: Guernica Editions.

Haddad, Yvonne Y., ed., 1991. *The Muslims of America*, NY: Oxford University Press.

Haddad, Yvonne Y. and Adair T. Lummis, 1987. *Islamic Values in the United States*, NY: Oxford University Press.

Hogben, W. Murray, 1991. 'Marriage and Divorce Among Muslims in Canada,' in Earle H. Waugh, Sharon Abu-Laban, and Regula Burckhardt Qureshi, eds., *Muslim Families in North America*, Edmonton: University of Alberta Press.

Lavan, Spencer, 1974. *The Ahmadiya Movement: A History and Perspective*, New Delhi: Manohar.

Lincoln, Eric, 1982. *The Black Muslims in America*, Boston: Beacon Press.

Din, Maulvi M. Jan., 1924. *The Moslem Sunrise*, vol. III, no. I.

Sadiq, Mufti Muhammad, Oct. 1921. *The Moslem Sunrise*, no. 2.

———, July 1922. *The Moslem Sunrise*, no. 5.

———, Jan. 1923. *The Moslem Sunrise*, vol. II, no. 1.

Schermerhorn, R.A. 1970. *Comparative Ethnic Relations: A Framework for Theory and Research*, NY: Random House.

Turner, Richard Brent, 1988. The Ahmadiyya Mission to Blacks in the United States in the 1920s', in *The Journal of Religious Thought*, vol. 44, Winter-Spring, no. 2.

———, 1990. 'Islam in the United States in the 1920s: The Quest for a New vision in Afro-American Religion', unpublished Doctoral Dissertation.

Walbridge, Linda, 1991. 'Shi'i Islam in an American Community,' unpublished Doctoral Dissertation.

Waugh, Earle H., Baha Abu-Laban, Regula B. Qureshi, eds., 1991. *The Muslim Community in North America*, Edmonton: University of Alberta Press.

The [Re-]Construction of South Asian Muslim Identity in Queens, New York[1]

USHA SANYAL

INTRODUCTION

In recent scholarship on race and women in America, it has been convincingly argued that we need to view categories such as 'race' and 'gender' as social constructs, historically rooted in and shaped by social experience. It is argued, furthermore, that such construction is subject to constant contestation between individuals and groups differentially situated in the power structure of societies, and that it is therefore part of a larger political process 'involving unequal relations of power'.[2] In this paper I extend this analysis to an exploration of questions of identity among certain Muslim groups in the greater New York metropolitan area.

There has been too frequently, I believe, a tendency to reify 'Islam', and in recent years, to conflate Muslim activism and religiosity with 'fundamentalism' (a term with which I am uncomfortable), when, in fact, we know that 'Islam' means many things to many people (particularly within the Muslim community, whether conceived as the world-wide *umma*, or as more locally-determined, particular communities of Muslims). Beyond the minimalist definition of a Muslim as one who believes in and practises the five 'pillars' or duties of the faith, much more is involved, obviously, in 'Islam'. Thus, I would like to argue, Muslims' own understandings of 'Islam' are historically rooted in and shaped by their social experience. In recent fieldwork I have tried to understand why some South Asian Muslims in America have renewed their commitment to their faith, what the social context of this commitment has been, and how they construct their 'Islam'.

ICNA

There are today a growing number of Muslim organizations nationwide in America attempting to bring Muslims together and provide a forum for community activities in an 'Islamic' manner. My fieldwork data comes from the Islamic Circle of North America (ICNA), mosque and community centre in Jamaica, North America. Founded in 1977, the center today has approximately a hundred full members, 1,000 associate members (half of these are called 'workers' to indicate their active involvement in ICNA affairs), and about 2,500 supporters who attend meetings and events on an irregular basis.[3] In terms of geographical spread, the organization is headquartered in New York City, and has branches in several cities throughout the country, as well as Canada. Its purpose is broadly stated as seeking 'the pleasure of Allah' and establishing an 'Islamic way of life'. More specifically, its vision is based on Maulana Mawdudi's *Jama'at-e Islami*, an organization particularly active today in Pakistan.

Maulana Mawdudi (d. 1979) led a movement with a simple message which has attracted educated Muslims in a number of countries outside Pakistan, its home of origin. Mawdudi's understanding of 'Islam' rested on a number of related propositions. The first of these is that sovereignty rests entirely with God, and society must be based on this principle. As Charles Adams says, from this follows Mawdudi's judgement that

> the moral evil of the age . . . consist[s] in having accepted sovereigns other than God—the will of the people, the law of rulers, the nation-state, custom, personal preference, or whatever—and . . . furthermore, that the sufferings of the age in their entirety are to be traced to this error.[4]

Mawdudi's second proposition is that the basis for human conduct is the divine law, accessible through the Koran and the model provided by the Prophet Muhammad through the *hadith* literature. According to Mawdudi, these two sources provide whatever guidance Muslims need. All that is required of the Muslim is that he or she apply reason and judgement to understand the texts, and then implement the guidance these provide in his or her life. Scholars of Islamic law (the *ulama*) may thus be dispensed with in the conduct of one's personal life.

Finally, Mawdudi insisted that Muslims must go beyond the personal transformation of the individual to the transformation of society. This in turn requires political power:

. . . common people . . . act according to the pattern ordained by those who possess power. . . . If [power is] in the hands of righteous people, worshippers of God, then it is inevitable that the whole of social life be God-worshipping. . . . None of the purposes of religion can be accomplished so long as control of affairs is in the hands of *kafirs* [unbelievers].[5]

The *Jama'at-e Islami* seeks to create 'a corps of disciplined, morally upright, ideologically sound persons who might occupy the crucial positions in the future Islamic state Mawdudi hoped to bring into being'.[6]

Here in America, ICNA sees itself as furthering the *Jama'at's* agenda, shorn of its political aspects. In the American context, ICNA has a clear message. On the one side stands a morally bankrupt America; on the other a small morally upright Muslim 'brotherhood'. The cover of ICNA's 1989-90 annual report presents a picture of stark contrasts: against a green background on the middle of the page large letters proclaim: 'Islam is the Answer'. Surrounding this slogan on all sides are the problems of American society: AIDS, poverty, alcoholism, crime, adultery, discrimination, suicide, child abuse, stress, pornography, homicide, drugs, homosexuality, abortion. In painting this picture, ICNA finds meaning and purpose in its crusade to 'Islamize' American Muslims and preach Islam to non-Muslims.

But ICNA's work starts, first, with its own membership. Like the *Jama'at*, the core membership is deliberately small. Members must sign an oath of loyalty, and pledge to make a number of important changes in their personal lives. Thus members are required among other things to 'abstain from major sins', and agree not to 'earn [their] livelihood by means which may be described as immoral, or sinful, e.g. involvement in riba (interest or usury), liquor, adultery, promotion of vulgarity, false witnessing, bribery, embezzlement, stealing, or gambling, etc.'.[7] Beyond this, members must strive to bring up their children in an appropriate manner, and even to try to reform the life-style of a spouse involved in 'un-Islamic activities' or making a living through 'forbidden means'. Finally, members are required to donate two and a half per cent of their monthly wages to ICNA's treasury (a new kind of *zakat* or alms-tax, one might say). Failure to observe the pledge can lead to temporary suspension and, eventually, expulsion (by decision of the central leadership as represented by the central Nazim and a two-thirds majority of the *Shura* (consultative council).

Beyond their personal dedication to ICNA and its cause, members must engage in efforts toward *dawa* (propagation) both among 'nominal' Muslims and non-Muslims. In the former group, a particular focus is youth-related work.

The fear of losing the younger generation to American culture is real, and undoubtedly grounded in experience. ICNA members do their best to provide in 'Islam' an attractive alternative to the young through youth outreach programmes, summer camps, media programmes, and the like. While the number of young people responding to these efforts undoubtedly represents a minority of the young Muslim population in America, these numbers seem nevertheless to be growing. Once they have been won over, they become part of a self-conscious Muslim 'vanguard' devoted to winning 'converts' from the large population of nominal Muslims.

In this connection, ICNA makes a great effort to propagate its message through the media. It publishes an English-language monthly magazine, *The Message International*, whose presentation is polished and attractive, and scope wide. Recent issues have focused on events in Iraq, Algeria, Bosnia, and the former Soviet Union, together with more local concerns. Moreover, a division of ICNA called 'Sound Vision' is engaged in developing computer software which allows one to call up any word or combination of words in the Koran and *hadith* literature; for children, it has developed several programmes consciously patterned on Sesame Street and other popular American TV shows, adding, of course, a didactic message.

Having sketched briefly the kinds of activities that ICNA engages in (there are many more, including Sunday school, a matrimonial service, a book service, etc.), let me turn now to questions relating to the ICNA members' efforts to reconstruct their identities at a more personal level. In doing so, I draw on field observations.

First, the people I observed at ICNA are part of the most recent wave of immigration, those who have migrated to America since the early 1970s. As other studies have pointed out, a notable characteristic of this wave of immigration is its attempt to differentiate itself from the host culture, rather than to assimilate with it. Many reasons are given for this: among them the fact that the facility of communications worldwide enables immigrants to simultaneously participate in, or at least be influenced by, the culture and politics of their home country (and, for Muslims, the wider Muslim world) while in America. In view of the larger number of Muslim immigrants in the US, moreover, no radical break is required with the past, and assimilation into

American culture can be more selective than it once was.[8] These immigrants are likely not only to pride themselves on standing apart from the host country and its culture but also from earlier Muslim immigrants.[9]

For the members of ICNA, this effort to differentiate themselves from Americans has meant, in effect, creating an identity in opposition to it. For them, this oppositional identity is articulated in terms of an increased emphasis on 'Islam'. In my conversations with a number of first-generation Muslim women immigrants, I was struck by the observation that their commitment to an Islamic identity has increased after coming to the US. One of my informants was a leader and active organizer of the women's wing of ICNA, who told me that before she came to America twenty-one years ago, she had never observed *purdah*.

Sakina (as I will call her) came to the United States in 1970 from Lucknow (India), following her husband here a few months after his arrival.[10] He had an engineering degree and got a job right away. Soon he joined an MBA programme on a part-time basis, going to school after work near their home in New Rochelle. Sakina, twenty years old, had just given birth to their first baby girl in Lucknow. Although still recovering from a painful and difficult delivery, she had left for America only days later because her American visa was about to expire. She remembered that trip vividly, for soon after her arrival she had to be hospitalized when her stitches became septic. A year later she was pregnant with her second child, and again went to India to give birth. This time she stayed with her parents for four months, returning when her husband came to collect her after performing the *hajj*.

Raising two more children in the coming years, Sakina never went to school in America nor has she worked here. Her life began to change when, out of curiosity and without any encouragement from her husband, she began to read books by Mawdudi, in particular his translation of the Koran into Urdu, books that were in their home because of her husband's fondness for reading. Gradually, she began to feel that she should change some things in her life, things that were in her own hands and power to change. As she saw it, saying the daily prayers, keeping the Ramadan fast, and veiling herself in public were things she could do if she could build up the strength and will to do so. Today in public she wears a slate grey garment that covers her from head to toe, including a mouth covering, leaving only her eyes exposed. In private, she is an attractive woman in her early forties, fond of jewellery and with feminine tastes in clothes, which continue to be Indian in style.

It is apparent that Sakina's lifestyle changed *after* her immigration to America. When she goes to Lucknow on family visits, she finds her family, as before, not observing daily prayers, not wearing the veil. Why, one wonders, did she make these lifestyle changes other than out of idle curiosity in Mawdudi? I think the timing of her involvement in ICNA affairs must surely be important: having raised her children to school-age, she must have had unaccustomed (and probably unwanted) leisure on her hands, and may even have been personally lonely. Although her frequent visits back home indicate that she continues to be part of an extended kinship network, in New York City she lives in a single family home with her husband and children. In addition, a South Asian Muslim couple and their two daughters (one of them divorced, with a little girl) live next door. I believe that association with ICNA has allowed Sakina to build a new network of social relationships with other South Asian Muslim women (and through them, with their friends and families more generally) that substitutes for the kinship-based network that she would have been a part of had she remained in Lucknow.

Thus, in Sakina's case, and that of other first-generation women like herself, 'Islam' and ethnicity (members of ICNA are predominantly South Asian and Urdu-speaking) have been privileged in the absence of extended family relationships. There is a social function to this as well: the sharing of a South Asian Muslim cultural past, as well as the opportunity provided for the children of such families to meet other immigrant South Asian children (with the possibility this provides of marriage alliances, as well as learning Urdu, and other social goals). And for someone as dynamic as Sakina herself, ICNA has also dramatically enlarged her field of activity. As a leader of the women's wing for several years, she has shouldered considerable responsibility and been geographically mobile. She has frequently travelled by air outside New York to report on the activities of branches of ICNA in other parts of the US and in Canada, accompanied by another woman like herself. In the course of a normal week, Sakina drives long distances from her New York City home to attend and lead women's prayer and meditation meetings either in someone's private home or at the ICNA community center, about twice a week. At these meetings, informal groups of married women and young girls read the Koran, reflect on what they have read, and exhort one another to be better Muslims.

In the course of her many years of leadership, Sakina has also acquired impressive public speaking skills. One of the special events organized by the women's wing is an all-night vigil at the Queens mosque twice a year—once to celebrate the anniversary of the Prophet Muhammad's birth, and again during the fasting month of Ramadan. This lasts from about eleven at night to six the next morning, and is an exclusively female event. The husbands drop their wives at the mosque, then return home to look after the children. Meanwhile, at the mosque there are speeches by the chief office-holders and active members of the women's wing, on topics ranging from the importance of prayer to current political events. On the night I observed the proceedings (in October 1991), Sakina delivered a ringing speech in Urdu on the American and Soviet role in opposing Muslim interests on the world stage (she referred to the *mujahidin* in Afghanistan, among other things), and compared present-day America with the *Jahiliyya* of pre-Islamic Arabia. Another woman spoke about the trials and tribulations of Sayyid Qutub, the famous Egyptian leader of the Muslim Brotherhood during the 1960s. Clearly, identification with and involvement in ICNA affairs has been a major source of empowerment for women like Sakina.

A somewhat different case of self-empowerment through religious activism (in that this involves a conversion) is that of the young Hindu woman from the Caribbean who came to New York to study accounting and converted to Islam about six months after her arrival:

> Ruhana [as I shall call her] came from Trinidad in September 1988 to study accounting at LaGuardia Community College. She is one of three children. Her family is of Indian origin, and lives in Trinidad and Tobago. They are Hindus.
>
> Ruhana told me that she had always prayed, and had been looking for something meaningful, something that would tell her how to live her life. . . . [But] nothing she read was meaningful to her in personal terms. When she came to New York, she was frightened about being alone in the midst of crime, drugs, and violence, and prayed even harder for help. Then one day she heard God tell her that she was a Muslim.

The decision to convert was obviously a source of strength to Ruhana. As with most of the Muslim women with whom I have talked, she was self-confident, proud of her new identity, and articulate. When I met her in October 1991, she was preparing to leave New York, having just taken the bold step of agreeing to marry an American Muslim she had never met, who lived in Houston. Her frail but apparently unflappable mother (who had no part in influencing any of Ruhana's important decisions) was going with her to attend the wedding.

Among second-generation Muslims that I have met at Rutgers University, New Brunswick, some women have suggested that a visit back to their homes of origin (Pakistan or India) have had a transformative influence in their lives. Aisha was a year old when her parents emigrated. She grew up without any special religious instruction. Then, when she was seventeen (and in her Junior year at high school), she went to Pakistan. Her experience of Pakistani culture and comparing it with her own lifestyle in America led to a gradual process of change in the direction of greater religious observance, though not in emulation of her Pakistani kin. Indeed, she was critical of them for being 'bad' Muslims. In an interview she told me:

> Three years after I came back from Pakistan, I started wearing the *hijab* [veil]. In Pakistan, wearing a scarf isn't very prevalent. People who grew up in their respective Muslim countries a lot of times just do what they're told because they assume it's right. What happens in America is that you really have to find out what's right and what's wrong. A lot of times you find out things that your parents don't know because they've grown up with what's been told to them. They didn't really bother to look into it. Over here, you have to do a lot of your own reading and research to find out. I think a lot of the older Pakistani and Indian women don't realize that you're supposed to wear a *hijab*. It states explicitly in the Qur'an and the *hadith* [prophetic sayings] that you do have to. I had to explain to my Mom, I had to show her, I had to have a little patience, but now, it's fine.

Aisha's account points to an interesting role reversal, and to a new kind of conflict between first-generation immigrant parents and their children who have grown up here.

One of the areas of tension is the conflict between the universality of 'Islam' and the particularity of South Asian ethnicity. As I have mentioned, the women at ICNA are overwhelmingly South Asian and Urdu-speaking. Their children's first language, however, is English, though most can speak Urdu as well. The importance of ethnicity appears to decrease for the second generation, primarily due to school and college and the exposure to American culture that this entails. However, even second-generation South Asian Muslims tend to marry someone from their parents' host country. To some extent, this may be explained by the fact that Muslim marriages are usually arranged or at least initiated by the parents. None of the single Muslim women that I talked to at Rutgers on the subject of marriage expected to marry someone of her own choosing, though they expect the final decision to be theirs. Given the continuing importance of ethnicity to the first generation, marriages between people of different racial backgrounds seem unlikely to become more common in this generation. In particular, marriages between South Asian Muslims and Black American Muslims seem very unlikely because the latter continue to be associated with negative South Asian cultural images. As long as ICNA remains largely South Asian in composition, however, this will probably not be a very important issue for its members.

The re-negotiation of gender and generational roles is a more immediate concern. On the whole, despite the continuing importance of South Asian cultural norms—expressed most visibly in the segregation of men and women in the ICNA mosque—I got the impression of a much greater emphasis on equality between the sexes than would be the case in South Asia. In this context I was particularly struck by the widespread use of the terms 'brother' and 'sister' (in Islam) by English-speaking South Asians when addressing one another. In the same vein, the ICNA annual report speaks of the activities of its women's wing as the 'Sisters' Wing: The Other Wheel of the Wagon'.

Likewise, when I tried to understand the significance to the women at ICNA and to college-goers of wearing the veil, it became clear that they saw it as a strong statement of identity and difference; that those who do wear the veil do so voluntarily, sometimes against the wishes of their elders, and find in it a means of personal liberation. In fact, women who have chosen to wear the veil (a step they take with great deliberation, for they see it as irrevocable) seem to develop a sense of superiority to their unveiled sisters, not to speak of the non-Muslim majority.

Clearly, these personal decisions are themselves an expression of the renegotiation for space and identity in the American context by Muslim women as women, both in terms of the non-Muslim majority amidst which they live, and in terms of their relations with their husbands, fathers and sons. This is not to say that first-generation immigrant women such as Sakina are frustrated in their traditional roles as wife and mother; in fact, for women such as herself such roles have not precluded an enlargement of their space through ICNA. From what I have observed, women who entertain a sense of grievance about their social roles *vis-a-vis* their husbands' tend not to be of South Asian ethnic origin. I heard heated and angry comments, for instance, from a Caribbean woman (not Ruhana, mentioned earlier) married to a Pakistani man; she questioned not only her exclusion from many male activities that her husband was engaged in (related to ICNA) but also the acceptance by other women at ICNA of what she saw as their secondary role in ICNA affairs. Another note of challenge was sounded by a woman writing in English in the ICNA womens' magazine (which latter is primarily in Urdu), raising the possibility of a Muslim woman going against her husband's wishes, if he were being a 'bad' Muslim. This woman wrote:

> Many Sisters must contend with nominally Muslim husbands, with husbands who drift away from Islam, or oppose their accepting Islam. . . . Asiya [the wife of Pharoah] is a model to all Muslims, male and female. She was the subject of a tyrant [i.e., Pharoah] whom she defied, and a victor over the lure of materialism, rejecting the petty riches of this world for the wealth of Allah. She rejected Pharoah for the Creator of Pharoah—the Creater of all Pharoahs—and their Destroyer as well.
>
> Asiya demonstrates that even the ultimate in human obedience—that of a wife to her husband—is strictly conditional upon his obedience to Allah. She rests in the Qur'an as a living reminder that women—that all human beings—are servants first and foremost of Allah. Only from this loyalty is allegiance to mortals—to husbands and fathers and families and leaders—derived. When push comes to shove, Allah comes first.[11]

While I doubt the women I have met at ICNA would break with their husbands when 'push came to shove', the fact that such sentiments are aired at all is interesting.

With regard to relations between parents and children, the student who felt she had to 'explain' to her mother and be patient with her in order to convince her that an injunction was placed on Muslim women in the Koran to veil, illustrates what may be a special kind of 'generation gap'. The context for her statement itself seems to be more 'American' than 'South Asian' (or 'Islamic'), given that age-based deference is a strong cultural norm in South Asia. The same article quoted above comments on this as follows:

> In some cases, a new twist on the classic 'generation gap' has spawned

conflict in Muslim families in which the children are more conservative than their Westernized elders. Parents who learned Islam in Westernized societies sometimes disapprove of their children's interpretations of Islam, and issues ranging from dress to the abandonment of un-Islamic cultural traditions assume the strident dimensions that they do in the families of reverts [i.e., 'new' Muslims].[12]

In a very different context, uneasiness of relations between the generations was illustrated for me at an ICNA meeting one day as I sat with the other women watching the mens' meeting in another part of the building on an internal TV screen. When a young male student introduced a much older Pakistani visitor to the men's group as 'Brother so-and-so', his mother commented in embarrassment, 'In Pakistan, he would have addressed him as "Uncle"!'

To conclude, let me reiterate that Muslim women who have chosen to make their Muslim identity definitive find in this identity a source of liberation, and see 'Western' women, correspondingly, as sexually defined by society and therefore devalued as human beings. By adopting the veil, which they see as a symbol of their return to 'true' Islam, and by making other changes in lifestyle (collectively best described as a form of 'social asceticism', perhaps, as these changes are family-oriented and involve considerable self-discipline) they are forging with each other and with Muslim men a common cause, that of Islam in an overwhelmingly non-Muslim environment. Indirectly I believe this may have led to an empowerment of the household, which is the womens' sphere. For those Muslim women who venture beyond the confines of the household, typically to go to school or work, their distinctive dress style creates a boundary between themselves and their non-Muslim colleagues, and promotes in them a heightened sense of moral worth.

NOTES

1. I am grateful to the Center for the Study of American Religion, Princeton University, for granting me a post-doctoral fellowship during 1991-2 to enable me to carry out the research on which this paper is based.
2. Joan W. Scott, *Gender and the Politics of History,* New York: Columbia University Press, 1988, p. 26. For an argument on race as a social construct, see Evelyn Brooks Higginbotham, 'African-American Women's History and the Metalanguage of Race', in *Signs: Journal of Women in Culture and Society,* 17: 2 (1992).

3. Figures based on *The Message. International,* XII 2 (July-Sept. 1988), 11; *Islamic Circle of North America: Annual Report, 1989-90,* 5.
4. Charles J. Adams, 'The Ideology of Mawlana Mawdudi', in Donald E. Smith (ed.), *South Asian Politics and Religion,* Princeton: Princeton University Press, 1966, p. 382.
5. Mawdudi, quoted in Adams, ibid., p. 389.
6. Ibid., p. 390.
7. Islamic Circle of North America, *Constitution* (March 1990), p. 6.
8. See Sharon McIrvin Abu-Laban, 'Family and Religion among Muslim Immigrants and Their Descendants', in Earle H, Waugh, Sharon McIrvin Abu-Laban, Regula Burkhardt Qureshi (eds.), *Muslim Families in North America,* Edmonton: University of Alberta Press, 1991.
9. Ibid., p. 23.
10. The details of Sakina's life-history are based on my field notes.
11. Karima Omar, 'Family Affairs', in *Behno kay Nam* ['In the Name of our Sisters'], Summer 1986, p. 26.
12. Ibid., p. 27.

REFERENCES

Abu-Laban, Sharon McIrvin, 1991. 'Family and Religion among Muslim Immigrants and Their Descendants', in Earle H. Waugh, Sharon McIrvin Abu-Laban, Regula Burkhardt Qureshi (eds.), *Muslim Families in North America,* Edmonton: University of Alberta Press, 6-31.

Adams, Charles J., 1966. 'The Ideology of Mawlana Mawdudi', in Donald E. Smith (ed.), *South Asian Politics and Religion,* Princeton: Princeton University Press, 371-97.

Higginbotham, Evelyn Brooks, 1992. 'African-American Women's History and the Metalanguage of Race', in *Signs: Journal of Women in Culture and Society* (Winter), 17.2: 251-74.

ICNA (Islamic Circle of North America), *1989-90. Annual Report.*

———, (March 1990). *Constitution.*

Message International, The (July-Sept. 1988), XII. 2.

Omar, Karima, 1986. 'Family Affairs', in *Behno kay Nam* ['In the Name of our Sisters'], Summer, 24-8.

Scott, Joan W., 1988. *Gender and the Politics of History,* New York: Columbia University Press.

Intertwining Religion and Ethnicity: South Asian Cultural Performance in the Diaspora

CARLA PETIEVICH

In North America, especially in Canada and the United States, there is a conventional ideology to the effect that our richness and success derive from the fact that we are nations of immigrants. Since it is not the purpose of this essay to render as full a deconstruction of this ideology as one is tempted to do,[1] I will merely preface my own discussion with the observation that 'richness in diversity' compels immigrant groups to blend in while maintaining, through various articulation strategies, what in particular they are contributing to that diversity.[2] Among the most commonly articulated particularities is religion, as several essays in this volume address.[3] Yet shared religious faith does not necessarily serve all the needs of community formation; indeed religion and culture—contrary to totalizing discourses of universalist religions like Islam or Christianity—are distinct entities and can actually serve to mark fissures in communities of 'the faithful'.[4] In Walbridge and Haneef's essay on the Ahmadiyya community in North America[5] the point was made eloquently, yet not incendiarily, that culture needs always to be negotiated; and that it is not coterminous with religious identification. But while the Ahmadiyya community addresses its need for cohesion by actively discouraging cultural prerogatives as some members attempt to assert them (as through the use of such ethnicity-markers as language) among certain other immigrant groups performing arts are the preferred and prominent markers of ethnicity.

The organization, patronage and performance of 'traditional' art forms are among the ways in which many South Asian immigrants assert their inherited cultural identity in a new space.[6] Taking this assumption as its basis, the following essay works toward a hypothesis to the effect that may characteristics of 'diaspora' must be recognized as simultaneously characteristic of contemporary post-colonial South

Asia as well. In other words, that which we call South Asian diasporic culture can also be called contemporary transnational South Asian culture. The following remarks by ethnomusiocIogist Harold F. Powers offer a point of reference:

> . . . the subsequent status of the traditional art musics of formerly colonial India and Indonesia in their now politically independent homelands has depended in large part upon the transfer of patronage to the new elites whose authority originated in their respective nationalist movements. It is only their acceptance of the music ascribed to the Great Traditions as an expression of indigenous cultural attainments in the newly independent nations that has ensured or can continue to ensure the transmission of these gloriously complex arts onward to the continuing enrichment of our common humanity.[7]

I think we can recognize in Powers' mention of 'the new elites whose authority originated in their respective nationalist movements' the parents of many cultural patrons who form the focal group for this essay. And it seems to me that the project of transmitting what Powers terms 'the Great Traditions' into a post-colonial time is remarkably comparable to the project of transplanting them to new soil across the world. That project may be understood as preservation or reinvention, or even in other ways, but the motivations behind them may be more similar than we would be inclined to suppose.[8]

Among the most compelling motivations, one might say, is anxiety. Anxieties surrounding 'loss of culture' among immigrants are not necessarily 'communal' or 'universal,' for they often reflect the *individual* self-identification and *personal* adaptation of parents to their new social spaces, rather than reflecting identification as members of social or communal groups (eg. 'Pakistani Muslim' or 'South Indian Hindu'). Yet it can be argued that particular religio-communal associations do impact cultural transmission from one generation to the next.

Two particular cultural forms are highlighted here—Karnatak music festivals and performances of Urdu ghazal poetry in North America and Britain. Through them, significant differences can be discerned in the extent to which religious identity and ethnic identity are simultaneously expressed, celebrated and transmitted by South Indian Hindu parents and by South Asian Muslim parents to their children raised in new spaces.[9]

Expressive differences among community groups reflect structural differences among the various institutions by which religion and ethnicity are transmitted (mosques, temples, cultural associations, etc.). Put another way, the kind of culture transmitted—and how it is shaped and what it is intended to offer—is determined by the nature of institutions chosen as vehicles of cultural transmission. The social functions of houses of worship may be as important in transmitting culture as the modes of worship themselves; and cultural associations, if housed separately from centers of worship, can focus culture in yet other ways. Because of the differences in established function between Hindu temples and mosques, music and dance work very differently in inculcating a sense of 'Indianness' or 'Pakistaniness' among the children of South Asian immigrants in North America and Britain.

Transnationalism, or this thing we call 'Diaspora', is reminiscent of the proverbial elephant which, when described by numerous people with a range of sensory abilities, each perceiving a different part of the elephant as its characteristic whole, can be represented and understood (not necessarily inaccurately) in multiple, sometimes competing, ways. Here attention is paid, on one hand, to difference in ethnic or religious or communal identification among those who have immigrated. On the other hand, and equally important when discussing the 'South Asian diaspora',[10] is how generational difference can shape different experiences between the generation of immigrants and their children, and that, too, is born in mind in this essay. Much recent literature on South Asian diaspora—indeed upon 'Diaspora' as a whole—focuses on children growing up in cultural spaces different from those in which their parents were reared.[11] By contrast, primary attention will be paid here to the cultural activities and productions of immigrant parents themselves rather than to those of their children; and to the implications of cultural transmission when viewed through the grid of these parents' experience rather than that of their children.[12]

DEMOGRAPHICS

Attempts to diagnose the patronage and consumption of various forms 'lead to social definitions, not artistic ones'.[13] The demographic of class within particular communities is also crucial to the types of cultural expression chosen by any given group within the broader categories of 'South Asian American', 'South Asian Canadian' or 'Asian Briton'. The class background of immigrants within their country of origin often influences which particular cultural forms are favored in new spaces. Thus, though there are exceptions to this rule,[14] consumers of Karnatak music in India, or of Urdu courtly culture in India or Pakistan, will be likely to continue identifying these forms as important to their cultural identity after migration. Indeed, the pressures toward upward social mobility for immigrants can lead them into patronage of these prestigious art forms where they might not have otherwise expended their resources. Simultaneously, pre-migration consumers of popular culture (such as cinema) will generally continue to identify with popular cultural forms in their new spaces. They may even become producers or entrepeneurs in the arts, patronizing artists of entertainments which cater to their own tastes; and they may encourage their children to cultivate these tastes as well. Thus, parents who had frequented *mushairas* (poetic assemblies) growing up in Pakistan or India will often make use of opportunities to recreate the *mushaira* atmosphere in North America or Britain and to include their own children in the audience whenever they can; while parents whose relationship to Urdu poetry was more closely associated with cassette recordings and television performances will continue to purchase and listen to commercially available recordings, though they may or may not buy tickets to live performances. All this is not to ignore that people have eclectic tastes, and that some patrons of 'high' culture enjoy popular culture as well. It is surely the case that some of those who purchase tickets to see variety shows featuring Bombay film stars also sometimes purchase tickets to *mushairas* or other 'high culture' functions.

Finally, a family's relationship to the English language before migration may also determine which cultural forms get expressed and which are passed successfully between generations.[15] Karnatak music and 'high' Urdu poetry have, for most of the twentieth century, attracted enthusiasts among classes of people who also embraced English-language education in South Asia. To the extent that these people write about and read about music and poetry in English, they have some chance of passing their enthusiasm on to the next generation who read only English comfortably, though they may understand and appreciate Tamil or Urdu or Telugu or Hindi.[16]

None of the trends outlined earlier is particularly surprising, yet all are worth noting. As to Indo-Muslim and South Indian 'high' cultural patronage, it may be said that what Karnatak music and Urdu poetry have in common is, to begin with, that they are both expressions of 'high culture': both require special training on the part of practitioners and audience. As 'high' cultural forms that demand specialized knowledge on the part of their audience, both these performance arts tend to rely for their continued survival on patronage rather than on commercial viability. Both these qualities, but especially the latter, strongly distinguish Karnatak music and Urdu poetry from popular culture. The resources necessary to patronize both forms—especially acquiring the requisite training for educated appreciation—have thus far proved to be found more among professionals of the immigrant generation than among those of the generation raised in new spaces. This condition stands in stark contrast to the recent commercial history of Bhangra, or even popular ghazal singing.[17] Accessibility—both of language and classical systems—also plays a part in patronage, because the most accessible forms will carry the greatest commercial viability. Thus patronage of classical performance arts can be expected to shift (perhaps even to diminish) as the educative structures that have been in place for several generations are affected by globalization and migration.

A form of Urdu cultural performance often referred to as 'classical' rather than popular, by people interviewed for this project, is the *Sham-i Ghazal* ('ghazal evening') which involves musical renditions of ghazal poetry. Performers such as Jagjit and Chitra Singh, Anup Jalota or Munni Begum are wildly successful, commercially, in both South Asia and abroad. The children of immigrants are present far more at their performances, in my experience, than at formal *mushairas*. But the cognoscenti agree that their performances, both musically and literarily, are more appropriately termed 'light classical' rather than classical *per se*.[18] And informal surveys of young people in New York/New Jersey/Connecticut—the region where I live—suggest that they are more likely to buy and listen to cassettes of this 'light' ghazal music than 'pure classical'—if they listen to ghazals at all. When asked to elaborate on these preferences, young people explained to me that they found the ghazals sung by Munni Begum and Jagjit Singh much easier to understand than those by more 'classical' singers like Begum Akhtar or Farida Khanum or Iqbal Bano,[19] artists whose work tends to make greater lexical demands of its audience. Musically, too, their ghazal renditions tend to be less challenging than the more classical musicianship of artists like Begum Akhtar and Farida Khanum.

RELIGIOUS AND SECULAR ARTS

Thus far, then, the patronage and consumption of Urdu cultural forms has centered around notions of 'classicism' or the specialized knowledge necessary for appreciation; or perhaps the prestige attached to this classicism, even in the absence of the specialized knowledge. Now another factor, that of religiousness vs. secularity, must be added to the equation. A question of especial concern here is, 'What particular difference does religion make to the artistic genres patronized and transmitted across generations?' More specifically, what bearing does the *Muslim* part of the term 'Indo-Muslim culture' have on patronage, consumption and transmission of music and poetry in the diaspora? How does this compare with 'non-Muslim' arts and culture?

In the case of Karnatak music festivals (especially those celebrating the poet-saint Tyagaraja)[20] there seems to be a near-complete, unproblematic intertwining of the classical music system with Hinduism as a religious tradition. The grammar of Karnatak music presupposes nothing about the content of song texts; indeed, it does not require song texts at all in order to be meaningful as music/sound. And yet, the song texts are overwhelmingly devotional. The child who studies Karnatak music will inevitably be exposed to some form of Hindu devotionalism, and so her/his musical training may also prove to be religious education of a sort.[21] Yet the devotional lyrics are not crucial to the musicology of Karnatak music. An *alapana*, for example, may employ no song text whatsoever and still be a full musical treatment of a raga. And although the voice is by far the most popular musical instrument, Karnatak musicians include violinists, percussionists, veena players and wind instrumentalists as well.

Nothing could be further from the case of classical Urdu poetry, at least on the face of it. Like the Karnatak music system, Urdu poetry employs a highly complex prosody, derived from Arabic and Persian poetry. But—to state the obvious—poetry is overwhelmingly dependent on word texts. Furthermore, what gives classical Urdu poetry its distinctive identity is the love aesthetic which forms the core of its texts. To paraphrase one authority, a ghazal that does not talk about unrequited love, employing the standard conventions, is not really a ghazal.[22] Furthermore, ghazal texts *per se* have never been considered sacred.[23] They can claim a certain spirituality and a philosophical depth, because of their strong historical association with Sufism and mystical love. But love poetry does not represent 'sacred text' to normative Islam of the kind enjoying a tremendous, continually growing, popularity in the diaspora and in South Asia. A child instructed in the appreciation of Urdu ghazal will certainly be inducted into a cultural tradition, but it will stand at distinct variance from Islamic *religious* instruction. Even more to the point, there is no reason to expect that a child being instructed in the fundamentals of Islam at a local mosque, by a maulvi, is simultaneously receiving instruction in how to appreciate classical Urdu poetry. And he (the pronoun is used advisedly) is unlikely to find encouragement there to cultivate an appreciation either of Hindustani classical music or of dance, though both art forms are appropriately credited with having developed under a significantly 'Muslim' population of artists and patrons.

Nowhere are such differences between Hindu/South Indian culture and Islamic/ Indo-Muslim cultural transmission more dramatic than in the case of dance. Bharata Natyam dance, tied to Karnatak music, relies heavily on devotional stories and myths involving deities, as has been alluded to already. Thus, a child learning a dance piece within this system will typically be taught a song text in Telugu, Tamil or Sanskrit; will receive a body of folk/cultural lore in the form of widely-held stories; and the fact that these stories are about the lives of gods, godesses and heroes contributes to her/his religious education. Furthermore, in North America new temples are being designed and constructed with facilities for dance instruction and recital on site. This amounts to bringing Bharata Natyam, formerly known and vilified as 'temple dancing' by British colonial officials and Indian reformers, right back into the temple for the first time in nearly a century, as has been noted by both Hansen and Waghorne elsewhere in this volume. It can be argued quite persuasively that the particular circumstances of the diaspora have expedited this reinsertion, this intertwining of Hindu religion and South Indian ethnicity; for we do not see its widespread occurrence in South India, where dance recitals take place overwhelmingly on the proscenium stage; and where *aficionados* of the arts are not necessarily religious-minded people.

Diasporic Islam, by contrast, especially as practiced by South Asians, represents a paradox when juxtaposed with Urdu cultural performance. On one hand a reformist, neo-conservative, universalist outlook may be said to characterize the highly organized, highly visible presence of Islam in North America and Britain. This religious approach claims to have little use for secular art.[25] Even more to our point, perhaps, is that secular art often draws its inspiration from specific local culture, and this might tend to compromise the universalist project of such organizations as the Islamic Circle of North America (ICNA) or other large organizations. While South Asians may be visibly active in ICNA or ISNA (the Islamic Society of North America), even taking leadership roles, and there has been a visible trend toward treating Urdu as an Islamic lingua franca for Muslims from South Asia, standard forms of Indo-Muslim expressive art play little or no part in this linguistic hegemony.[26]

Compare Bharata Natyam's blending of dance with religious site to the case of Kathak, the North Indian dance form developed at Muslim courts, tied to Hindustani classical music. Never, to my knowledge, has this dance been welcome at mosques, nor can it claim any place in Muslim devotionalism. On the contrary, its great practitioners were historically *tawaifs* (courtesans) whose cultural status was high but whose social status was not 'respectable'. Many of Kathak's song texts are Hindu and devotional; and even when secular (and Kathak has the capacity to tell secular stories), the primary audience is assumed to be the patron or king, not Allah. This stands in marked contrast to the practice of Bharata Natyam, wherein dancers are theoretically making an offering of their dance to the god(s). But Kathak, popularly and uncomplicatedly understood as 'erotic' dance, is generally anathema to religious elites and other Muslim conservatives who deem visual arts depicting the human form to be blasphemous. While Muslim culture in North India can be credited with developing the Kathak aesthetic of grace and sensuality, there is nothing specifically Islamic in it (where 'Islamic' refers to religious content). I can recall not a single instance in which a cultural group organized around mosque affiliation produced or sponsored a Kathak performance in North America or Britain. Even in contemporary Pakistan there are very few accomplished classical dancers who perform publicly, and they tend to be decidely secular in personal orientation and social milieu. Indeed, the visible tension between court culture and mosque throughout Islamic history seems alive and well here, despite the disappearance of 'courts'. Harold Powers, in a slightly different yet relevant context, has said:

> It is true that where other factors are favorable, a high musical art can flourish in a Muslim society. Nonetheless, Islam is at best ambivalent about music, which is always at least potentially under suspicion as detrimental to

religion. Where there are other communities attaching a positive value to music (as in Hindustan), or where autochthonous cultural uses for music have not been submerged (as in Java), a high musical art has little to fear from an onslaught of Islamic Puritanism alone. But where other factors are not propitious for art music it will certainly get no help from Orthodox Muslims.[29]

Although Powers' remarks are addressed primarily to what he calls 'the core Islamic countries'—in which I would include Pakistan, though not unproblematically—much of their substance pertains to Islam in North America and Britain, too.

There remains, however, the phenomenon of *qawwali*, an art form from within Islamic tradition that does seem to blend religion and ethnicity.[30] One thinks particularly of such *qawwals* as the late Nusrat Fateh Ali Khan and the Sabri brothers, whose song texts blend one kind of devotionalism with classical, erotic themes. Preliminary observations suggest that many people subscribing to reformist, Sunni Islam (historically antipathetic to the mysticism and heterodoxy of Sufism) are avid fans of *qawwali*, an art form developed by, and completely the province of, Sufis. If popular consumption levels are reasonable indicators, recorded and commercially-purveyed *qawwali* has become more normative a South Asian Islamic art form than classical Urdu poetry.[31] Certainly Nusrat is the only Pakistani artist to have attained tremendous international superstar status and to have enjoyed remarkable concomitant commercial success. The presence of music and percussion, not to mention the energy generated by the *qawwals* themselves, provides a mood—an emotional space for cultural identification on the part of audience members I have interviewed—which is capable of bridging gaps in comprehension at the simple level of language. One person spoke of her admiration for Nusrat Fateh Ali Khan, saying that just his repetition of the name 'Ali' could move her into such an emotional space; and that in this space she felt the pride and beauty of her 'own' culture (by which she meant Pakistani culture).[32] The contribution of Nusrat should not be underestimated in terms of popularizing and legitimizing what had been previously, in South Asia, a marginalized music both socially and socioeconomically.[33] In the diaspora it appears to be a performance art growing as rapidly under the rubric of 'family entertainment' as under that of 'spiritual expression'.[34] In Pakistan, too, in the late 1990s it appears to be enjoying the sanction of 'high' Islamic art, if the frequency of sponsored, quasi-public performances can be seen as a reasonable indicator. One is tempted to see in both spaces—the 'West' and Pakistan—a comparable search for cultural authenticity.[35]

Mushairas do not command the audience and commerical market claimed by *qawwali* in North America and Britain. *Mushairas* with an audience of a hundred people or more are typically attached to even larger cultural events, such as Eid, or academic conferences. Those boasting a *Sham-e ghazal*, featuring musical renditions of poetic texts, draw far more people than *mushairas* featuring only non-musical recitation.[36] Indeed, such evenings usually open with the *Sham-e ghazal* and move on to the more 'serious' poetry only late in the evening, by which time the crowd has thinned considerably, and gender and generational composition has become all but monochromatic (i.e. middle-aged or older, predominantly male, and of the migrant generation rather than North American or British-born and -raised).[37] This 'hard core' group, I would argue, are participating in a performance of cultural identity that is secular through and through. While the evening may have opened with the recitation of a Quranic verse by a local mullah, both the mullah and overt expressions of piety by now will have long departed, as will most of the women and children. (An exception can be made in the case of those women who are themselves poets—they are rarely unaccompanied by their husbands or other male chaperones, and almost always beyond child-rearing years.) An evening advertised to begin at 8:00 p.m. will typically get off the ground around 9:30-10:00 p.m. and, if fire wardens permit, carry on until 2:00-3:00 a.m. The success of the event will often be assessed by how late it has lasted.[38] All this is not conducive to family participation, and tends to reinforce the generational divide between the arts consumption of parents and their children.

Take, by contrast, a Tyagaraja Aradhana Utsava. Though the crowd may be a bit thin at the opening *arati* around 8:30-9:00 a.m. it thickens during the course of the day, peaking somewhere in the late morning, before the home-cooked lunch feast is served. These events are designed for full family participation, with programs for children as well as adults, and age-based competitive categories delineated for judging and the awarding of prizes.[39] Kathryn Hansen has described such events elsewhere in this volume, offering fulsome description of various Tyagaraja festivals, and I will not rehearse all that here. I will, rather, point to a few characteristics of program and audience content to highlight the comparison being made between these festivals and Urdu *mushairas.*

Nothwithstanding the limited expertise of some of the younger children, there are participants of all ages from 5-6 years to the most senior members of the community. All are singing songs composed by Tyagaraja (whose *oeuvre* accounts for an overwhelming proportion of the Karnatak repertoire). In the past several years there has also been an essay contest among the children at the local festival in my own area (that of the North Jersey Music Lovers). One award-winning essay in 1994 compared the centrality of melody in Karnatak music with the notion of harmony in Western classical music (with fair expertise on the topic demonstrated by its 11 year-old author). The essayist spoke of the need for appreciation of both Indian and Western culture as well as the importance of spirituality in the songs of Tyagaraja.

Because of the daytime scheduling of the event, the entire family can participate, with childcare being provided in a separate space for those children who become restive as the day progresses. The event usually culminates in an evening performance by an accomplished artist, either local or, in the case of really big festivals like Cleveland or Pittsburgh, brought in from India. In New Jersey, the artist is usually local, and the event lasts no later than about 9:00 p.m. Disruption to normal family routines is thus kept to a minimum. While Euro-Americans such as myself are welcomed politely, are remembered from one year to the next, and are dutifully sent mailings of events throughout the year sponsored by the New Jersey Music Lovers, these events seem clearly to be staged with an 'internal' audience in mind, consisting primarily of the music society's members and their families. There is neither any apparent self-consciousness *vis a vis* the dominant society nor any particular interest or hostility toward it. But that winning essay reflects a clear understanding that the primary audience for Tyagaraja Aradhana Utsavas is bicultural, *Indo-American.*

In the case of Indo-Muslim cultural events combining religion and ethnicity, there can be a multiple and complex audience in the mind of the organizers, where an evening begins by presenting itself to an external audience and ends up with a much more internal audience as the hours pass. At an event advertised as 'Eid Dinner & Mushaera' in March 1993, also a family event for the first half of the evening, there was a rich and variegated agenda. Since Eid is marked as a religious celebration, the event opened with a prayer and the hall was gender-segregated. There was also a political agenda, the event having been organized by a group called the Islamic Public Affairs Council. Former Governor of New Jersey James Florio, his wife, and several other public servants were awarded plaques lauding their vigorous prosecution of hate crimes; they were also instructed on how to refer to Islam and Muslims, including the Council's preferred pronounciation and spelling of various terms relating to Islam (e.g. 'Makkah' as pronunciation of the geographical center of Islam was announced as preferable, actually as 'correct', over the more Orientalist spelling and pronunciation of 'Mecca').

In other words, up to this point, the gathering had been an assertive, public event. That ceremony having concluded, however, the organizers reoriented their projection inward. The language of discourse changed to Urdu, in keeping with the switch in intended audience. After dinner (for which the Governor was not apparently expected to stay, and he did not) came the *mushaira.* The hall held perhaps one third of its original audience by that time, approximately 10:00 p.m., and there was a new compere (master of ceremonies), now a member of the literati, rather than the official spokesman from the Islamic Public Affairs Council. The mullah, too, had long departed, and there were fewer *dupattas* drawn over female heads. My presence was noticed far more dramatically than at North Jersey Music Lovers events, and my credentials checked thoroughly. Indeed, much to my mortification, I was not allowed to simply sit in the audience once my credentials had passed muster, but was called to the stage to sit with the poets and used as an excuse for parents to exhort the few children in the audience to follow my example and learn Urdu![40]

While this event had opened as a joint ethno-religious occasion, by now it had become strictly ethnic. I suggest that the particular expressions of Islam among its organizers left the intertwining of religion and ethnicity far less seamless than in, for example, the case of a Tyagaraja Aradhana Utsava. There was no 'children's program', nor any other visible address toward the inclusion of children that I could discern than the exhortation alluded to above. I feel confident that efforts on the part of young people to join in the *mushaira* would be welcomed, but there was no apparent infrastructure to facilitate such participation. There was no hypenated 'American-ness' in this event. By the time the *mushaira* was in full swing, this was a South-Asian-Muslim event, not Pakistani-American; and it was almost exclusively Pakistani at that. Whereas one might argue that South Indian children in New Jersey are being energetically inducted into the propagation of 'Karnatak' culture, Muslim children of South Asian ethnicity are being inducted into the propagation of Islām, but not necessarily into Indo-Muslim culture in its historically secular manifestations. If each ethos is being inculcated in children, the inculcation is being effected at distinctly different events and spaces.

With these remarks I have wished to engage with some of the dilemmas of cultural transmission that capture members of minority cultures in larger, dominant societies such as we find in North America, where demands for the assimilation of immigrant groups is strong. On the face of it, the intertwining of the sacred and secular in South Indian 'high' culture seems to demand fewer distinct institutions to parents concerned about passing on to their children their own ethnic identity in terms that seem appropriate to them, the parents. While the diaspora has facilitated the reinscription of Hindu temples as sites of performative art culture, this has not happened, by and large, in the case of the diasporic mosque. The mosque does not appear to provide South Asian Muslims with the easy combination of Indo-Muslim (ethnic) and Islamic (religious) culture embodied in the North American Hindu temple. Islamic institutions, while highly organized and impressively assertive in the public sphere, rarely take as part of their provenance the education of children in traditionally 'mythic' Urdu culture.[41]

LANGUAGE AND ETHNICITY

Vernacular language remains one marker of ethnic identity whose future is difficult to imagine with confidence into the near or the extended future. Sandria Freitag has observed, in the context of late-nineteenth century popular participation, that

> Perhaps the most important point to make . . . is the lack of congruence between religion and language. [A number of essays in the volume whose introductory essay this quote draws from] provide no evidence at all for equating Urdu with Muslims, or Hindi with Hindus . . . there were moments when the congruence in public expression exactly fit this equation, but these are small in number throughout the period [of the late 19th century]. *If Urdu is not to be seen simply as a language of religious identity, then, how should it be analyzed in the contestations that entwine culture and politics throughout the 19th and into the 20th century?*[42]

If we are to truly pursue and understanding of the interplay among religion, culture and politics, we must also add that the temporal extension highlighted above should be extended to include the geographical expansion of the twentieth century South Asian diaspora. Perhaps unsurprisingly, the limited scope in which it comes into play in the context of diaspora can direct one's attention back to the language politics of South Asia itself. As noted earlier, in diasporic mosques Urdu has sometimes come to serve as a South Asian 'Islamic' lingua franca, where Bengali Muslims (or African Americans[43]) are obliged to bow to the hegemony of Urdu; on the other hand the Urdu language to which great prestige has been attached in South Asia for the past century or two—that of secular, North Indian courtly culture—is apparently on the decline. Even in Pakistan, where Urdu is the national language, one could argue that it serves less as a marker of ethnicity than as a lingua franca employed in the project of nation building to bridge linguistic gaps between Pakistanis from divergent linguistic regions and potentially competing ethnicities.[44]

If we take the first case, we see Urdu approaching status as a 'sacred' language because of its ubiquity in diasporic mosques that cater primarily to South Asians. This connection reinforces certain of the dominant ideologies pertaining in Pakistan. Primary among these is the connection among Urdu speakers, Islam and the Pakistani nation. In other words, Urdu is a langague which, lacking any particular regional or geographic roots, signifies a *qaum* and one that is territorially boundless, like Islam itself. In Pakistan this absence of geography serves the national ideology; though its use retains only a tenuous, rather abstract connection with the sacred *raison d'être* of the nation state. In the diaspora, by choosing Urdu, Pakistani Muslims have the opportunity of reinscribing onto a new landscape the essential nexus among being South Asian, being Muslim, and being Pakistani. This allows regional identity—if not strictly ethnicity—to stand in the face of the more hegemonic Islamic language, Arabic.[45] Ethnic reinforcement in this case does not, however, protect such secular arts historically associated with the Indo-Muslim *qaum*, as poetry.[46]

This particular 'loss' of secular Urdu culture is not exclusively a diasporic phenomenon; a loss of secular culture can be charted throughout the twentieth century in South Asia as well, both in India and in Pakistan.[47] It is quite likely that the 'idea' of Urdu would last a generation or two longer than its currency as a spoken medium among those identifying in some way as 'Pakistani' and/or as 'Muslim'. But at present the international *mushaira* scene attests to a transnational Urdu culture that is simultaneously expanding geographically even as its numerical place in the lives of South Asian Muslims may be diminishing.

WHOSE DIASPORA IS IT?

The problematics of essentializing what the South Asian diaspora is continue to intensify as one reads such scholars as Gayatri Gopinath[48] and Sunita Mukhi,[49] whose work is permeated by the question, 'Whose diaspora is this?'

Bhangra in Britain, cultural shows at New York University, Eid functions in northern New Jersey or Montreal; Tyagaraja festivals, Nusrat or Jagjit at Alice Tully Hall—all these are part of the current landscape. All are absolutely contemporary and simultaneous, though not necessarily intersecting one another. The creative and evocative assertions discussed by Gopinath and Mukhi both reflect a generation of youth fiercely resisting the efforts of various groups to inscribe them into any particular definition of 'Indian-ness' or 'Pakistani-ness' while at the same time holding onto some aspect of that essential also recognized by their parents in order to sustain some acceptable notion of cultural continuity. For this group the term 'South Asian' seems to be more comfortable than the terms 'Indian' or 'Pakistani' or 'Bangladeshi'.

The diaspora is everybody's and nobody's in particular. The impulse toward ethnic identification is not time-bound, it endures from generation to generation. What we can say as the third millennium of the Common Era approaches is that forms and genres of cultural expression in transnational South Asian cultures do not necessarily reflect territorial boundaries so much as generational shifts in milieu. As religion, on a global scale, reclaims public space lost over the course of a fiercely secular twentieth century, South Asianness will doubtless find itself renegotiating Hindu-ness, Muslimness, or Sikh-ness again. It will be interesting to see how the hyphens in identity reshape and recoalesce; where, if at all, terms like 'Pakistani' or 'Indian' or 'Punjabi' or 'Bengali' will appear in relation to the hypens; and what it will mean for such expressive cultural media as language and the expressive or performing arts.

NOTES

1. But which, nevertheless, most of the essays in this volume do either directly or indirectly.
2. For a more specific discussion of this dilemma, see below Saloni Mathur's remarks in 'The Second Generation Speaks: A Panel Discussion' in this volume, where the competition for 'ethnic broadcasting' time is highly contested among various South Asian groups in Vancouver, Canada.
3. See especially the essays of Waghorne, Sanyal and Walbridge & Haneef.
4. This was found to be the case in Walbridge and Haneef's survey of the Ahmadiyya community in North America (see Chapter 6). Ahmadi leadership, especially the community's spiritual guide, have taken serious and sensitive pains to draw together one such community whose faith was not in question, but whose culture was diverse.
5. Linda Walbridge & Fatimah Haneef, 'Inter-Ethnic Relations within the Ahmadiyya Muslim Community in the United States.' Chapter 6, this volume.
6. The following remarks are based on research which included interviews and participant observation at performances in Britain, Canada and the United States between 1991 and 1997.
7. Harold F. Powers, 'Classical Music, Cultural Roots, and Colonial Rule: an Indic Musicologist looks at the Muslim World' *Asian Music* 12.1 (1986): 19-20.
8. One must bear in mind, however, that the expressions of generational divide between parents and children are likely to differ in South Asia and North America. The difference might be explained by parents as a loss of culture on the part children raised as cutural minorities outside South Asia. This in turn would suggest that geography is more important than some theorists of diaspora might like to consider it; but I think it makes as much sense to give great weight to the condition of being either in a cultural minority or ethnic majority as to factors of geography.
9. In this essay I assume that the grammars of religious and ethnic, or cultural, literacy are not necessarily one and the same. One can be a secular person manifesting strong cultural identification; or a person strongly schooled in a religious tradition but less so in the secular aspects of cultural tradition.
10. For illustration of the problems surrounding terminology when discussing 'diaspora' and 'transnationalism' see especially the transcribed Panel Discussion which concludes this volume. While concerned about the implications of naming and defining the experience of others, I continue to await the advent of a language of greater precision and sufficient range before abandoning the admittedly limited language currently employed.

11. Cf. Gayatri Gopinath, 'Bombay, U.K., Yuba City: Bhangra Music and the Engendering of Diaspora', in *Diaspora* 4, 3 (#303), Winter 1995; and Sunita Sunder Mukhi. See also the welcome plethora of recent anthologies of fiction, poetry and essays by North Americans and Europeans of South Asian descent represented by e.g. Maira & Srikanth, *Contours of the Heart: South Asians Map North America* (NY: Asian American Writers' Workshop, 1996); or Fauzia Rafiq, ed., *Aurat Durbar/ The Court of Women: Writings by Women of South Asian Origin* (Toronto: Second Story Press, 1995) and Makeda Silvera, ed., *Piece of My Heart: A Lesbian of Colour Anthology* (Toronto: Sister Vision Press, 1991).
12. But see also the transcribed panel discussion in this volume, not unproblematically entitled 'The Second Generation Speaks'.
13. Powers, p.11.
14. See, for example, Kathryn Hansen's discussion of Bharata Natyam as a pan-Indian cultural icon in the diaspora, not bound to the same regional affiliations one tends to see in India.
15. I use the term 'successful' transmission advisedly, as what particularly concerns me is not the attempt to transmit culture from parents to children—that appears to be universal—but rather which forms are successfully transmitted, in other words, the degree(s) to which they are embraced by generations growing up with divergent family and public cultures.
16. One such example would be found in the journal *Sruti* which is published in English by the Madras Music Academy—that 'high temple' of Karnatak culture—and which is relatively easy for North Americans to subscribe to and receive. On the other hand, and quite understandably, very few publications concerned with Urdu literature publish in any language other than Urdu itself, with the notable exception of the Pakistan Academy of Letters, which makes a point of maintaining a journal in English as well. There is also the *Annual of Urdu Studies*, published in English from Chicago (vols. 1-7) and the University of Wisconsin (vols. 8-13). Its subscribership is international, and though it tends to be either scholarly or from among the Urdu literati, it represents a possible link between generations in order to realize which there would need to be more outreach to the second and third generations. The predicament of Urdu literature is addressed by this author in greater detail in other work in progress.
17. An important distinction must be made here between the two cultural forms known as *sham-i ghazal* and *mushaira*. The former, the more commercially viable of the two, also tends to demand far less specialized knowledge from its audience than the latter.
18. Indeed, some of the cogoscenti—those schooled in classical Urdu literature to a high degree—would hesitate to even call the ghazals

performed by the artists mentioned earlier anything other than 'popular'.

19. See below for further discussion of *sham-i ghazal* events *vs. mushairas.*
20. See Kathryn Hansen's 'Singing for the *Sadguru*' in this volume.
21. But it is not at all clear that performing or listening to Carnatic music is entered into consciously and primarily as a devotional activity.
22. The authority invoked here is Prof. M.A.R. Barker. There is a history, during the past century, of experimenting with the ghazal's content; and with interpretation and symbology to render the genre 'relevant' to the modern political milieu; but these experiments have not substantially altered the core themes and topics of Urdu poetry. Indeed, the most successful innovator, Faiz Ahmed Faiz, was arguably successful precisely because he employed canonical motifs. It was his personal genius to create effects of a profoundly political nature, and his peers are few, if not nonexistent. But the real point here is that politically-colored Urdu ghazal has never achieved, nor less sustained, the popularity of the unabashedly romantic love lyric.
23. *Qawwali* represents an interesting variation on this theme, and will be taken up below.
24. Much good research has been published on the vilification of *devadasis* and the outlawing of temple dancing in British India. See especially Amrit Srinivasan, 'The Devadasi and her Dance', *EPW*, 2 Nov. 1985.
25. Especially among the followers of Maududi and the Barelwi movement discussed by Usha Sanyal.
26. It is worth noting that a parallel role for Urdu has also developed in Pakistan since 1947, as a lingua franca not tied to expressive arts like music and dance. On the other hand, the notable exception is that Urdu literature is prominently patronized by the Pakistani state, though less so than is Urdu as lingua franca.
27. The great Kathak artist, Nahid Siddiqui, told me that she has to be very careful in selecting pieces for public performance in front of Asian audiences in Britain.
28. For a fuller elaboration of this tension, cf. Ira M. Lapidus, *A History of Islamic Societies* (Cambridge University Press, 1991) passim.
29. Powers, p. 19.
30. For the authoritative full-length study of *Qawwali* in English, see Regula B. Qureshi, *Sufi Music of India and Pakistan: Sound, Context and Meaning in Qawwali* (Cambridge 1986; republished by Chicago, 1995).
31. As mentioned below, typical attendance at a *mushaira* will be small and select; while the last Nusrat Fateh Ali Khan concert I attended took place at a nearly-full Alice Tully Hall in Lincoln Center, New York (14 Nov. 1993).
32. This was ascertained by the interviewer through a follow-up question to her statement (Interview: 14 May 1994).
33. In this way Nusrat Fateh Ali Khan may be compared to Vishnu

Digambar in the early years of the twentieth century in Hindustan. By introducing Hindu devotional lyrics into thumri, and employing popular but 'classical' ragas like Bhairavi and Pilu, Digambar opened up a space for the reentry of Hindus into what had become the overwhelmingly Muslim-dominated world of Hindustani music; and for acceptance by the urban middle classes of what had been viewed as a courtly, erotic, less-than-fully-respectable, music. See Powers (1986: 24-6).

34. It will be most interesting to see if *qawwali* continues to remain as popular as it has been during the early and mid-1990s, given the untimely demise of Nusrat Fateh Ali Khan (in September, 1997). If the expanded recordings on offer at mainstream commercial music retail outfits in New York City are any indication, Qawwali has made significant inroads as the designated genre through which Pakistani music enters the category of 'World Music'.
35. Based on this author's research in Pakistan between November 1997 and May 1998. By quasi-public I mean events at venues such as the National College of Arts in Lahore, or in hotel function halls, in addition to events produced in private homes.
36. The issue of *tarannum* recitation—since it is not seen as 'music' *per se*, does not enter into my formulation, although it may be observed that *tarannum* reciters are informally understood to be disguising weaker poetic texts with the appeal of their chanting.
37. One notable exception to this is the British singer Najma, who seems equally comfortable presenting herself as a pop singer or ghazal artist. I would note, however, that her ghazal singing does not impress this listener with its classicism or deep knowledge of 'high' culture either in respect to text or musical treatment.
38. I attended—but not to the end—one such particularly successful event in Montreal in May 1992, as part of the 2nd World Urdu Conference. Due to the success of the *mushaira* on the Saturday night, the morning academic session was cancelled because everyone, organizers included, slept in on Sunday.
39. See Hansen, 1993.
40. I mention this awkward event to underline the dilemma of cultural transmission rather than for self-aggrandizement.
41. While it is true that in some mosques there is some instruction in the Urdu language, the texts tend to reinforce the religious orientation of the mosque rather than the 'high' culture of secular arts with which Urdu has been linked in the past several centuries.
42. *Culture as Contested Site: Popular Participation and the State in the Indian Subcontinent* (unpublished).
43. See Walbridge and Haneef on the Ahmadiyya community in the US, Chapter 6.
44. To date best available treatment on the subject from a Pakistani

perspective is Tariq Rahman's *Language and Politics in Pakistan* (Karachi: Oxford University Press, 1996).

45. This is a problem suggested by the phenomenon of diasporic mosques catering largely to South Asians, wherein Urdu definitely seems to be the language of choice for all discourse other than prayers. While it allows Pakistanis and some Indians to reinscribe Urdu as a 'Muslim' language, it puts pressure on Punjabi, Bengali and other non-Urdu-speaking South Asian Muslims to conform to the linguistic hegemony of Urdu speakers. At the same time, one notes in Pakistan these days, that there is an increased Arabicization of Urdu. This is probably accounted for by the large population of Pakistanis who work (or have worked) in the Gulf states during the past couple of decades and learned Arabic there. Some sources in Pakistan identify this trend with Zia ul-Haq's formal and legalized process of Islamization during the 1980s.
46. Ironically, then, the way is paved for those who assert that one can imagine a time in the not too distant future when we will have little reason to associate a particular Urdu culture with Islam.
47. The process is also apparent in Hindu nationalists' attempts in India to repress free expression if what is being expressed is deemed 'not Indian'. Cf. the December 1998 vandalism by Shiv Sainiks of cinemas showing the film 'Fire' which centered on a lesbian relationship within an extended middle-class urban family. Reported in the *New York Times*, 8 December 1998.
48. Cf. 'Bombay, UK, Yuba City: Bhangra Music and the Engendering of Diaspora', in *Diaspora* 4, #3 (Issue #303), Winter 1995.
49. 'Performing Hybridity at New York University', in Risa Morimoto, ed., *Asians in America 1995: Conference Proceedings*, NYU.

REFERENCES

Annual of Urdu Studies. Edited by M.U. Memon (# 8-13) and C.M. Naim (#1-7). Pubished by the Center for South Asia, University of Wisconsin-Madison.

Barker, M.A.R. 1968. *A Reader of Modern Urdu Poetry,* McGill University.

Freitag, Sandria B., ed., *Culture as Contested Site: Popular Participate and the State in the Indian Subcontinent* (unpublished).

Gopinath, Gayatri. 1995. 'Bombay, U.K., Yuba City: Bhangra Music and the Engendering of Diaspora', *Diaspora* 4, 3 (#303), Winter.

Lapidus, Ira M. 1991. *A History of Islamic Societies,* New York: Cambridge University Press.

Maira, Sunaina and Rajini Srikanth, eds. 1996. *Contours of the Heart: South Asians Map North America,* New York: Asian American Writers' Workshop.

Mukhi, Sunita. 1995. 'Performing Hybridity at New York University', in Risa Morimoto, ed., *Asians in America 1995: Conference Proceedings*, NYU.

Powers, Harold F. 1986. 'Classical Music, Cultural Roots, and Colonial Rule: an Indic Ethnomusicologist looks at the Muslim World', *Asian Music* 12. 1.

Qureshi, Regula B. 1986. *Sufi Music of Indian and Pakistan: Sound, Context and Meaning in Qawwali*, New York: Cambridge University Press.

Rafiq, Fauzia, ed. 1995. *Aurat Durbar/The Court of Women: Writings by Women of South Asian Origin*, Toronto: Second Story Press.

Rahman, Tariq. 1996. *Language and Politics in Pakistan*, Karachi: Oxford University Press.

Sanyal, Usha. 1996. *Devotional Islam and Politics in British India: Ahmad Riza Khan Barelwi and His Movement*, New York: Oxford University Press.

Silvera, Makeda, ed. 1991. *Piece of My Heart: A Lesbian of Colour Anthology*, Toronto: Sister Vision Press.

Srinivasan, Amrit. 1985. 'The Devadasi and Her Dance', *Economic and Political Weekly*, 2 November.

Sruti: India's Premier Music and Dance Magazine. Monthly Publication of the Sruti Foundation, Madras.

Identity, Kinship and Community: Bangladeshis in the United States

DOROTHY ANGELL

Almost exactly ten years ago, I returned from several months of research in Dhaka and Calcutta among the families of emigrants to the United States. That period followed roughly two years of ethnographic study of Bengalis in five US cities; it also obliged me to rethink the writing I had already begun. No longer could I treat the issue of identity as one of many salient features of this diaspora group: it became the central and organizing issue. This rethinking was not my choice; it was the imperative within what people told me and what I observed. This conference is an appropriate venue in which to revisit the ethnographic present of 1983-4 as I begin a new research venture on Bangladeshis in the United States in a new decade.

In this paper, I re-examine my findings on what one Bangladeshi friend and colleague frequently calls the 'identity crisis' which Bangladeshis face in the United States and to consider the theoretical and methodological approaches to identity that I have employed to understand the South Asian diaspora. Toward the end of the paper, I outline very briefly the questions I wish to ask in the new work in progress.

In early treatments of the South Asian diaspora (e.g. Tinker 1977) and of South Asians in the United States (e.g. Hess 1976; Melendy 1977), and even in a recent volume on the South Asian diaspora (Clarke et al. 1990), the concept of identity is not part of the focus; if the term is used at all, it is applied only to groups or categories—that is, identity becomes inferentially synonymous with ethnic group membership or diffuse and other-ascribed ethnicity. In more recent work in which identity has become the explicit focus, attention to it has gone in two principal directions: to the ethnic features of groups, and to the intra-psychic identity of individuals.

Identity, as the characteristics of ethnic groups

An early example of the first, or ethnic group, direction is Maxine Fisher's work (1978). Her study of Asian Indians in New York City focuses on Indian immigrant voluntary associations, distinguishing between groups formed around religious, natal state or linguistic affiliations—which she styles 'parochial identities', and the emerging pan-Indian movement—in which she finds evidence of a 'fused' identity. The identities of individuals are understood as extensions of this group allegiance: thus someone who has relinquished ties to home region or language is thought to have a broader identity base than someone still closely tied to the meanings and relationships of home. As I shall try to document below, this equation does not hold for Bangladeshis—or for Bengalis as a whole.

Saran and Eames (1980) similarly confine identity to the question whether Indian immigrants in the United States retain or modify Indian (especially Hindu) cultural features while participating in American institutions. The criterion of identity maintenance or change thus becomes the presence, absence or alteration of externally observable cultural practices and symbols from the homeland.

Karen Leonard is currently engaged in 'cross-national' research on the social networks of South Asian international and inter-regional migrants—most recently, from Hyderabad—their construction of a 'remembered homeland', and their 'constructions of personal and national identity in the diaspora' (1992: 1). She makes use of historical and survey research and focuses on interviews and oral 'experience narratives' (1992: 2). Within these narratives she finds two principal emphases: the ways the homeland has actually changed as compared to the emigrants' memory of it; and the differences emigrants observe between themselves and members of the adopted culture and between themselves and those they left behind.

Identity as the intrapsychic experience of individuals

As premier examples of the second or intrapsychic approach to identity, I cite the work of Sudhir Kakar and Alan Roland, both practising psychoanalysts. Kakar focuses on the cultural categories and contents of his patients' psyches, but does so against the background of psychoanalytic categories and developmental sequences which he holds to be universal and in that sense normative. Within that theoretical framework, the Indian self becomes an inferior one, constituted—as Kakar sees it—by weak ego boundaries and dependence on outside authority figures. While the distinctive cultural features of this self are central to Kakar's interest, the concrete social contexts and relationships in which individuals are grounded are much less so.

By contrast, Alan Roland's aim (and here I paraphrase the paper he gave at the 1992 Wisconsin South Asia meetings) is to examine how the contents and norms of identity vary across cultures, and only then to develop a comparative psychoanalytic theory without implications of inferiority to any cultural self. In his work on Indians in the United States, he focuses on their development of a 'bicultural self' and on the differences in interactional styles and in expectations for various kinds of relationships between Indians and Americans.

Another approach to identity

Rather than approach identity from the outsider's view of a group, as was my own original research plan, I have taken the view to which the Bangladeshis themselves brought me: the stance of the person—the social actor who reflects on her field of activity. In this concern with the person, I am grounded not in psychology but in British social anthropology and its French ancestors Durkheim and Mauss. The formulation of this stance which I have found most useful is that of Meyer Fortes (1978: 24):

> To be adequately a person . . . one needs at every stage both to know for self guidance and to show for orderly social relationships to be possible, who and what one is within one's culturally specified social universe.

Fortes' phrasing helps clarify the particular problematic of identity on which I have focused: the challenge to personal identity coherence which is presumably inherent in all forms of social dislocation, and perhaps especially so in migration to a radically different culture where it is by no means certain that one can continue to show to others the same person one knows oneself to be. Exactly how this process works out for particular Bangladeshis in particular social locations within the United States, and which contexts of their lives appear to be associated with identity congruence or dissonance, is what interests me.

Distinguishing between 'person' and 'self'

In the good company of such anthropologists as A.I. Hallowell (1955), T.N. Madan (1982) and Milton Singer (1984), I make a distinction between 'person' and 'self'. I take it that each of us is, minimally, both person and self—that is, both the social actor and the private being who can observe that activity and reflect upon it in dialogue with either the self or another listener. In other contexts (e.g. Rutherford 1984) I have spelled out at length both the dimensions of the person/self distinction and some of its important implications. In this paper, I focus on the social person, only briefly noting where Bangladeshis themselves invoke the self as refuge when their personhood is in flux or in danger.

Since so much of what adheres to 'person' and 'self' for Bengalis belongs to the realm of personality for Americans, it is necessary to underline that the formulation of identity in this context here has nothing to do with personality and indeed subsumes extraordinarily different personality types. Bengalis themselves are fond of saying, of this person or that one, 'he [or she] is a real character!'—calling attention to idiosyncracies of temperament and personality. But the identity features to be discussed in this paper are all very widely shared within Bengali culture.

Considering the relationship between identity and community, I am also interested in the United States Bangladeshi community, both nationally and locally, as a collectivity of these persons, and in their organizations and activities and the changes in them over time. But I do not find the term 'identity' helpful in characterizing these changes or in speaking of individuals' connections to the community and its institutions. Rather I refer to persons' 'identification' with or 'participation' in groups and organizations, and I hold open the question of the nature of the relationship between any particular Bangladeshi's identification with or participation in her ethnic community, or in the larger American community, and the vicissitudes of her own identity as a human person. I have analysed this relationship at length elsewhere (Angell 1986).

This theoretical and methodological stance appears heuristic in a number of respects, summarized in the closing discussion. For the present, I simply want to point out two consequences of this approach for the following argument: first, there is a shift of attention from any preconceived boundary between Bangladeshis and Americans and thus from any treatment of Bangladeshis as a closed ethnic group. If the person's field of activity is what we hold in the viewfinder, the field may cross the Bangladeshi/American 'border', be located entirely within the Bangladeshi community or—conceivably—be wholly in American 'territory'. Indeed, there are examples of all three.

A second consequence of this approach is to suspend any *a priori* notion of what identity change would look like for this category of persons, or even to assume that we know what are the salient elements of their identity. A Bangladeshi man who worships at the mosque daily in Dhaka but only occasionally in Washington DC has not necessarily undergone an identity change—unless that observance was a critical component of his own personhood. A Bangladeshi woman who chooses not to wear a sari to work in the United States may or may not feel this as a compromise of who she is. As Steven Vertovec (1990: 107) points out, 'ethnicity is not a quantitative matter'—not a question of 'more' or 'less'. I suggest the same is true of identity. The only way to know whether the members of a given immigrant group are having trouble showing themselves as the same persons they know themselves to be is to listen to them, to hear their stories. And it is to those stories that I turn.

Bangladeshis define themselves as Bangladeshis and as persons

There are two principal arenas of discourse and practice in which Bangladeshis articulate their understanding of who they are. In the first they define themselves as Bengalis from Bangladesh, thus setting themselves apart from Indian Bengalis. In the second, they define themselves as distinctive human persons, simultaneously setting themselves apart from the collectivity of Americans (or from 'American culture'). It is worth underlining the latter: Bangladeshis use precisely the same set of salient features to characterize themselves as a particular kind of person—relational, affective, moral—and to draw the contrast between themselves and the culture in which they now live. I shall return to this crucial matter.

What we may think of as the distinctive markers of Bangladeshi culture—religion, language, passionate political interests and debate, food, music, apparel—enter their discourse only as they distinguish themselves from Indian Bengalis (with whom they in fact share most of these features, albeit in degrees of variation) or as they describe activities they share with friends in their homes or in gatherings of the larger Bangladeshi community. These 'ethnic' characteristics are not part of their definition of themselves as human persons, not what they see as being at risk when they settle in the United States, not central to the 'identity crisis' of which my friend speaks. A discussion of that identity and that crisis follows. Two levels of data inform this analysis: Bengalis' explicit discourse and the implicit cultural meanings which inform their activity.

Bangladeshi core identity: two sources of understanding explicit discourse about distinctive personhood

Simply put, Bangladeshis collectively regard themselves as being 'a certain sort of person', and they see this essential identity as being threatened by life in the United States and especially by what they frequently call 'Americanization'. At the heart of this identity are several crucial markers: feelings, sharing, and human relationships. It is almost impossible to talk about any of the three in isolation, as each implicates the others. Yet each is also distinctively nuanced.

Bangladeshis understand themselves as persons who have a rich emotional life: to 'have feelings' is at the heart of being human. The feelings cover the emotional range and are experienced deeply. They are to be freely expressed to those with whom one is 'close'. The latter is crucial: feelings are at the centre of the self but also create and prove one's bonds with others. And thus the realm of sharing.

When Bangladeshis talk about their close relationships, 'sharing' is the central characteristic of those ties. Everything, potentially, is to be shared; nothing is to be held back. In addition to one's feelings—'both the sorrows and the joys', one shares news, gossip, food, activities from the homeliest to the most special, and perhaps most important of all one shares one's family life. Whoever is part of one's household is included in invitations from close friends: all the ages and generations attend together.

About relationships, it is not quite adequate to say that Bangladeshis value their ties to kin and friends, although of course they do; it is more cogent to say that they know themselves—as both social person and private self—through these ties. One's identity is formed through relatedness, not through individuation. It is taken for granted that individuals are distinctive: this uniqueness is not something people need to strive for. But precisely what makes them distinctive is the sum of all their relationships. Any story told by a Bangladeshi about herself will be simultaneously, and indeed primarily, about all the people who make up her life. Even in the unusual instance when many important social ties are broken all at once, personal identity can be repaired through identification with others, potentially even others whom one does not know. Thus a woman who had lost friends through an unpopular marriage comforted herself by consciously identifying with 'all women everywhere', and with her own 'humanity', and recommended those sources of identity to her teenaged daughter. In this and a number of other stories, there is a clear indication that selfhood can become a strong refuge when one's familiar social personhood is called into question. But even this selfhood, it is important to note, is relational—not individualistic.

Such an identity—formed and grounded in human relatedness, acted out through sharing, and expressed through feelings—is thought to be under direct threat in the United States. The key features of American life said to endanger this identity are 'individualism' and 'materialism'. A Bangladeshi mother of two complained that her nine-year-old son resisted giving up his room when his father's brother from Bangladesh was coming to visit: the boy said, 'But it's MY room.' His mother commented to me, in some distress, 'Too much of "my this" and "my that"—too much of individualism and selfishness.' She wants her children to share what they have, but more than that she wants them to want to share. The same boy asked his mother on the same occasion, 'Are all Bengalis our relatives?' Of course his mother told him no, but she wants him to feel a part of the 'widespread net' of relationships to which he does belong.

Bangladeshi parents characteristically worry that their children will become 'another sort of person'. Given that personal identity is constituted by relatedness, especially with one's family, a threat to that identity carries a double danger: that the person will become so different as not to 'fit' in the family any longer, and that the three-generational nature of the family will thus be ruptured. If children raised in the United States are no longer able to talk to their grandparents in Dhaka (which is a question not only of speaking Bangla but of knowing what to say and how to behave), their parents will lose the sense of generational closeness and continuity which is reciprocally the bedrock of both the family and the identities of its individual members.

The sense of danger to the younger generation, coupled with parents' awareness of the advantages they sought in coming to the United States, gives rise to an identity-maintenance strategy of 'recognize and choose' in which many Bangladeshis say they instruct their children: 'To recognize what is best and worst in both cultures, and to choose the best in each', as one young father put it and others echoed. Almost without exception, people sort this out as a choice in favour of American institutions and what they typically call 'Bengali values'. Parents are glad to have employment advantages for themselves and good schools and colleges for their children, but they hope the children will keep the personal qualities and family-centred loyalties of a 'real Bangladeshi' boy or girl. For the young people, then, good choices will lead them to take advantage of United States education and training while remaining essentially unchanged as a person: thus an elaborated rather than a contradictory identity. But for the parents themselves a kind of split identity is often the uneasy result—split between their daily lives in the United States and their ties to Bangladesh. As many say, their minds are constantly in both countries yet they are now fully at home in neither.

Along with this explicit discourse about identity, there is also an implicit understanding and practice of identity which can be derived only by observation and analysis. I am not suggesting a dichotomy between these two dimensions: both are 'true'. For this second dimension of understanding about Bangladeshi identity, one must have in mind several of their implicit cultural concepts, especially those of the household, the family, and kinship.

Implicit cultural categories informing identity

The household, in its narrowest definition those who live under the same roof, comes closest to matching American categories. But a Bangladeshi household is unlikely to be limited to the nuclear family (however defined) or even to persons related through blood or marriage. At any given moment it may also contain family or friends visiting from Bangladesh or from other parts of the United States or Canada, or the child of friends from Bangladesh on a year-long stay to pursue a degree. It will certainly include unmarried sons and daughters, whatever their age; it may include elderly parents. But it is not just that the members are different from the 'mainstream' American household; so is the sense of what a household is and how it relates to the rest of the world.

The household in Bengali cultural understanding does not stop at the door: it takes in its immediate surroundings, both the human environment of neighbours and the green environment of garden and trees. The metaphor of 'open doors' is used very often by Bangladeshis to describe what they had at home and miss in the United States: the visiting back and forth with neighbours and family members in other households, and the going in and out of doors—to take a stroll, to admire the garden, and to chat with the neighbours. Many tales of physical and psychological distress among immigrants have the common denominators of closed-in housing units (such as high-rise apartments), isolation from the passing human scene, and prolonged cold weather. One woman, newly alone in an apartment during the day, tells of going to shopping malls just to see and be near other people.

A good deal has been said in the literature about the disappearance of the extended family when South Asians emigrate; the observation of South Asians living as nuclear families in their countries of immigration has been taken as diagnostic of the breakup of the joint or extended family and its replacement by the nuclear family (Nandan and Eames 1980: 199, 213). But evidence from intensive study of Bangladeshi families in the United States, and their relatives in and near Dhaka (Angell 1992; Rutherford 1984), does not support this interpretation. Certainly one may find, in both countries, an apparent equivalent of the prototypical Western nuclear family: husband and wife and their minor children. And indeed this may well be the most common residential pattern of middle-class Bangladeshi immigrants in the United States. But just as the household is not limited to the family, so the family is not limited to those who live together. And this means more than simply reckoning others (a sister in Dhaka; a brother in Canada) as part of one's family. It typically means including them in planning and in important decisions; it almost always means behaving as if those who were part of the family in Bangladesh are an active presence in it in the United States. A Bengali woman scholar based in Calcutta has proposed calling these 'economically joint' and 'emotionally joint' families, and the construct fits well. In instances where such joint behaviour is not the case—where a nuclear family really is a separately functioning unit—family histories show that the separation almost always preceded emigration from South Asia. And indeed there are cases of economically joint families, with a multi-generational residentially joint core in Dhaka, even after three generations of emigration to the West.

The Bengali understanding and practice of kinship is hinted at in what has been said about the household and family, but now requires an explicit exposition. Fully analysed by Inden and Nicholas (1977), Bengali kinship defies any effort to be brief, but several salient points are indispensable for an adequate understanding of the Bangladeshi experience in the United States. In Bengali culture, kinship is established through 'shared substance'—that is, persons are said to be related because they share one or more culturally salient substances. 'Substance' is understood non-dualistically, and thus it embraces what we Westerners are used to separating into physical and spiritual. Persons are related through the sharing of bodily substance, thus creating the familiar category of consanguinal kin. They are also related through the sharing of ordinary daily activities, thus creating the category of affinal kin.

Further—and thus significantly extending the reach of Bengali kinship beyond the frequently named category of 'relatives and in-laws'—persons may become related through sharing particular, long-term activities like attending the same school, going on a pilgrimage, or being neighbours over time. Persons included in this larger reach of kinship are indeed considered kin (*attiyo*) or like kin (*attiyo-moto*). A Bangladeshi woman in Maryland, seeking to explain Bengali kinship to an American anthropologist, held her arms as far apart as they would go and said 'we spread the net of kinship very wide—like this!' It is by now obvious that the Bengali understanding and practice of kinship fosters many relationships which we in the West would more often label 'friendship'. Bengalis, too, speak often of friends, but the most common Bangla word for friend, *bondhu*, which shares its root with the verb meaning 'to bind', itself underlines the deep and lasting nature of the tie.

Persons who share kinship also share feelings and attitudes appropriate and distinctive to the particular relationship: adults owe their parents respect, filial love, and care; they owe their children friendship, parental love, and guidance. Brothers and sisters give each other friendship, fraternal love, and help. All of these relationships are grounded in love and in the 'close' feeling generated by sharing. And these relationships—hierarchical between the generations, egalitarian within a generation, and all created through repetitive sharing—are the models upon which Bangladeshis form their new relationships in the United States, or try to.

A distinctive matrix of identity

What I am suggesting is that Bangladeshis articulate, in their self-understanding and in practice, what I am calling (until we can invent a more satisfactory term) a distinctive matrix of identity. I mean 'matrix' in parallel with the geological term: the substrate. The explicit discourse about feelings, sharing and relationships points especially to the qualities Bangladeshis understand to be distinctive to themselves; their implicit shared understandings about household, family and kinship point to the meaningful social field—the particular contexts—in which they enact their lives. And this matrix both enables and constrains their activity in these contexts.

It seems to me that the distinctive Bangladeshi working out of identity is of considerable descriptive interest. But I suggest that it is more: it has explanatory power. As argued elsewhere (Rutherford 1984), no other variable, singly or in combination, goes as far toward explaining the outcomes of Bengali lives in the United States—who does well and who does not. Each component of this identity matrix may be examined fruitfully in this respect. I have already alluded to the trouble almost certain to accompany the lack of 'open doors' in this country. Let us now focus on the implications of the imperative toward 'extended kinship' in this country, and in particular the gender differences to be found in that practice. Some of these differences are not merely interesting or surprising but perhaps also counterintuitive.

Implications of extended kinship for identity and community

The grounding of personal identity in the 'net' of kinship relations, coupled with the fact that most Bangladeshis are not able to bring this net with them to their countries of diaspora, puts a premium on their understanding and practice of extended kinship. This understanding and practice provide them with both a potential resource and a potential source of profound disappointment in the

United States. If they are able to make friends with whom they can find the kinship experience of shared activities, emotions and responsibilities, these new friends can become kin—and 'fill in' for the missing relatives. Since most Bangladeshis do not reside in ethnic clusters, these substitute kin must be sought within a widely dispersed Bangladeshi community or among the Americans closer at hand, in the neighbourhood or at work.

But this is where the findings, notably those on gender differences, may surprise us—at least to those of us imbued with American (that is, United States) cultural notions about friendship. Since most Bangladeshi men have come to the United States as professionals, one might expect them to have many opportunities for friendship with their American colleagues. Since most women, whether professionals or not, do not work outside the home, one might expect their opportunities for new friendships to be more limited. The reality is almost the obverse.

Among women, the few who work outside the home do not typically report friendships made there; rather women refer to these relationships, somewhat wistfully, as acquaintances, or friends, but not close friends. In general it appears that women who stay at home with their young children and live in friendly middle class neighbourhoods with other young families stand the best chance of making new friendships that pattern on the kin they have left behind. And it is the compelling nature of this kin patterning that appears to leave out other potential friends (including Americans who make a more radical separation between kin and friends) and to explain what might otherwise appear somewhat surprising or even anomalous choices. Thus a highly educated Bangladeshi woman, suffering extreme loneliness in an apartment complex where most of her neighbours are at work during the day, makes a deep friendship with an American neighbour, a woman half her age (and with half her education) whose husband is away on military duty. With her she shares the ordinary activities shared by a mother and her unmarried daughter or by sisters: cutting up the food, cooking it, gossiping, caring for younger children.

Among men, those in demanding professional jobs in corporations or government report few work-related friendships with Americans, presumably because those contexts present scant opportunity to make friends on the Bengali pattern. Those men who came here as graduate students, or who now work in universities or in their own businesses, report more friendships made in these contexts. The Bengali notion of shared substance seems explanatory, as men in these latter work settings tend to have the most sustained and potentially close relationships with other men. But American cultural expectations of friendship between men do not usually include the intimate sharing of emotions; there are many stories of disappointment and profound sadness in this regard. A Bengali physician in a large hospital who relates that his colleagues regard him as 'foolish' or 'too lenient' or 'weak' because of his 'enormous investment' in his friends and his openly emotional attachment to his family is perhaps the epitome of an identity-disturbing conflict between knowing who one is and showing that same person to others. It is not surprising that men's stories characteristically include vivid memories of and longing for their old 'family friends' and 'school-day friends' from Bangladesh; it is these friendships based on close, frequent, family-related contacts over many years that Bengali men value most and that they depend on to bolster their identity, even in absentia.

When such 'like-kin' friendships are not to be found and, perhaps worse, when they are apparently found but then come to an end, the resulting sense of disappointment is great, sometimes extending to depression or to chronic physical illness. Indeed it would not be far-fetched to say that the successful establishment of at least some 'replacements' for the absent kin is a condition of emotional health in the new country. Essentially all stories of emotional breakdown, severe depression, and 'madness' revolve around the lack or loss of such kin-like ties.

Thus the successful sustaining of identity does require the replacement or re-creation of a salient field of relationships—a widespread net of kinship, to use the metaphor offered to me—and a community in that sense. This vital resource need not be found within the Bangladeshi collectivity itself. But for these friendships to work, and to endure, they must be built on the 'Bengali model': informal, emotional, diffusely sharing, and patterned on kinship. If this much can be established, even though other aspects of life in American culture are distressing and alienating, the person's core identity can remain intact. Of course relationships on the 'Bengali model' are not exclusive to Bengalis: they may not be normative in most sectors of American society, but they are to be found. And, in a delicious irony, what is perhaps most distinctive to Bengalis about themselves can, in the right circumstances, lay the groundwork for enduring bonds with persons apparently very different from themselves.

Whether Bengalis are unique in this practice of 'kin replacement' remains to be established (comparative research along these lines would be rewarding), but it is already clear that not all South Asians in diaspora follow a similar practice. A brilliant piece of research (Meemeduma 1988) has clearly established that Sri Lankan women in the United States are most unlikely to make new friends in this country, even with other Sri Lankan women, and the perhaps expectable consequence is a high incidence of psychological distress, loneliness, and even physical illness—precisely the experience of Bengalis when the 'kin replacement' doesn't work. But when it does, the replication of bonds formed in intimate family sharing has the potential to create a very wide and secure base for their familiar identity in a vastly unfamiliar culture.

Ten years after the initial research in Bangladesh and the United States which this paper recapitulates, these are the major questions I want to ask: (1) Are the recent changes in the composition and organization of the Bangladeshi community in the United States associated with new dimensions of identity construction among those who were the subjects of the initial research? (2) How do members of the generation now in their late teens and early adulthood articulate their identities, in their discourse and in other forms of practice? Do they find in themselves the characteristics and do they undertake the practices which their parents understand as the indispensable signs of a Bengali identity? How does each understand his personal identity, as one containing conflicting elements or synthesis?

By and large, explicit interest in identity in the South Asian diaspora has centred on one of two definitions of identity. The first is ethnic identity—that is, the distinctive cultural features, practices or institutions thought to characterize the emigrant group and especially to set it apart from other ethnic groups and from the society of migrants at large. Thus attention has gone to features such as wearing apparel, practices such as ethnic celebrations, and institutions such as voluntary associations and political organizations. It has been relatively little considered whether the members of the group in question regard these elements as markers of their own identity as persons.

The second focus, the identity of the intra-psychic self, has been the province of psychoanalytic theory. Here there are at least two directions: to prejudice the 'Indian self' against a universalizing normative definition of the mature self, or to document distinctive cultural selves as a prelude to a general and comparative psychoanalytic theory.

My own approach to the identity issues of a particular group of South Asians in diaspora has been to interpret the way they construct and practice their personhood and selfhood and to analyse the implications of these constructions and practices for the concrete contexts of their life in the United States. But I am not a clinician. I do not understand the content of what people tell me to be intrapsychic except insofar as it is simultaneously culturally mediated and socially meaningful and thus a particular manifestation of shared understandings. Not only are the individual subjects of the inquiry social persons with [cultural] meanings in their heads—most Westerners would find this a commonplace observation—but the very way in which they come to be distinctive persons and selves is a social process which has been informed in a particular culture and is now being transformed in still other cultures, a perspective much less agreeable to members of societies whose members are certain of being self-made.

It appears that the research approach to which the Bengalis led me can afford a bridge between our several disciplines, as it permits us to hold in view simultaneously the relevant social landscape, the multiple and contested cultural understandings at issue there, and the unique persons whose stories are only beginning to be heard and whose struggles for meaning, belonging and power are scarcely understood by those among whom they now live. A distinctive identity matrix is presumably discoverable for each of the groups in this diaspora; we do not know yet in which respects these matrices overlap and in which ones they diverge. That discovery can take us far toward a more satisfactory understanding of the highly particular contexts—from the most intimate and personal to the broadest social and political—in which dispersed South Asians engage their lives in their new lands. And this discovery will lay a solid base for studying changes in these persons and collectivities over time: what endures; what is transformed; what is left behind.

Bangladeshis construe themselves both as bearers of a distinctive culture, whose symbols they use primarily to organize their own community's events and to distinguish themselves from Indian Bengalis, and as a 'certain sort of person'—a relational, affective and sharing one who is at the heart of their identity. The distinctive Bengali cultural symbols are evoked and manifested with great flexibility, and any one of them may or may not be central to the identity of a particular individual. But the construct of personhood—the distinctive moral being—can be abrogated only at peril to both individual coherence and family continuity. A successful replication of the most salient kin relationships is associated with both identity coherence and family continuity. When that replication fails, persons—and potentially their families—are threatened with an identity diffusion which Bengalis often refer to as a process of 'deconstruction'.

Especially in the emotional and relational aspects of their personhood, and in the manifold ways those aspects are elaborated in social practice, Bangladeshis (and Indian Bengalis, too) understand themselves to be unique among South Asians in their countries of diaspora. What if they are right? What if each of us really is the sum of our relationships and the meanings we find there? There are suggestive leads and even compelling evidence from semiotics (Singer 1984) and from particle physics (Capra 1991) to name just two scientific fields. After all, as Dumont has wonderfully clarified, our impression of being an Individual, a separated entity, is the product of a familiar Western cultural ideology, not a universal human experience.

REFERENCES

Angell, Dorothy, 1986. 'Bengalis in the United States: patterns of participation and identity', in *Tradition and Transformation: Asian Indians in America*, Richard Harvey Brown and George V. Coelho (eds.), *Studies in Third World Societies*, no. 38. Williamsburg: Department of Anthropology, College of William and Mary.

———, 1992. 'Those Who Go "Outside" and Those Who Remain "At Home": the view from Bangladesh', 21st Annual Conference on South Asia, University of Wisconsin-Madison, 6-8 November.

Angell, Dorothy and Enayetur Rahim, 1993. 'The Bangladeshi Community in the United States', unpublished manuscript. Files of the authors, Washington, DC.

Bertaux, Daniel, ed., 1981. *Biography and Society: The Life History Approach in the Social Sciences*, Beverly Hills, CA: Sage Publications.

Bertocci, Peter J., 1981. 'Marriage Alliance and Dyadic Solidarity in Rural Bangladesh', *Asian Thought and Society*, 6: 104-21.

Bhattacharyya, Deborah, 1981. 'Madness as Entropy: a Bengali view', in

Women, Politics, and Literature in Bengal, Clinton B. Seely (ed.), South Asia Series, Occasional Paper no. 10, East Lansing: Asian Studies Center, Michigan State University, 31-40.

Capra, Fritjof, 1991. *The Tao of Physics: An Exploration of the Parallels between Modern Physics and Eastern Mysticism,* third edition, Boston: Shambhala.

Clarke, Colin, Ceri Peach, and Steven Vertove, eds., 1990. *South Asians Overseas: Migration and Ethnicity,* Cambridge: Cambridge University Press.

Dumont, Louis, 1970. 'The Individual as an Impediment to Sociological Comparison and Indian History', in *Religion/Politics and History in India: Collected Papers in Indian Sociology,* Paris/The Hague: Mouton.

———, 1980. *Homo Hierarchicus: The Caste System and its Implications,* Complete revised English edition, Chicago: University of Chicago Press.

Fisher, Maxine, 1978. Ethnic Identities: Asian Indians in the New York City Area, Ph.D. dissertation, Anthropology Department, City University of New York Graduate Center.

Fortes, Meyer, 1978. 'An Anthropologist's Apprenticeship', *Annual Review of Anthropology* 7: 1-30.

Hallowell, A.I., 1955. *Culture and Experience.* New York: Schocken.

Hess, Gary, 1976. 'The Forgotten Asian Americans: the East Indian community in the U.S.', in *The Asian American: The Historical Experience,* Norris Hundley (ed.), Santa Barbara, CA: Clio Press, 157-77.

Inden, Ronald B. and Ralph W. Nicholas, 1977. *Kinship in Bengali Culture,* Chicago: University of Chicago Press.

Kakar, Sudhir, 1978. *The Inner World: A Psycho-analytic Study of Childhood and Society in India,* New York: Oxford University Press.

Kohli, Martin, 1981. 'Biography: account, text, method', in *Biography and Society: The Life History Approach in the Social Sciences,* Daniel Bertaux (ed.), Beverly Hills: Sage, 61-75.

Kromkowski, John, 1981. 'Review of The One and the Many: reflections on the American identity', by Arthur Mann, *International Migration Review* 15: 785-7.

Leonard, Karen, 1992. 'A Remembered Homeland: Hyderabad, Deccan', 21st Annual Conference on South Asia, University of Wisconsin-Madison, 6-8 November.

Madan, T.N., 1982. 'The Ideology of the Householder Among the Kashmiri Pandits', in *Concepts of Person: Kinship, Caste, and Marriage in India,* Akos Ostor, Lina Fruzzetti, and Steve Barnett (eds.), Cambridge, MA: Harvard University Press.

Meemaduma, Pauline, 1988. 'The Support Networks of Sri Lankan Women Living in the United States: a study of settlement and adaptation', D.S.W. dissertation: School of Social Work, Howard University, Washington, DC.

Melendy, H. Brett, 1977. *Asians in America: Filipinos, Koreans, and East Indians,* Boston: Twayne Publishers.

Nandan, Yash and Edwin Eames, 1980. 'Typology and Analysis of the Asian Indian Family', in *The New Ethnics: Asian Indians in the United States,* Parmatma Saran and Edwin Eames (eds.), New York: Praeger, 199-232.

Rahim, Enayetur, 1990. 'Bangladesh in the Perception of the Bangladeshis in the United States', Asiatic Society of Bangladesh, Dhaka, 18 August.

Roland, Alan, 1990. 'Indians in America: adaptation and the Bicultural Self', 19th Annual Meeting of the Mid-Atlantic Region of the Association for Asian Studies, Rutgers University, 19-21 October.

———, 1992. 'The Issue of Psychoanalytic Universalism: The Self in India, Japan, and America', 21st Annual Conference on South Asia, University of Wisconsin-Madison, 6-8 November.

Rutherford, Dorothy Angell, 1982. 'Bengalis in the United States: The Domain of friendship', 81st Annual Meeting of the American Anthropological Association, Washington, DC, 5 December.

———, 1984. 'Bengalis in America: Relationship, Affect, Person and Self among those 'Away from Home', Ph.D. dissertation, Department of Anthropology, The American University. Ann Arbor: University Microfilms International.

Stigler, James W., Richard A. Shweder, and Gilbert Herdt, eds., 1990. *Cultural Psychology: Essays on Comparative Human Development,* Cambridge: Cambridge University Press.

Tinker, Hugh, 1977. *The Banyan Tree: Overseas Emigrants from India, Pakistan, and Bangladesh,* New York: Oxford University Press.

Singer, Milton, 1984. *Man's Glassy Essence: Explorations in Semiotic Anthropology,* Bloomington: Indiana University Press.

Vertovec, Steven, 1990. 'Oil Boom and Recession in Trinidad Indian Villages', in *South Asians Overseas: Migration and Ethnicity,* Colin Clarke, Ceri Peach and Steven Vertovec (eds.), Cambridge: Cambridge University Press.

The Second Generation Speaks: A Panel Discussion

DAVID LELYVELD

In our preliminary session, it emerged at the outset that we wanted to question the concepts associated with the title 'The Second Generation Speaks' and also, perhaps, with the word 'diaspora' in the conference. 'The Second Generation Speaks' sounds like a call for personal testimonial, confession, autobiography, or, most uncomfortably, playing the role of informant. That raised questions about who gets to talk in what kinds of settings, and how such talk is framed. There is much to be said about this. Some of the things that may get said here will be autobiographical and personal, but they are framed in a more analytic and academic context than perhaps the original title suggested. The members of the panel will be speaking informally, but attempting to do something rather different than presenting 'authentic', unmediated, raw testimony. They are all graduate students in history, anthropology and the Human Rights programme in the School of International and Public Affairs here at Columbia University.

The term 'second generation', which was new to some of the members of our panel, derives from what can safely be called the 'master narrative' of American immigration history. That narrative is that there is a 'first generation' of uprooted immigrants, drawn or pushed to the American shores but forever ill-adapted—in language, values and cultural practices—to the transition. Their hopes lie in the second generation, the children who master the language and ways of the new society, conceived [of by] itself as otherwise integral ('my son the doctor', etc.). But these children make their adaptation at the cost of rejecting their parents' way of life, or at least by subordinating it. The story may go on to a third and fourth generation that tries to recover the 'lost' culture and, in some cases, carries it back to the land of origin (the bringing of chopsuey to China and pizza to Italy, etc.). But they are more likely to lose all but the most decorative and epiphenomenal characteristics of the worlds their ancestors came from. This master narrative has been challenged by much more complex and pluralist histories such as we have heard in the last two days. Yet its power is exemplified in the title of the panel. It will be further challenged here.

There is another narrative, in the word 'diaspora', in some sense intentioned with the narrative of the 'second generation'. The term itself derives from a longstanding history specific to Jewish ideas of exile and redemption. It speaks of an entire, self-consciously unified population driven out from a land of origin, and dispersed throughout the world, and of messianic hopes for an eventual return. How is it that such a word has come to be used to refer to people who have come from South Asia? Not that the word is wrong, but the question is, 'how has that word come to seem right for so many people?' What sorts of interpretations of experience does such a vocabulary imply? And are there alternative ways of speaking and understanding the lived and various experiences of *this* time in this very different world and set of circumstances to which the people from South Asia have migrated? Such are the questions that the panelists will discuss.

Our first panelist is Ritu Birla, who is a graduate student at Columbia University in the history of South Asia.

RITU BIRLA

I will start by talking about my situatedness and its relationship to the kind of work that I do, but I want to backtrack a little bit and think about the conference so far. Most of the papers have focused on immigrants, that is, what we would think of as a first generation, and we thought we would sort of facetiously call this panel 'Can the Second Generation Speak?' This question asks about our place in the framework of the conference. We are all concerned with being kinds of 'native/diasporic informants', that is, 'specimens of the second generation' and will speak about what it is like to be in the second generation. The first thing that I think we're all going to address is that the second generation has to be problematized.

What does 'the second generation' mean? The term implies a scattering, from a homeland, an origin, an authentic place which defines identity singularly and essentially. And this is my entrée into thinking about authenticity more specifically, and debates around authenticity, which I think most of us in the 'diaspora' have had to confront and negotiate as we grow up. So I want to open up the discussion first by just talking about the different kinds of authenticity debates. The first one might ring true for most of us who are of South Asian descent and have grown up in cultures that are non-South Asian, cultures in which there is not a large awareness of what South Asia is, of what its terrain is like, what its multiplicity of cultures is like; and we've all played roles of 'native informants'. This means being asked to be a specimen, and also an essentializing anthroplogist who catalogues, categorizes and 'creates' an authentic picture of South Asia. The kind of question you would be asked is, 'Why do Indian women wear dots on their heads?' or you're in a classroom and you happen to get turned to because you're expected give the Third World point of view because you happen to be the only non-white person in the room. Or, you tell someone you're from India and they tell you that they really enjoy curry—curry is, of course, generic at this point—so the assumption behind these kinds of questions (and I'm being a little facetious, but not really) is that we can represent an Indianness that is authentic, as opposed to that which one would read in a book. And so we have 'the diasporic' as authentic, as an essence.

There is also another dynamic of cultural authenticity that we've had to deal with, and that is being treated as an absence, as inauthentic. Here I'm going to bring up a term that's kind of controversial, which I heard only last year (I was told that it had been in use for quite a long time): 'ABCD'. It stands for 'American-Born Confused *Desi*'.

The whole notion of *desi* is about claiming an authenticity. This reminds me of what Carol Breckenridge said yesterday about India not being able to let its diaspora go. We're all *desis* even if we haven't been there. However, the 'A-B'—the American-Born—sort of implies that you're not really authentic. I mean you are, when you can be appropriated, but you're not really authentic, not the 'real Indian'. 'Confused' is meant, I think, derogatively, the sort of double inscribing of identity of South Asian ethnicity within a Western experience. I'd like to think of this confusion—the 'C' in 'ABCD'—not as confusion but as 'complexity'. Confusion denotes an inability to choose between two cultures and we need to rethink that, to question whether asking to choose is necessary in the first place, or even possible. On this point, the classic sort of question that you get asked if you're in a position, like I am, of someone who is born in India—I'm actually not second generation, I'm first generation, born in India and really grown up here since the age of two, as you can probably tell by my accent—is 'Do you feel more Indian or more American?' For someone like myself, it's an unanswerable question. It's about not really being able to place yourself within the boundaries of nation. There's a sense of being supra-national. I certainly feel, personally—this is the confessional part of my talk—that this has informed the way I look at my work academically, and my interests have been, from the beginning, communalism and nationalism in the subcontinent. I was attracted to communalism because it seemed natural to me that people had multiple identities, that we were all double, triple, quadrupally inscribed. And this seemed to me starkly apparent in the Indian context, especially, where you have caste, class, region, linguisitic and religious affiliation (religious also not just being monolithic Hindu or Muslim, but Vaishnavite/ Shaivite, etc.). So I was always attracted to thinking about communalism: why is it that religion, or one aspect of religion, becomes emblematic, and gets privileged out of all these identities in the public and political spheres?

The sense of super-nationality is also about questioning discourses of nation. Another part of my work addresses the symbiotic relationship between communalism and nationalism as part of the same thing, not as two polarized opposites, but really supplemental to each other. This sort of perspective comes from having to question national boundaries and, thus, identity and think of it, as Frank Korom said earlier this morning, as multivalent.

DL: Our second panelist is Gita Srinivasan, who has come all the way from California. She is a graduate student in anthropology at Stanford University, and is about to go off to Trinidad to do her Ph.D. research.

GITA SRINIVASAN

I would like to affirm that there are more subject positions available to us on this panel, and in other places when we're talking about these issues, than the sort of confessional, autobiographical, 'tell your story, tell your life' on the one hand; and the academic on the other. I think there is a third position, which I feel keenly as a writer, in which one can draw on personal experiences yet refract them in a certain way in which what is drawn out is more than just personal. This is an important point to keep in mind because we often fall into a binarism in the academy which valorizes the confessional but frames it very strictly within a certain boundary and limits its potency in some ways.

A lot of what Ritu said rang true for me. I'm doing my work in Trinidad, among East Indians there. I'm looking at ethnic identity and popular cinema, basically at how Indians over there watch Hindi films as a way of connecting with India, a way of inventing India, a way of imagining India. I've had an interesting experience as a sort of second generation Indian, and even the idea of myself as a woman of colour was not something that I naturally grew up with, but was a very specific intervention in my academic training that arose at a certain point. I remember going home—I had just joined a group named 'Colour', and saying I was a woman of colour—where the response was that I had gone to college and become very uppity, and where did I get off thinking of myself as a woman of colour? So it's something that is mediated through various discourses within the academy, as well as just my experiences being labelled because of how I look. So I have this interesting thing happen to me, where in school there is this idea of being reified as a Third World subject—that I could speak on certain issues, and that there is this hierarchy of identities which I felt very strongly in my graduate career, where 'Woman of Colour' somehow won out, and this is how I felt I was constantly positioned. It's a definite part of who I am, but it's a part, and I often felt this 'inauthentic Indian' feeling.

However, when I go to Trinidad, I have the experience of people looking to me, somehow because my father is directly from India and not four generations back, as more in touch, more real, more purely Indian. And I study them, so there's this hall of mirrors effect, which I find poignant and also interesting. And it is a hall of mirrors in that there is no point of origin, necessarily. So coming back to the point about the diaspora, and problematizing whether the term always has to be [used] in reference to a point of origin. My work is more concerned and interested with fantasy and invention, that may be refracted from this point of origin, but may have little or nothing to do with practices going on today in India.

Let me give an overview: I'm going to explore how local ethnic identity and a relationship with Indian homeland are constructed through a consumption of popular Hindi films. In this process of invention the popular traditions intermingle with the mass imaginary, the notion of imagined community engendered through print capitalism is brought to transnational communities connected through video images. Indo-Trinidadians perceive themselves as in some way Indian, but their experience is Trinidadian. Typically their most recent contact with India was in the late-nineteenth century. There have been, in the last fifteen years, more people going back, but even then, I suspect from my initial conversations with people, that their experiences of India were somewhat through the veil of these films and their narratives. So the films are characterized by elements of fantasy and spectacle. They arrived in Trinidad in 1937, and have played a vital role in strengthening Indian language skills and a sense of continuity with India. There's chutney soka music; there's dance music which was taken from the films and used in Hindu cultural revivals; people look to the films as educational tools, in a way: copying architecture, costumes. And the fact that they're movie sets, that they don't have a clear referent in India is not of paramount importance. I found that discussing viewers' personal involvement and responses to these themes embedded in characterizations, plot lines, is a way of accessing the larger dynamics of ethnic identification. So in the films I'm going to look at how discourses of culture and nation in the media texts construct particular forms of knowledge and pleasure, making available particular identities and identifications; then [at] how viewers' different social positionings, awareness of culture and the context of the viewing affect these interpretations, and the uses of their knowlege; and then [at] the specific political and social ramifications of these identity constructions in a national and transnational context.

DL: Our next speaker is Farhad Karim, who is a graduate student in the School of International and Public Affairs, in the field of human rights. He has done fieldwork in Pakistan.

FARHAD KARIM

I think I will begin by describing the lens through which I see all these issues. On one level I definitely see it in my work—I'm focused on human rights and humanitarian issues—and I'm always interested in issues of rights and claims. My work particularly focuses upon these issues in a post-colonial context, and in a transnational context.

On a second level, I think my work, or my opinions and discussion of this situation, is rooted in growing up in Vancouver, Canada, which has a very different system than here; [in] going to elementary school in the 1970s when it was in vogue to be free to be you and me (laughter) and a very different system, where multiculturalism since 1971 has been a state-sponsored policy. And [my work is] also [rooted] in a South Asian community which has been in Vancouver for over a hundred years. That was very different from the experience that I've seen and am getting to know in New York City, and that is the kind of the lens I see things through.

I think the word 'diaspora' is problematic. It masks the heterogeneity of the people involved: you're talking about ex-patriates, exiles, immigrants and second generation, third generation, fourth generation. As we heard yesterday, we have groups of people who are multiple-migrants. My family is four generations out of South Asia, which, in a way, is a very different experience. You also have different classes, you have gender, all these other issues which are masked by this idea of 'diaspora'.

'Diaspora' carries a lot of baggage, especially for me in the human rights world, because it is associated originally with the Jewish diaspora, and the idea of the claims one has on an original homeland. In the case of the Jewish community you have the rectification of one displacement by causing another displacement, a sort of 'domino effect'.

What rights, what claims, do South Asians in the diaspora have over South Asia? We've heard yesterday about transnational capital flows influencing BJP party politics. Territorially, the claims are not that strong, but where I've seen a South Asian community diaspora going back and claiming their rights is in the case of Uganda. They are going back to get 'their' property, and then the people who are living in 'their' houses and running 'their' factories and plantations will be displaced in their turn.

Why are South Asians being asked to come back to Uganda to claim this property? It's an interesting alliance, on the one hand, with an African elite in Uganda that wants to see capital flows come into the country; it's an alliance with transnational groups like the IMF who want structural adjustment (and therefore policies); it's an alliance with South Asian groups who want 'their' property back, to make 'their' money again. So this whole idea of what claims one has back on the authentic place, the place of origin, is something I wish to raise.

I wanted to raise also the master narrative of immigration: that we came to this country poor, from India or Pakistan, stayed indentured labourers or petty entrepeneurs, worked harder, made more money, and now have become doctors and dentists and lawyers and members of parliament; and you see in this a great march forward, as if there had been an evolution, so that we can now assert our identity. This narrative is viewed in a very progressive way. In Canada, you see that very much, at least in the state-sponsored rhetoric that I was educated in. You know, you had groups—there's a very famous incident in British Columbia which constitutes a marking point—the Komagata Maru incident, where a boat [carrying] mainly, in fact, all Punjabis, but mainly Sikh Punjabis, was turned away and not let into the country. And it's juxtaposed against the [fact that] today, the head of the Immigration and Refugee Board is a South Asian woman actually born in Kenya. So, you see this [progression]: people uses to be 'Hindoos', then they became 'Punjabis and Pakis', then 'East Indian' . . . now they're Indo-Canadian, and maybe we'll become South Asian soon. And on another level, in terms of Officailspeak, we went from Asiatics and Visible Minorities to now being 'new Canadians' (laughter). And with the construction in our new homeland of masjids and mandirs, gurudwaras, jama'at khanas, and imambaras, it's as though we've 'gone for it'. And I think this all masks the multiple sides of the domination that prevails.

I give three examples of different areas of my work where I've seen this. First, there are people who have come from South Asia, like us, and inhabit the same geographic space in Canada, but don't have this thing called 'papers', or 'citizenship'. What does that mean? We may want to be transnational with our identities, but unfortunately, rights are extended to individuals qua members of nation-states. So what does it mean if you don't have citizenship? I see particularly how it affects labour groups.

There is also the issue of what happens with women. The group I worked with, women who were beaten, women who wanted divorces—the community set up organizations so it could be dealt with within the community, because, you know, we're this model minority, we're going a long way, we want to show a good face, so we can't show that we're mean to our women. So what happens is that communities set up organizations to mediate the difference, and women definitely lose out.

The third point is also along the line of women, and I'll take an example from the Gulf, and my work in human rights in that area. The Gulf, again, is looked on as a great land of opportunity with a wonderful economic system, and people from India and Pakistan and Sri Lanka and Bangladesh go there and make money and bring it back home, and improve their quality of life. I can talk later about what happens transnationally, when it gets related back to South Asia, but right now I want to talk about a particular case with women as maids, giving the example from Kuwait. The labour laws, for example (and this goes back to my point about citizenship rights): maids are house servants and do not, as a rule, get protected under labour laws, flimsy as they may be for foreigners. As a foreigner in the Gulf, particularly in Kuwait, you have very few rights. And the cases with women are, basically, that they show up through agencies, having paid a lot of money, and have to pay money back, so they don't have the money to leave. Their passports are taken—this is a very general phenomenon. I hate to generalize, but in the case of maids I think one can. Their passports are taken away, they're treated badly, beaten, raped, assaulted (you have cases of debt bondage), and it's been very well documented including the complicity of Kuwaiti officials and other South Asians who basically trade in these women. I'll give you two examples—I really have to read them.

The first case is that of a woman named Singhala Bulasi—and I'm reading from a report put out by the Women's Rights Project and Middle East Watch:

> Singhala Bulasi, a 20 year old Sri Lankan woman, told us that on the day she was admitted to the hospital her employer had followed her into a room she was cleaning, locked the door, and raped her. After he had raped her, Ms. Bulasi said that he threw her off the balcony and she landed on the ground several stories below. Ms. Bulasi was admitted to al-Razi Orthopedic Hospital. Both her ankles were broken, she was bleeding vaginally, and there were lacerations to her labia and rectal area that required stitches. We observed that she had a tear that extended from her vagina to her anus, an injury consistent with having been forcibly raped by someone using a sharp object.

The cases go on, but I'll read one more. There's a case of Mamta Sharif, another Sri Lankan woman, 19 years old, who was sexually assaulted by her employer's son; she was punched in the head repeatedly by her employer whenever the infant she took care of misbehaved. After two months of this treatment, Ms. Sharif told us she drank two glasses of Clorox bleach to try to kill herself. Her employers took her to the hospital for treatment, from where she was arrested for attempting suicide, following her treatment. And then once she was taken to jail she was beaten repeatedly, by sticks, by police officers . . . and there are other cases where police officers end up raping these women. Then they can't go back, and end up living in the compounds of the various embassies. When we look at this narrative, we have to realize that there are multiple sites of domination and exploitation going on.

DL: Our next panelist is Saloni Mathur, who is a graduate student in anthropology at the New School for Social Research.

SALONI MATHUR

'What does it mean to speak about a second generation?' I am going to push the question a little bit more. A personal experience that informs the beginnings of a response to that question for me comes out of my location as a Canadian graduate student in anthropology, doing research within South Asian Canadian collectivities in Vancouver.

This research looked at the cultural politics involved in the production of South Asian television broadcasting in a number of Canadian urban centres. That is, I was looking at the practices of individuals who produce what is also known as 'ethnic media' or South Asian 'minority broadcasting'. In Canada it is a federally regulated landscape: the television cable company in Vancouver, Rogers Cable, is legislated by the CRTC, the Canadian Radio and Television Commission, to provide at least a half-hour per day of 'ethnic programming', cultural programming for all of Canada's ethnic groups. The intention of the state by legislating that is to supposedly reflect on an Anglo-dominated media the full range of Canada's multilingual and multicultural groups.

Who does and doesn't get constituted by the state as having access to air time and being an ethnic group is a very tricky business. Thus access to television air time is itself a very political and contested site. South Asians in Canada are defined by the state as an ethnic group, and so in Vancouver they were allotted four hours of air time a week on public access. This air time in Vancouver for the past twelve years has been controlled by one broadcaster who used to be with the BBC in Britain but is originally three generations from Kenya, a South Asian woman, Sushma.

Sushma produces a Hindi programme called *Indradhanush*, which, ironically, means 'rainbow'. The irony will become clearer as I continue. Over the last ten years of her dominating that four hour time slot, she has been contested by various Sikh, Muslim, and Fijian Canadian groups who feel that Sushma doesn't represent their interests on that show. In this case the interests concerned were political, religious, and linguistic, but it has been much more than that. The way in which these groups have contested her show has been articulated in a variety of sites, through very personal threats; through construction of a public hit-list after 1984; through organized boycotts of a programme headed by the Fijian Indian group, public demonstrations (one particular Muslim group); and through very complicated interventions into regulatory environments to try to demonstrate a breach of her license to operate. So [her opponents] were going to the CRTC to suggest that she was breaking copyright by showing Indian films, and so on.

The goal of all of these groups has been to have Sushma's license revoked, through whatever means it would take. They have failed to accomplish this specific task. She is still producing, but the point I want to emphasize is that these disputes are still ongoing while we speak, and they have been going on for ten years. Sushma, on the other hand, who has been hired by the cable company as the 'Indo-Canadian producer' for the region, says to me that she has been doing (in her own words) 'As good a job as humanly possible to try and appease all of the diversity of interests in the South Asian collectivity in western Canada. Did you know,' she said to me, in just total exasperation, 'that there are sixty-two South Asian organizations in Vancouver?'

It's a very complex set of disputes, but I am trying to outline some of the contours of it, to make an obvious but very important point about the nature of ongoing frictions and tensions between South Asians as they have been played out in this context of broadcasting. What I have found is that cultural and political claims to 'difference' is a very important aspect of the production of South Asian (in this case) broadcasting, which in turn is a reflection of the collectivity itself. In fact, South Asians are known for their continued internal tensions, whether it be over air time (in this case) or political office, or the boundaries between countries. They have a history of contesting for public space which extends well beyond this context in contemporary Canada. Differences among South Asian Canadians extend across geographical, regional, political, linguistic, religious, class, caste, and gender boundaries. While South Asians of Canadian origin may have in common a 'South Asian origin', what constitutes that part of the label is radically divergent and always competing. The term ['South Asian'] assumes a certain internal consistency when, in fact, South Asians include Caribbeans, Indians, Bangladeshis, Pakistanis, Sri Lankans, as well as people from East Africa, etc. What became increasingly obvious to me through watching these disputes that South Asian ethnicity, or culture, or community, is evaluated differently by men and women; in this case by Fijians and Sikhs, by East Africans, by Muslim Canadians, and by the state. South Asian ethnicity in the Canadian context is profoundly contested, with as little consensus about what it really is as in debates about what constitutes 'Canadian culture'. The most recent example of that was a Sikh young man in Alberta who wanted to become an RCMP officer (Royal Canadian Mounted Police), so all of a sudden the image of an RCMP officer with a turban got radically challenged. It ended up going to the Supreme Court because [that image] was sufficiently not-Canadian.

Many writers have made this point, that notions of 'culture' or 'community' are not self-evident. They are, and frequently can be, as complicated as each position within them. In my opinion, the notion of an ethnic community as it has been set up in a variety of state and academic master narratives, and the ensuing assumption of a single South Asian experience that is ethnic, does not reflect any lived reality so much as it expresses and legitimates a singular dominant perspective shaped, consciously or not, by its own agenda. And, in addition, coming of age in the political context of a federal multicultural bureaucracy in Canada has increased my suspicion of this kind of pluralist impulse to reconcile all the details in a radically diverse landscape. Further, I have come to maintain a very cautious scepticism about the need to speak of a unified South Asian culture or community without also asking the contingent questions of whose interests that [notion] ultimately serves. As to why these kinds of categories are important to me, it is because they are linked to my sense that uncritical thinking about marginal groups can itself be a source of marginalization.

So, having said all of that, it is with a deliberate sense of sustaining these tensions that I want to come back to ask the initial question of what it means to speak with any coherence about a category called 'second generation'. And not only that, what does it mean to be asked to speak as part of a category called 'the second generation'—as David said, in the terms of someone else's story? What does it mean to be asked to participate on a panel in which somehow knowledge has been organized demographically if we consider our own panel in relation to the one just prior to us, for example. And how do we in academics reproduce—certain configurations of power in terms of the relationships between subject and object? Acknowledging at the same time that even our best academic categories are provisional, shifting, unstable, and contested, my concern is how the notion of a second generation—as part of what has been recognized by dominant language concerning US immigration history—tends to eclipse a lot of the complexity of what it means for me to have come of age as a South Asian subject in a transnational space. And how does it fail to account for what Farhad has also suggested, how does it fail to account for the different national frames (in this case the difference for me between Canada and the United States) in which a subject formation takes place? And how does it tend to forge an assumed unitary generational experience out of a much larger landscape of lived racism and sexism in which any generation comes of age? All of these remain questions for me.

The last thing I'll do is consider another very different sense in which all of us on this panel may constitute something called a 'second generation', the sense in which we are also all graduate students doing Ph.D. research around South Asia. To that extent, in the most general sense, if we are seen to be representative of something, we may be seen to represent a second generation, an upcoming generation, of graduate students doing intellectual or scholarly work around South Asia. I am not too sure how to develop that thought, except to simply suggest in relation to the title of this conference, 'The Expanding Landscape', that it might also be relevant to think about an expanding intellectual or professional, institutional landscape that is expanding precisely because of the kind of knowledge being constructed by the presence of a generation like ourselves. May anything be said to uniquely inform our location as a second generation of academics that might ask the kinds of questions that we ask? How are they shaped by a particular positionality that comes out of being both located as investigating subjects as well as the subject of investigation?

One more thought: the kind of politics of positionality that I am talking about in relation to how knowledge gets constructed is, for me, to have a different kind of stake in the subject of our studies; whereby, for example, an orthodox Hindu temple, or a particular festival or cultural performance, are not only syncretic expressions and performances of culture or ethnicity, but also exist for many of us as part of a larger topography of structures of oppression that regulate for us codes of gender and sexuality and assist in mobilizing some very dangerous Hindu fundamentalisms that may brutally determine the conditions under which we live as Canadians or Americans of South Asian origin. I am suggesting that the positionality of being both subject and object does, for me, rest on a very urgent political stake in what we are up to. And if we are thinking about transnationality, or diaspora, as a framework for thinking about opening up new forms of agency, how are we to do that?

DL: Let us now focus on one thread in this, which is itself a large subject: political usages of identity, and the construction in particular of the concept of 'multiculturalism'. One of the things that developed in our earlier discussions is the concept of multiculturalism. Here in New York City we just lost a chancellor of schools to the cause, possibly, of multiculturalism. In 1993 the New York City Chancellor of Schools was drummed out of office by those who opposed the inclusion of gay families in NYC's school curriculum on social studies. In the Canadian context, as Farhad pointed out the concept has very different meaning and politics. One might also say there is an Indian context. How do alternative perspectives, group identities, get constituted and how do they play out in modern political settings?

RB: I wanted to address the issue of identity politics. My most recent work has been on communalism, and I wanted to build on some of the transnational ties in terms of Hindu identity construction, and the construction of the Indian nation as a Hindu nation. The point I wanted to make—and I think it is just an example of how we might be able to think transnationally—is about communalism in India. I have to situate myself very specifically, because my personal experience is rooted very much in the tri-state area [NY, Connecticut and New Jersey] of urban professional North Indians who, as far as I can tell, have done a great job of reconstituting India as a Hindu nation. There are very few Muslims in any of the gatherings I have been to—none in fact—and these gatherings are also very caste-specific, the [people I am talking about] are general merchant-caste professionals. Religion is used in the diasporic context as a kind of reconstruction of a kind of faith. I think that we ought to think about religion in the Indian context not just as a benign faith, but also as very much about a reconstruction and a reinvention of a certain kind of Hindu tradition where there are processes of reification and freezing going on. And you have to look at this within the context of identity politics in the United States. What I see going on is that we have the idea of 'Hinduism as tolerance', as syncretic, as all-absorbing. Interestingly, this is what is used by the BJP also to put forward a model of the Indian nation as Hindu. Thus Muslims are really Hindus, because Hinduism has this way of taking everything in.

I think that kind of rhetoric is being used also in the diaspora, but it is being used [in connection with] the idea of Hinduism as a religion that is tolerant and assimilative. Such rhetoric is, in fact, a way to address multicultural issues within the US context. Again, I am very much informed by the New York debate on multiculturalism, which may not apply to California or the Midwest. This new diasporic version of Hinduism is in fact an erasure—it is about a series of different erasures.

The first erasure [occurs when] you see 'tolerant Hinduism' being put forth as a version of multiculturalism. The question is, 'what role does Hinduism play in terms of its reinvention in the identity politics of the US for Indians?' Interesting here is that when we think about identity politics, we think of the politics of difference. I am thinking specifically about the African American model—at least in recent years. Perhaps we need to rethink what the politics of difference means for South Asian—Hindu—cultural identity.

Hinduism is used to talk about assimilation, which is part of the American dream, and this is the kind of Hinduism that is being put forth by urban professionals. Hinduism is also used to talk about a certain kind of tradition of family values that sounds a lot like the [tradition which] Republican administrations of the past eight years have been talking about. My point is that religion and its reinvention, in this context is used to mark difference—you know, we are Indians in this great multicultural rainbow of the Untied States—but [it is] also [used] to assimilate at the same time.

This is what I mean about rethinking the politics of difference: we're not just talking about difference, we're talking about marking difference and sameness at the same time. It's the same space. I think that's indicative of the way in which, if we think transnationally, we're getting a certain kind of break.

How does the reconfiguration of the Indian nation as a Hindu nation get sent back to India? That's the second question. Organizations like the BJP and the VHP are being funded by the very groups that talk about Hinduism as a focal point for family values. So there is an economic tie, certainly, and there is a cultural tie. I think that there is a great irony in Hindu Indians in this country building on the model of multiculturalism and diversity from the subcontinent [in order] to reify the idea of a nation in a particular framework and to send it back. So multiculturalism in fact becomes a kind of erasure of a variety of different identities.

The final point that I would like to make is that, if we throw the question of race into all of this—we've all been very quiet about the racism in our community, or at least the professional Hindus—if you throw race into it, then multiculturalism really does stand for a kind of erasure, because it means we can include everyone but somehow there is a kind of exclusion going on, as well.

FK: Concerning the politics of identity and multiculturalism in a transnational context, the South Asian community and the diaspora stand out in two ways. One is the fact that South Asians have come out of a colonial relationship. This is very, very different from Italian or Ukrainian immigrants. And it comes along with a lot of ideological, political, economic, and social baggage. So that's the first thing we have to remember that's common [to the South Asian diaspora in general].

The second point is that in different places and in different parts of the diaspora, the South Asian community goes in and then reinhabits different positions in the world capitalist system and joins the system at different levels.

So those are two points of similarity. In terms of difference of identity politics and multiculturalism, you have to realize, for example, we grew up in a sort of state-sponsored multiculturalism in Canada which is very different from the eugenically dictated policies of multiculturalism in Singapore, where balance-by-reproduction is sort of encouraged. The ways in which certain identities then are reified are very different.

This was underscored for me by an experience I had in a small village in northern Pakistan—a remote tribal area of Kohistan. I spent time researching and doing work, trying to find out men's views of women's rights there. There was one individual who decided he wanted to bond with me and he said, 'You have to prove yourself and shoot my gun.' Being extremely scared of guns, I couldn't shoot it. I tried to be a native informant for Canadians and said, 'You know, in our culture we don't do this sort of thing.' The irony of it all is that he said, 'No, that's because you're not black.' I said, 'What do you mean?' He said, 'I saw the L.A. riots'—he doesn't understand English and that's his only vision, he's never seen an African American . . . he's never seen a white person, for that matter—'only blacks shoot in your country'. That's one way the media are carrying American racism overseas. Secondly, there is a community in Baluchistan, in the Makran area, called the Zikris. The Zikris are rooted in a very syncretic tradition of Islam, and the practices are rather different. They have been there for a very long time, and within the same families you have [either] Zikris or more orthodox Muslims, whom they call Namazis—they do the sort of mainstream Sunni practice.

What has happened in Baluchistan is that a lot of workers have gone to the Gulf, and have come back with money; particularly from Saudi Arabia, there is a lot of financing of madrasas (Islamic schools), and it's the only educational opportunity for people there. So they come back and a new, non-syncretic, textualized, Wahabi vision of Islam is reimposed on this area and, sadly, the group that suffers are the Zikris.

You see more movement coming back from the Gulf. You see major racist attacks. You see beatings. [You hear:] 'You are not Muslim.' You see new authenticity within a Muslim world being created. [People are] told 'you are not authentic'. And this then plays out within party politics in Pakistan. This movement back from the Gulf affects women, who are being forced back into purdah. [You hear people say] 'We learned about the true Islam', as if the closer you get to Mecca the closer you get to the 'real' Islam.

In terms of Canadian politics *vs.* the United States, Bharati Mukherjee made a comment after slamming Canada for three paragraphs, where she said: 'No dark-skinned person has the right to feel comfortable inside American history.' So far one could agree, but she continued, 'yet *I* do.'

This panel is 'Indian Americans speak' [sic]. How does one become Indian American? This identity is being ascribed to you. If my family left before Partition, for example, am I Indian? Being here for as many years as she has, is she American? As the Indian nation increasingly becomes regarded as a Hindu nation, does a Muslim suddenly become Pakistani or Bangladeshi? And—going back to Canada and the various identities: I can talk about 25 Muslim organizations in Vancouver all fighting over what it means to be Muslim. How? Because you have a state bureaucracy there to maintain that.

And the last issue is dot-busters. A 'dotbuster' said—'every time I see a Hindu I feel sick. I feel like beating them up and killing them.' [What about] Muslims who were in Canada during the Gulf War?

Different things, different themes. What's definitely needed is a space to be able to renegotiate. What is needed is to remember that all these communities within themselves, the South Asian community, are of course fractured, but then are refractured among gender, class and linguistic lines. I want to end with my favourite quote. It rings true on so many different levels. [It's] from Mira Nair, being herself, acting as herself, in *Mississippi Masala.* When she is talking about something else, the figure at the end is Hari Patel and I think he was just re-quoted for the quintessential American dream. She says, 'You can be dark and have money, or you can be fair and have no money, but you can't be dark and have no money and expect to get Hari Patel.'

RB: I just remembered another example to caution us in terms of transnational thinking and identity politics. When I talk about Hindu tolerance and Hinduism being a wonderful syncretic culture, this is of course also a replication on the part of Indians in this country of a colonial orientalist stereotype. I think we need to be aware that we do this in expressing ourselves or making ourselves objects of tourism. India does this and we do this in this country. Another very good example of that was a group that was organized around VHP people in Great Britain recently who collected—I wish I had the exact amount—a sum of money that was over 10,000 sterling pounds for a bricklaying ceremony. This was funded partially by local British Councils, the British Government, because this was part of their tokenism and multiculturalism: 'Give them a few thousand pounds to lay bricks. We don't know what it means.' Well it means, as you know, a hell of a lot in another context.

SM: I don't have much to add. I think I might just pass the microphone in the interest of opening it up for others. But poor Farhad.

A few weeks ago I said to him, 'I don't think I'm second generation because I came to Canada when I was five years old.' He said that he's not second generation or Indian or American, so there are some truly impossible categories.

GS: In Trinidad as well, the Indian community is very highly segmented and divided over what it means to be Indian. Politics are pretty clearly ethnically and racially polarized and there is a history of Indo-Trinidadians not feeling as if they have had access to equal political representation. This has spawned, as someone from Trinidad recently told me, a regular cycle of Hindu revival. What happens each time is that a new authenticity gets created, and [there is] especially an interest in creating an Indian identity which is a Hindu identity similar to some of the things Ritu was talking about. One interest I have in looking at films is that they cross-cut several boundaries of this segmented community in terms of religion, political affiliations, and class; and the readings of the films will be very different and very revealing as to different interested perspectives on defining what it is to be Indian. In Trinidad there is this national slogan for a plural community, and the slogan is 'All the we is one.' So, 'All of us live in this country from different backgrounds, different races, different ethnicities, but we're all one.' And I have experienced different levels of discourse that I encounter when I talk with people about this.

At one level, people will stand by this and say, 'You know we are all one. We all celebrate each others' festivals. We all eat each others' food.' There's a great sense of a messy hybridization and flow which is initially presented as unproblematic. But there are also areas within the Indian communities where you find huge differences between very small groups of people who have different agendas on how to define themselves. The National Hindu Women's Association in Trinidad presented itself to me as *the* Indo-Trinidadian women's association, and there's a popular leader who calls himself Raviji. He is a sort of priest, community psychoanalyst, grassroots leader who writes weekly columns in the major Trinidad paper and sprinkles his columns liberally with words in Hindi. These words have taken on the import and cultural resonance of Sanskrit words. They are seen in this new reification of being Hindu and what that means. These Hindi words are seen as like the sacred texts, and they hold power, because people don't speak Hindi.

Concerning cultural production, I wanted to talk a little bit about something that was brought up earlier: the fact that is there a diasporic aesthetic. We have often been talking about things that have a reference point within India; can we talk about cultural production and expression that may really not have any reference point within India, but which speaks to an experience which is essentially outside of it? For example, in California I recently witnessed a local Indian fashion show and beauty contest which was billed as a second-generation kind of event. It was very interesting to see the kinds of clothing. Each young woman was asked what kind of role models she had, who was her role model, what were her plans for the future. I felt that it was a very MTV-influenced format. The way the women walked, the kind of clothes they wore, the very stylized poses that they got into were very influenced by images you see in *Cosmo* and *Vogue*, yet when they were asked who were their role models, the answers went like this: 'Gandhi'; 'my husband'; 'Gandhi'; 'Brooke Shields'; 'Gandhi'; and 'my father'. It was held in a large upper-middle-class restaurant, a very ostentatious display of material success, yet these were the values that were sort of symbolically being enshrined.

That's my point about a diasporic aesthetic. What they were searching for and who won the contest could be described as 'a modern girl, a girl who wanted a career and had ambitions, but who still had these kind of role models and didn't contest them in particular ways'. We might look at that as a way of talking about a diasporic aesthetic.

RB: Were they all the same Gandhi? Just another funny little story about a beauty pageant—and I can't believe I'm admitting to this large audience that I actually watched the Miss World Pageant two years ago, but I did only because I turned it on late at night and Miss India was a semi-finalist—Just a funny, funny tale of cosmopolitan Indianness: She answered one question by saying that she wanted to bring back Indira Gandhi because she thought she was one of the greatest figures in modern Indian history. Her answer to the crucial question, which would have gotten her the crown, was, 'If you had to change one thing in India, what would you do?' She said that she would build a national sports centre. She didn't win the crown.

But before Farhad gives an example of a new kind of cultural production through music in the South Asian diaspora, I want to, as a counterpoise, do a bit of historical periodization and say that the kind of music that Farhad is presenting is actually a recent phenomenon. It's interesting, as someone in their late twenties growing up and watching the ways in which you, as an Indian or a South Asian, get represented in mass media. Our first introduction to being represented was Merchant/Ivory. There is a dynamic of people going through phases of being represented in different ways. First you are Dr. Aziz in *A Passage to India.* That's the person that you associate with. And then maybe you become a more modern person, you read *The Buddha of Suburbia,* and then comes *Mississippi Masala.* Now you have a new kind of cultural production which, I think, is about responding to the kind of space which Indians inhabit in the Merchant/Ivory world, and that is a kind of neo-colonial world.

FK: I'm faced regularly with what my personal role, my relationship, is with (and how do I represent) South Asia? It comes into so many aspects of my work. This was radically underscored in a class I teach—[consisting] of six-year-old African Americans and some Latino kids—on India. Every week, I deal with this textbook full of *dhanyavads* and *namastes* and try to fill it up with some *sukriyas* and *salaam aleikums* while missing out *'Sat Sri Akal* and a hundred other things, so that's something problematic. And when reading to them stories from the comic books, it becomes problematic because all the bad guys are dark, all the women are dumb in some of these things. What does one try to do? Do you mask certain things? These are certain forms that have been produced and there are certain things that one has access to in the school system. How do you represent what you want to mask and what you want to show? In a way my problems were solved when the kids were getting very bored with me and wanted to play musical chairs. The teacher, of course, was great. 'Play some music. The Indians are such a spiritual people. I think it will make the kids more tranquil.'

I decided not to make the kids more tranquil, and played some music for them that is being produced more and more outside of South Asia, but rooted in South Asian communities. I have heard this music being critiqued from the right as inauthentic, and just a bad version of it, from the left as just a deterministic product of the late capitalist world. In a way, it is an appropriation of certain styles, but who is appropriating whom any more? It's changed. It's not the Beatles with a little bit of sitar, it's appropriation of black popular culture. It's appropriation of bhangra styles in Punjab. To me it is an exciting space where new forms are being negotiated. Who is appropriating whom? It is going back and forth. Thank god it's not the sort of karma cola, granola, India that you see at all the folk festivals. This is something new that's being represented.

Allow me to play some music, giving three examples. The first two snippets are from bhangra music. I was forced to hear it in college at South Asian functions. You're listening to 'normal' music, and suddenly this music comes on and all these people start to bhangra. My first reaction was 'Did they just come from India?' But no, it emerged mainly from the Punjabi community, and seems to be going all over. This Christmas in Vancouver there was a bhangra acid rave New Year's Eve party. I'll give you two snippets of this. The first is an earlier style. There are bhangra festivals now that are more techno-oriented. [music]

What's also interesting in terms of showing of wealth among communities—I've seen this in Vancouver—where once the big thing was to bring in a music party of Zakir Hussain or Nusrat Fateh Ali Khan (if one could) the new thing is to find a person who can do great bhangra from some small place in Vancouver.

Next is Nusrat Fateh Ali Khan and what's been done with him. You have 'Nusrat Fateh Ali Khan goes heavy metal', Nusrat Fateh Ali Khan techno, Nusrat Fateh Ali Khan reggae . . . and it's a lot of Punjabi as well as qawwali music. You have latter-day Sufis now as whirling dervishes in night clubs. This piece is a very Sufic qawwali about a pir (spiritual preceptor) who is probably rolling in his grave now, called Shahbaz Qalandar. It's made by the House of Shah in England. [music] Yes he was invoking Ali.

The last piece is by a man who calls himself Apache Indian. He is from London [sic]. It is a mix of Indian styles and reggae. It's very interesting in the way that he breaks down national boundaries, depending on the song. He also replicates orientalist stereotypes. Sometimes he comes flying in on a magic carpet from Delhi or Amritsar or Karachi or Dacca or he talks about Sri Lankans. It's really neat to see how he is imagining the new India or South Asia. This song is called '*Movie Over India*'. [music]

GS: To end things, I would just like to read a small essay with some general thoughts on identity and meaning, called 'The Landscape of a Body'.[1]

In Salman Rushdie's *Midnight's Children*, Dr. Aziz is made to carry out a series of medical examinations by peering through a seven-inch hole that's cut in a sheet that swathes the body of a young woman. Her father's sense of modesty demands that she not flaunt her body for strange men, doctor or not. Aziz becomes fascinated over years of such consultations, over the glimpses of stomach, shoulder, ankle. He falls deeply in love with the woman who, glued together by his imagination, accompanied him on all his rounds.

This image rises up before me as I reflect on the politics of identity and meaning, the landscape of a body, a geography, a map of the skin. When I was young my German-Jewish mother with landscapes and diasporas of her own to draw around me, made a film about the *sandhya* (evening) prayer ritual in India and narrated the smoky daybreak (?) scenes in her cool, quiet voice. In rare moments, my Madras-born father would tell me of pulling on new clothes Diwali-dawn, and I could smell them, cotton and coal. In my nine-year-old mind's sensuous eye, India was a place that happened in the morning. Later, as I grew, the afternoons came, the dusks, and I became aware that I collected glimpses up inside of me.

Three years ago in a Jakarta bus terminal an Indian ticket vendor drew me aside to tell me I must visit India because, you know, in India (he gestured with the money in his hand) you put the money in the water and it sinks. I imagined the ocean. He contemptuously rattled the Indonesian change so I could hear how flimsy it was.

An aged woman of South Asian descent, completely deaf, sat next to me in a Singapore institution for the elderly, looking into my face. Suddenly, she seized hold of my nose. 'India nose,' she said. 'Like mine.' She wouldn't let go.

In Bali, a Hindu tour guide sat me down in his dusty roadside office. There, among the ads for package deals, bus tours, days of sightseeing, he spoke quietly, in fervent tones, impressing upon me the importance of going back. Of visiting the temples. For myself, and also—his glance silently said—for him; for others I could not see.

The stories are endless. The stories of image collectors. For none of the people who spoke to me had ever been to India. Indias of the mind follow me. Always these moments of longing shared with strangers in which the images wash through me. They evoke the political and the mythical nature of my history and my identity and connect it to that of others. To collect images, or even to invent them, yet not to let that invention change the nature of the believing. This is a documentary imagination, a tendency toward fabulation that empowers through making and contesting meaning.

Whatever the expressive mode, my challenge is to bear witness to those experiences which lie in between, as I do, to those radical disjunctures in culture and consciousness which seem to yet be impossibly contained in lives. 'Sit up straight like a Brahm Jew', my mother admonished us at our kitchen table. I think that our intellectual and artistic processes both move more like a refracted translation than a clear and distinct peering into the centre of matters. The metamorphosis of translation making knowledge flex in different forms lies at the heart of my work on the meaning of Indianness in the diaspora. I approach this as an anthropology of the imagination, since so much of it has to do with inner discourses of memory, fantasy and invention. Translation between cultures and lives involves probing the unseen links between discourse and ideology, with the goal of revealing the subject, the process, that makes or unmakes that link. Individuals translate public culture into private truth by passing it through race, gender, class, desire, lived experience. Understanding what happens through this passage seems to me to approach some enlarging of one's scope of empathy, one's scope of identification.

My cousin Gopi tells me I am American, but my sense of smell is Indian. And recently in Trinidad, people looked at me longingly and said I had eyes like the girls in the Hindi films. When the Indo-Trinidadian bank teller in Port-of-Spain had to write my name over and over, filling out the forms, she drew the letters slow, with a kind of reverence, impressed that both my first and last name sounded real, from India. She looked at the letters and my face watchfully. I felt like a living memory.

NOTE

1. This essay appeared in *Our Feet Walk the Sky: Women of the South Asian Diaspora,* S.F.: Aunt Lute Press, 1994.

East Indians in the Diaspora: Fragments for 'The Second Generation'

GITA SRINIVASAN

A panel at an academic conference entitled 'The Second Generation Speaks' immediately strikes at disciplinary insecurities and issues of authority in anthropology. What seems to be at stake is the very status of lived experience, that complex and dangerous heart. Rather than having panelist/informants stage a confessional in the midst of an academic conference, I believe that individuals speaking of and interpreting their own experience might position themselves to make a fruitful and disruptive intervention. They might purposefully tangle the voices of experience and theory. As a first generation South-Indian-German-American-Jewish woman, the place I speak from is one in which theories are felt and named, and experience is interpreted in the living of it. Perhaps there are uneasy theories, hopeful theories, protective ones. Perhaps there is such a thing as raw theory, and data that is always already interpreted.

I'm most interested here with *how* such a subject speaks and names her experience. My words here will, I hope, neither confess a subjectivity nor reinscribe the standards of academic exposition. Perhaps there is another possibility: what I have learned and thought is in a sense what I have become, and this becoming clings insistently to its own form. It is at once an analytic stance and a mode of perception. For me, like many others, the question 'where are you from?' has multiple answers. I have never directly known the cultural and geographic points of reference from whence I arise. In me, the disjunctures and the particular silences of the migrant are twice inscribed. The re-territorializing of inner spaces and narratives, that central nerve of postmodernity, has marked my very senses.

II

I grew up in America, in placeless suburbs of the north-east. They had names like Somerset, Annandale, Fairfax, Meadow Lane

Apartments. We lived in neat two-storeys with lawns in housing subdivisions. On Friday nights we'd light a candle; on Sundays we sang a sloka. Beneath this accomodation, however, lay something as yet unglimpsed. Having flirted briefly with Unitarianism, my family began attending a Reform synagogue when I was a teenager. I remember the perfectly round face of our robust rabbi. My confirmation class once visited the home of our ancestral roots, New York's Lower East Side, and I peered down into a vast wooden barrel on the sidewalk at huge raw green pickles floating in brine. For me it was a comfortable Judaism, one that demanded little.

My younger brother had a Bar Mitzvah and, inexplicably, an investiture of the Brahmin sacred thread. A slender white cord was looped round his torso. He slipped it off easily after the ceremony instead of wearing it the rest of his life—the ritual was done, my father explained, for the experience of it. Our knowledge of Hinduism at that age (my brother's and mine, for then we formed a secret society together) was based largely on the Amar Chitra Katha comic books that we read voraciously for one year in the mid-1970s, in New Delhi. We rented them, grimy and frayed, for a week at a time from a man who had a small shack in the market. Comics were stacked up to the ceiling in ragged towers there; you could pull faded Archies and Richie Riches from all around. In the mythologicals we followed the stories of the blue gods with long eyelashes. 'O Lord grant me a boon!' we'd wail, parodying a thick Delhi accent. We'd grovel before each other and fall over laughing. It was one of our games. We returned to the north-east after the year with a gluttonous appetite for America, gorging ourselves on meat and television.

Later on my father and I travelled throughout south India, visiting temples and doing puja for the experience of it. In each one the pandit, whom my father had paid with a tourist's flourish, would usher us ceremoniously to the head of the line of hundreds of waiting supplicants. Cameras dangled from our necks as we strode past the multitudes of brown backs, the bare feet that had walked miles to reach. I found it difficult to look at them. I had never been part of an Indian community in the US; my knowledge of the culture was made up of fragments. I still have the embarrassing habit of forgetting whether I am Iyer or Iyengar. My father politely slept through the Friday night Shabbat services for years, remaining secure in his enigmatic pronouncement to me, 'You are more Hindu than you know.'

In graduate school I learned to talk about cultural authenticity. I travelled to Trinidad to study the Indian community there. A student greeted me warmly at the university, 'It's good to meet a real Indian', he said with a confidential glance. People watched me with a certain reverence, introduced me with pride. *She come from India. Her father a true-true India man.* I was assured that it was my father's blood that I carried. The utterance of my full name pleased people greatly. It has the name of an Indian village in it, and I was made to repeat it over and over for different people. *She have a nose like Nargis.* People assumed I neither ate meat nor drank—I was, after all, from India, a purer, mythic place where children obey their parents like they do in the 'Indian pictures'. Bollywood films flood Trinidad, giving glimpses of an India glowing with beautiful stars, singing and dancing. *If she from India at leas' she could sing us a song.* I was looking for my first immersion in an Indian culture, and people were looking to me for a validation, a reason. Over and over we searched each others' faces for traces of ourselves, gazing past the face, beyond, far, deep. It is a hall of mirrors where the image dissolves; all that remains is the motion of the gaze.

III

I began at an early age to disbelieve the appearances of things. Not because they concealed, but because they shifted unaccountably. Leave something in one place, and the next time you went to pick it up—well, you never knew. Not only was authenticity constructed, as I would write later on in graduate school, but the seemingly objective, even bodily characteristics on which these constructions hung were tricky.

In college I was introduced to a way of speaking about identity and joined a group for women called COLOR, initially finding it somewhat of a happy accident that I was accepted. I'd never had South Asian friends before. When I told my family on a visit home, there was great amusement—I'd become self-important in college, using fancy labels to describe myself. 'You don't look Indian at all' my mother remonstrates, even when I tell her how Americans approach me in the street and proffer photographs of their gurus for my approval, how Indians fall into quick intimacies with me on the train, assuming something I barely recognize in myself. 'A typical South Indian face', pronounces my father. My face the floating signifier, the open question people seem eager to answer with their stories. 'I don't know where you get this idea you look Indian', the exchanges with my mother underscore a certain familial anxiety over origins. She sent me off to Trinidad with a rather absurd admonition, or perhaps a plea, that still rings: 'Don't forget the West.' Which is why it was a matter of some surprise to me when I discovered that in crossing the *kala pani* (the black waters, as nineteenth-century indentured labourers from India had called it) over to Trinidad, I had in fact become white.

He stood in front of me, a young man on the make, making offerings. A ride home, an ice cream, a walk. *You more like a white girl.* In the streets, along with the hissing behind my back—the sound of Trinidadian males in public—I heard 'whitey', just under the breath. Here, in contrast to my home in self-consciously multicultural San Francisco, I am constantly reminded of my skin. Clear skin, paw-paw skin, fair skin, pink like the star-girls from India. *Gyul, you shoulda see how she pink-pink, and if yuh see how smooth*! 'Boys like red girls', says my sixteen-year-old neighbour matter of factly, turning her face up to me with the look of absolute certainty. A local character who considers himself an itinerant Hindu teacher was thrilled to meet me. 'Indian and German—so you are Aryan on both sides!' He pumped my hand, congratulatory, beaming.

I have had to develop a new self-perception in this context. As I live out my own identity in different situations, foregrounding certain aspects or having them chosen for me, what strikes me is the importance of looking at 'performance' through the eyes of the agent, not for its effects or results. Performing identities, for me, is not merely expedient—it can be a disorienting process in which my features subtly rearrange themselves, where some part of my reflection becomes unknown even to myself.

I am dressed to go out. My landlady in Trinidad pauses to look at me approvingly. 'Nobody would guess you have white in you. You look like a highclass Indian.' She chucks me under the chin fondly. *Don't forget the West.*

IV

Cultural authenticity is typically defined with reference to some point of origin. In my research on the impact of Indian popular cinema on Indo-Trinidadian conceptions of identity, I have come to see how people view themselves, as well as an India they have never known, refracted through the celluloid frame. This refraction, I think, problematizes in startling ways the notion of a centre or beginning. My fieldwork took me one afternoon to a high school in Central Trinidad. In an open air auditorium, hundreds of sweating Indians took lively part in an 'Indian Cultural Programme' of film songs and dances by local artists. *Top-Class entertainment in Top-Class auditorium for Top-Class audience, ladies and gentlemen!* An appreciative murmur would go up as the orchestra struck the first notes of an old sentimental favourite.

It is a convention of Hindi popular cinema that songs are actually sung by 'playback singers', and that on-screen actors lip-synch the words. This 'shadowing' of the song, as it's called in Trinidad, is often done without the artfulness of the Western music video, producing the effect of a somewhat disembodied voice. The song issues from the mouth of the hero or heroine who is at the same time running through a field of flowers, bathing abandonedly under a waterfall, or performing other strenuous acts of romantic devotion. Throughout, the voice rises magically from slightly moving lips in its own hyper-real realm of audio perfection.

Watching the show, I noticed that the young women who mounted the stage to sing stood immobile, arms held stiffly at their sides, expression never betraying the soaring melody. It seemed an awkward performance style, lips barely moving . . . unless, I realized, they were imitating what they'd seen in the movies, replicating with their bodies precisely the disembodied 'original' they'd seen hundreds of times on screen.

V

I grew up with the knowledge that certain stories were not being told in my house. Stories of the past, before America. They weren't hidden, exactly; it was just that there was no place, no time at which they were naturally summoned out of silence. Reverie is not a particularly productive state; it never had a great place in our American household. The Tamil ghost stories my father used to believe, my mother's loneliness growing up in New York City—the narrative bits I carefully collected were wondrous to me. They evoked lost worlds. They also rang curiously flat at times, because, I think, the lives we now led were not truly marked by these histories. I saw our present lives in the bright glare of America, each memory standing out in relief. No shadows. I found traces of these histories all around me, but the glimpses of word and image seemed somehow unmoored from their resonances. Their echoes were far away.

Even the Holocaust stories which could seem so tangible slipped out of my grasp at times, unfathomable in a flash. The stories were real to me; I knew them by heart—stories garbled by age, my *Omi* speaking German and English at once. At times, though, I was unable to step inside of them to allow them to live in me, demand of me, make me accountable. This is when I discovered that the absent points of reference had to be made, fashioned, by an act of will and imagination. A true and disciplined imagination, not a random inventiveness. By fully imagining them the lost spaces fill and the fragments come alive. They begin to cast a shadow, pull at me and ask me questions that are difficult to answer. Even my own experiences can have an insubstantial quality about them until I write them, tell them, imagine them fully, drawing out colour and smell. They *become* my own. And this, it seems, has become my way of perceiving, living, and binding myself to the world. Not the blood, not the land, but the frame.

Rushdie conceives of the migrant as a metaphor for the human condition, and it is perhaps at the level of metaphor that I can best understand displacement, diaspora, the 'second generation'. *I wanta marry my daughter to a nice boy from India.* Displacement can nurture a desire for a forever absent point where all things converge, a point which is yet, paradoxically, the vanishing point.

Contributors

DOROTHY ANGELL holds a doctorate from American University, Washington, DC for her research on Bangladeshis in the United States. A charter member of the Independent Scholars of South Asia, she currently works as a consultant for CSR in Washington.

PARMINDER BHACHU is Henary R. Luce Professor of Cultural Identities and Global Processes at Clark University in Massachusetts. She has published extensively on both sides of the Atlantic. She is the author of *Twice Migrants* (Tavistock, 1985) and is co-editor (with Sallie Westwood) of *Enterprising Women: Ethnicity, Economy and Gender Relations* (Routledge, 1988) and co-editor (with Ivan Light) *of Immigration and Entrepreneurship: Culture, Capital and Ethnic Networks* (Transactions, 1992). She was Senior Simon Fellow at Manchester University, England in 1996 and is currently working on a book for Routledge entitled *Dangerous Designs: Diaspora Fashion, Style and Images.*

FATIMAH HANEEF holds a Master's Degree in Near Eastern Studies from Columbia University.

KATHRYN HANSEN is a Visiting Scholar at the Institute for Research on Women at Rutgers University. Among her recent publications are '*Stri Bhumika*: Female Impersonators and Actresses on the Parsi Stage', in the *Economic and Political Weekly of India* (1998), 'Fifty Years After Partition: Dance in Pakistan', *Sruti* (1996), and *Grounds for Play: The Nautanki Theatre of North India* (Manohar, 1993).

DAVID LELYVELD is Executive Director of the Einaudi Center for International Studies at Cornell University. He is the author of *Aligarh's First Generation: Muslim Solidarity in British India* (Princeton University Press, 1978); and has published widely on the cultural and social history of North India since the eighteenth century, with special reference to Muslims and Urdu language. He is a member of the Independent Scholars of South Asia.

KAREN LEONARD is a Professor of Anthropology at the University of California, Irvine who works on caste, ethnicity, family and life history. She has published on the social history and anthropology of India and Asian Americans in California in *Making Ethnic Choices: California's Punjabi Mexican Americans* (Temple University Press, 1992) and in *The South Asian Americans* (Greenwood Press, 1997). Currently, she is researching the construction of identity in the diaspora by emigrants from Hyderabad, India, who are settling in Pakistan, Britain, Canada, the United States, Australia, and the Gulf states of the Middle East.

JOHANNA LESSINGER, an anthropologist, is a research associate at Barnard College, Columbia University and a visiting scholar at the Center for the Humanities, University of New Hampshire. A charter member of the Independent Scholars of South Asia, she recently published *From the Ganges to the Hudson, Indian Immigrants in New York City* (Boston: Allyn and Bacon Publishers, 1995).

CARLA PETIEVICH is Associate Professor of History at Montclair State University, New Jersey. In addition to her interest in South Asian arts in the Diaspora, she also writes about Urdu literature. In 1992 she published *Assembly of Rivals: Delhi, Lucknow and the Urdu Ghazal* from Manohar. From 1992-5 she served as President of the Independent Scholars of South Asia.

USHA SANYAL has taught liberal studies and religion courses at Western Washington and Rutgers universities. Her book, *Devotional Islam and Politics in British India: Maulana Ahmad Riza Khan and His Movement: 1880-1920* (Delhi: OUP, 1996), deals with the early history of the 'Barelwi' movement (referred to by its members as the '*Ahl-e Sunnat wa Jama'at*'). Among her other published works are articles in *Contributions to Asian Studies and Modern Asian Studies*. She currently works as a freelance editor and lives in Charlotte, North Carolina.

ESTELLE F. STRIZHAK is an officer of the US Government Justice Department and has been working in the field of refugee services for more than 25 years. An Inde-pendent Scholar of South Asia, she did M.A. and Ph.D. work in Telugu Literature from the University of Wisconsin, Madison.

JOANNE PUNZO WAGHORNE is Associate Professor in the Department of Religious Studies, University of North Carolina at Chapel Hill. She has published *The Raja's Magic Clothes: Kingship and Divinity in England's India* on the former Princely State of Pudukkottai (Pennsylvania State University Press, 1994) and co-edited an anthology of work on Hindu divine images, *Gods of Flesh/Gods of Stone* (Paperback, 1996).

LINDA S. WALBRIDGE, an anthropologist, teaches in the Department of Near Eastern Languages and Cultures at Indiana University. Her book *Without Forgetting the Imam: Lebanese Shi'ism in an American Community* was published by Wayne State University Press in 1996.

Index